Somebody in Charge

Somebody in Charge

A Solution to Recessions?

Pierre Lemieux

palgrave
macmillan

First published in 2011 by
PALGRAVE MACMILLAN®
in the United States—a division of St. Martin's Press LLC,
175 Fifth Avenue, New York, NY 10010.

Where this book is distributed in the UK, Europe and the rest of the World,
this is by Palgrave Macmillan, a division of Macmillan Publishers Limited,
registered in England, company number 785998, of Houndmills, Basingstoke,
Hampshire RG21 6XS.

Palgrave Macmillan is the global academic imprint of the above companies
and has companies and representatives throughout the world.

Palgrave® and Macmillan® are registered trademarks in the United States,
the United Kingdom, Europe and other countries.

ISBN: 978–0–230–11269–8

Library of Congress Cataloging-in-Publication Data

Lemieux, Pierre.
    Somebody in charge : a solution to recessions? / by Pierre Lemieux.
      p.   cm.
    Includes bibliographical references.
    ISBN 978–0–230–11269–8
    1. Recessions.   2. Financial crises—Prevention.   3. Economic
    policy.   I. Title.
    HB3711.L57 2011
    338.5′43—dc22   2010037347

A catalogue record of the book is available from the British Library

Design by Integra Software Services

First edition: March 2011

10 9 8 7 6 5 4 3 2 1

Printed in the United States of America.

Contents

List of Charts

Acknowledgments

I wish to thank a few colleagues who have read parts of the manuscript of this book: Christian Calmès (Department of Management Sciences, University of Québec in Outaouais), Mark Brady and Jeff Hummel (Department of Economics, San Jose State University), and David Henderson (Naval Postgraduate School and Hoover Institution). I spent the winter of 2009–2010 as a visiting scholar at the Department of Economics at San Jose State University, where many colleagues suggested useful ideas during informal conversations. Alex Tabarrok of George Mason University's Department of Economics as well as an anonymous referee provided useful criticism on a previous version of the manuscript. I also want to thank the Aurea Foundation (Toronto) and its advisor George Jonas for a grant that allowed me to spend time away researching and writing this book. Of course, none of these colleagues, friends, or institutions is responsible for any mistake I have made, nor do they necessarily share the opinions I express.

A Few Acronyms

Introduction: Adult Supervision

On August 9, 2007, at about 9:30 Eastern time, traders knew something very wrong was happening.

Traders buy and sell securities (stocks, bonds, etc.) for their own companies or for their customers. JP Morgan Chase, for example, has a number of trading rooms in its headquarters tower on Park Avenue in New York City. Its credit trading room, which deals with credit instruments (as opposed to stocks), has several hundred trading desks, each with two or three computer screens, and occupies a whole floor of the tower. At that time, some traders started shouting in a general brouhaha: they had never seen what was happening in the money markets. The money market is the part of financial markets where short-term credit instruments—that is, credit instruments with maturities of less than 13 months—are traded. This market had been tense for the whole summer, and the situation had worsened during the previous two days. Now, suddenly, money market interest rates were shooting up by several basis points (or hundredths of percentage points). Especially hit was asset-backed commercial paper (ABCP). Commercial paper is made of short-term (maximum of nine-month maturity) promissory notes issued by large companies. ABCP is a sort of commercial paper backed (guaranteed) by some specific underlying assets like mortgages, and generally has maturities of 30–90 days. The rates on ABCP went up from 5.35 percent to 5.95 percent. Moreover, as commercial paper matured (as loans became due), many borrowers could only roll them over for a period of one day.[1] Banks which had been willing to lend to each other overnight (banks with temporarily excess reserves lend to those with temporarily low reserves) at slightly more than 5.25 percent now required as much as 6 percent.[2] These increases in short-term interest rates were required by lenders to cover a mysterious new risk. The scare was simultaneously spreading to trading rooms around the globe.

What could look to an external observer as small increases in money market rates or a temporary freeze on the commercial paper market was a manifestation of a deeper—a very deep—problem. Analyzing this problem will take us much beyond the economic crisis that started in 2007. This book is about more than economic crises.

But in order to start, we need to understand a few concepts in finance. We have just seen what commercial paper, interbank loans, and the money market are. A few more concepts are necessary to understand what finance is and what it does.

A "security" is an instrument that gives its holder a claim on a stream of future revenues produced by real assets (factories, for example) or by other securities. The stream of revenue can be expressed by an interest rate or yield on a bond (or other form of loan), or by a dividend on a share of stock. One way or another, a security is a claim on real resources, that is, goods or goods producing goods. Negotiable contracts on securities, which give the right to buy or sell securities, or the latter's flows of revenues, belong to a more complex type of securities called "derivatives." We can view securities as sophisticated forms of loans, since a loan also gives the creditor a claim on some of the debtor's revenues. By conceiving securities as loans, we can better see the whole point of finance: it is for people who want to save, that is, to consume less today and more tomorrow, to transfer their actual claims to real resources to those who want to consume more today and less tomorrow or to producers who want to produce more for the future.

These transfers of claims are often done through "financial institutions." Banks are financial institutions that borrow money with one hand and lend it with the other—that is, they engage in *intermediation* between savers and borrowers. We can distinguish two kinds of banks, although the difference is a question of degree. *Commercial banks* take deposits from the public and relend part of those, in order to pay interest to their depositors and to make a profit. A commercial bank's depositors are its main lenders. *Investment banks* do not take deposits from the general public but finance themselves mainly by borrowing large amounts of money from investors and corporations. They are involved not only in commercial loans to businesses but also in purchasing the latter's securities, brokering securities, and advising their customers on their financial structures and activities— including such things as mergers, acquisitions, and IPOs ("initial public offerings," that is, when a firm first issues stock on an exchange). In the broadest sense, investment banks can be defined as including securities brokers and dealers. A bank can be and is—in most times and countries, with rare exceptions like the United States—a mix between a commercial and an investment bank; such a bank is called a *universal bank*. As intermediaries, banks have one distinctive feature: they borrow short and lend long; the loans they get from their depositors (or other short-run lenders) can be called back with a very short or no advanced notice, while the loans they make are callable only over a certain period of time. You can take your money out of the bank at any time, but the bank can't make you pay off your loan before the agreed maturity and outside the agreed repayment schedule.

At the center of the crisis that started in 2007, we find residential mortgages, and especially the so-called subprime mortgages (or simply "subprimes"), sold to borrowers who did not meet the usual credit standards. By the time the crisis struck, more than half the residential mortgages had been securitized, that is, transformed from normal loans carried on the balance sheets of the issuing lenders to mortgage-backed securities (MBSs). The technical name for MBSs backed by residential mortgages is "residential mortgage-backed securities" (RMBSs), but since these are the main type of MBSs involved in the crisis, I will refer to them simply as "MBSs" in this book.

Understanding MBSs is crucial. Start with a simple, real-life example, documented by financial journalist Roger Lowenstein.[3] In the spring of 2006, a certain mortgage lender had issued 2,393 subprime mortgages for a total value of $430 million. The data were provided to the journalist but the names of the institutions involved were removed to preserve the confidentiality of the contractual relationships. The mortgage lender sold this pool of mortgages (call it "Subprime XYZ") to an investment bank. The investment bank designed a special purpose vehicle (SPV), a company designed only for this purpose, to which it sold Subprime XYZ. To finance the purchase of this mortgage pool, the SPV issued bonds backed by the mortgages, meaning that the bond holders had a claim on the revenues flowing from these mortgages. Interest paid and principal reimbursed by the mortgage borrowers were flowed through to the owners of the bonds. These bonds were MBSs, and the investment bank was their "sponsor."

Sponsors often offered credit guarantees or, through third parties, insurance on their MBSs. They often kept some of the MBSs they issued as part of their own assets on their balance sheets.

The SPV typically issued different classes or tranches of bonds on a given mortgage pool. The most risky category of tranches, equity tranches, would absorb the first losses in the underlying mortgage payments and thus carry a higher interest rate to compensate investors for this risk. The second category of tranches, mezzanine tranches, would cover the next losses. The third tranches, senior tranches, which would share in losses typically exceeding 12 percent of mortgage payments, were less risky and thus paid the lowest interest rate.[4] To go back to our actual example, Subprime XYZ was divided into 12 tranches or classes of bonds, from the most risky to the least risky. The lowest equity tranches were to start defaulting if and when losses in the underlying mortgage reached 7.25 percent. As this loss was forecasted to be 4.9 percent for Suprime XYZ, even the most risky MBSs looked like a bargain.

There were more complex securities built from mortgage pools. A collateralized debt obligation (CDO) is a tranched claim on MBSs (or other securities).[5] It can be considered as a more complex sort of MBS, as it is an MBS backed by other MBSs (or other securities). One level of complexity higher, CDOs-squared are made of pooled and tranched CDOs. But we will concentrate on simple MBSs to follow our story.

Banks often created another sort of entity or "conduit," called "special investment vehicle" (SIV), that acquired MBSs and financed these purchases by issuing ABCP.[6] On the eve of the crisis, at least 10 percent of outstanding commercial paper was backed by residential mortgages.[7] This is how the commercial paper market came to be related to problems in residential mortgages.

In August 2007, investors realized that a large proportion of the mortgages underlying MBSs and ABCP would be defaulting. With mortgage default rates jumping up (more than 13 percent or Subprime XYZ were delinquent in the summer of 2007, a proportion soon to double[8]) and even senior tranches being threatened with default, investors became suspicious of anybody who could own MBSs or commercial paper backed by these securities. Since it was not clear who owned what sorts of MBSs backed by what sorts of mortgages, and which ABCP was backed by risky MBSs, uncertainty spread like wildfire.

Later during this dramatic month, Countrywide, one of the largest mortgage lenders, had to secure a large emergency loan from a group of banks, and the Fed cut the discount rate (the rate at which it lends to banks as lender of last resort) besides establishing a special lending program. The autumn of 2007 saw more dramatic financial events, including the bankruptcy of Netbank. Many financial dramas were to mark the following year: the purchase of failing Countrywide by Bank of America, the expansion of Fed loans to banks, dramatic drops in the Fed's discount rate and short-term rates, further bank failures, the demise of investment bank Bear Stearns and its purchase by JP Morgan Chase, the seizure of Fannie Mae and Freddie Mac by the federal government, the bankruptcy of investment bank Lehman Brothers, and the creation under President George Bush of the $699-billion Troubled Assets Relief Program (TARP).[9] The recession that had started at the end of 2007 would last until well into 2009. And even at the time of writing this book, in mid-2010, the recovery is fragile.

A recession is characterized by reduced production, increased unemployment, and a drop in the general price level or in the rate of inflation. A depression is simply a longer and deeper recession. Recessions and depressions are a matter of degree, from shallow recessions like in 1990–1991 or 2001, to deeper ones like in 1980–1982, up to depressions like in 1929–1933. (Note that, in dating a recession, the first date always marks the peak of the previous expansion, and the second date the trough of the recession.) The generic term is "recession"; "depression" marks one extreme of the spectrum. Many people—including economists—thought that the 2007–2009 recession would degenerate into a depression of many years. "We are in a depression," Richard Posner wrote at the beginning of 2009 in a book whose subtitle was *The Crisis of '08 and the Descent into Depression*.[10] We now know that the recession has fallen far short of a depression, although mistaken policies could produce a second dip.

Compared with the Great Depression, the recent recession was minor. During the Great Depression, real gross domestic product (GDP) (the total of all final goods produced in the United States) declined by 26.7 percent, unemployment shot up to some 25 percent of the labor force,[11] and the Dow Jones Industrial Average (an index of the share prices of the 30 largest U.S. industrial corporations) dropped by 86 percent. In the 2007–2009 recession, the corresponding numbers were 3.7 percent, 10.1 percent, and 41 percent. In some respects, the recent recession was worse than the one that hit in 1981–1982: in the latter, real GDP decreased by 2.6 percent, and the Dow Jones dropped by 23 percent. If we add to the 1981–1982 recession the one that occurred shortly before in 1980, then the combined, double-dip 1980–1982 recession looks worse than the recent one. An indication that the Great Depression was deeper is that that the general price level decreased by 24 percent, while it continued increasing slowly through most of the recent recession, and was subject to relatively high inflation in 1981–1982.[12] Yet, the 2007–2009 recession has been a memorable recession, whose political consequences will be major. Many people clamored for government intervention, and the government was happy to oblige.

Can recessions and depressions be prevented, and how? Most people seem to think that policymakers can. Alan Greenspan, the Fed chairman from 1987 to 2006, was hailed as a thaumaturge who could control the money supply such as to smooth the cycle and prevent recessions. Journalist Bob Woodward wrote a book about him entitled *Maestro*. John McCain, when he was running in the 2000 presidential Republican primary, joked that he would reappoint the aging Fed chairman even if he were to die: "I'd prop him up and put a pair of dark glasses on him and keep him as long as we could." Greenspan would sit in his bathtub to read statistics and determine what should be the price of all goods in terms of money.[13] But, as *The Economist* noted, "[o]ne day, investors will realise central bankers are not magicians." The magazine added, "That might be another Black Monday," referring to October 19, 1987, when the Dow Jones Industrial Average dropped by 23 percent.[14]

When confronted with depressions and depression scares, people wonder if there is somebody in charge, and hope that there is. In the run-up to the 2008 presidential election, *National Review* editor Ramesh Ponnuru said, "what people above all are looking for right now is a sense that there's somebody in charge."[15] The British Foreign Office Minister, Lord Malloch-Brown, hoped that the April 2009 G20 London summit would demonstrate that "there's someone in charge out there."[16] Nobel Prize-winning economist Paul Krugman hails the "macroeconomic managers."[17] References to "adult supervision"[18] are another expression of this appeal to authority, as is the proliferation of administrative "czars"—from the energy czar to the AIDS czar, the drug czar, the intelligence czar, the regulation czar, and up to the recent remuneration czar (aka Special Master for TARP Executive Compensation). Is it time to appoint a top czar, the czar of czars, *the* Czar? The phenomenon is not new: "There is a sense people are getting that no one is in charge," says Professor John Nye to explain the reaction against the growth of impersonal markets in the eighteenth and nineteenth centuries.[19]

The need for somebody to be in charge seems obvious. Or is it? Can somebody really be in charge? In Chapter 1, I will consider the limits of authority. Yet, if somebody is, or tries to be, in charge, can we expect more good than harm? I address this question in the rest of the book.

Consider the many complex fields of human endeavor where everything works better for most people when nobody is in charge. Language is a complex and changing set of nuanced words, abstruse syntax rules, and fuzzy meanings which allow for the expression of a near-infinity of sentiments, emotions, images, concepts, and ideas. Although purists regularly invoke the specter of language corruption, who would think that putting a committee in charge of forcibly regulating language would yield useful results?[20] Love relationships provide a similar example: millions of men and women meet in a systemic disorder with great risks to themselves and their potential offspring. Shouldn't there be somebody in charge, some authority that would pair the best matched couples? Shouldn't the Russian state prevent the emigration of Russian women intent on marrying Western men, as the Liberal Democratic Party of Russia proposed? "Our wonderful women are the best in the world," declared the proponent of the measure.[21] Other complex areas where the same arguments for some central authority to be in charge would seem to apply include the rearing of children, moral rules, religion, and science. What is different between these fields and the cycle of booms and recessions? Why shouldn't someone be in charge of all complex problems and opportunities in life?

One answer is that economic problems are different and that some, like recessions, need to be controlled by authority. In Chapter 2, I will consider what recessions are, and whether or not they are self-correcting without somebody in charge. Think of that chapter as a crash course in macroeconomics, but one that the noneconomist can understand with a minimum of jargon and effort.

Whether or not the authorities can or should be in charge of the economy, we must ask what happens when they try to be. In chapters 3–5, we will see that before the 2007–2009 recession, somebody *was* in charge. The authorities were trying hard to be in charge of the economy in general (Chapter 3), of banking and finance (Chapter 4), and of the mortgage and housing market (Chapter 5). Chapter 6 inquires into whether the policies adopted by the monetary authorities before the crisis bear some responsibility.

Is it really more absurd to talk about "our women" than to expect somebody in charge to save "our markets," as the Securities and Exchange Commission claims?[22] Saving our economy is what the federal government was and is proposing. In his January 27, 2009, State of the Union address, President Barack Obama talked about "our people," "our jobs," and even "our First Lady."[23] Who are "we"? What is the "we" that will be in charge? Chapter 7 will examine such questions—and many other related issues. It will try to look in a realistic way at how the authorities make decisions.

I ask my reader to forget what he has been hearing and reading about the economic crisis and to be prepared for surprises. Let's keep our minds open to all sides of the ideological debate. Let's not be afraid to ask fundamental questions, and try to see what underlies the economic crisis. Perhaps it is a different crisis than what we thought it was.

CHAPTER 1

The Limits of Authority

. . . in the great chess-board of human society, every single piece has a principle of motion of its own, altogether different from that which the legislature might chuse to impress upon it. If those two principles coincide and act in the same direction, the game of human society will go on easily and harmoniously, and is very likely to be happy and successful. If they are opposite or different, the game will go on miserably, and the society must be at all times in the highest degree of disorder.

—Adam Smith[1]

A modern economy is an incredibly complex system. Can Authority manage it?

By "Authority" I mean political authorities—"the state," in the sense of organized political power at all levels (federal, "state," and local) and in all branches (legislative, executive, and judiciary). American usage—unfortunate usage, I think—takes "state" to refer mainly to the federation's basic entities, which diverts attention from the general use of the term, as the whole apparatus of government. Using the generic "Authority" in this chapter will allow me to emphasize better the "somebody in charge" that many have been calling for. Paradoxically, in an epoch supposed to be marked by freedom and individualism, the concept of authority has taken a nearly sacred connotation provided it is dressed in democratic clothes. Witness the ubiquitous "the authorities" and "czars." The capital "A" I use for "Authority" in this chapter will remind us of this quasi-sacred character of political authority.

Social Complexity

Society, in which the economy is imbedded, is a very complex system. The first source of complexity lies in the diversity of individuals and their preferences. Think of people like Paris Hilton and Sarah Palin, Madonna and

Leonard Cohen, Bill Gates and Hugh Hefner. Think of the individuals you know who share personality traits with the celebrities just mentioned. Think of urbanites and rednecks, Christians and atheists, wine drinkers and tee-totalers, amateurs of French cuisine and consumers of fast food, geeks and technophobes, smokers and vegetarians, old and young consumers . . . Think about the richness of individual personalities, their life experience, their goals and desires. All these individuals have to live together and peacefully compete for resources. A simple social system will not accommodate all this diversity.

A second source of social complexity lies in the production system that responds to diversified individual preferences. In 2008, final goods and services worth $14 trillion were produced in the United States. Of these goods and services, households consumed $10 trillion (the rest was consumption by government, exports, and capital goods for investment).[2] Ten trillion is a very big number. Counting to 10,000,000,000,000 would take 317,000 years at one number per second. Ten trillion seconds ago, man was just appearing on this planet. These 10 trillion dollars of goods and services cover millions of different goods and services: food and drinks, clothing, housing, health, transportation, communications, recreation, education, financial services, et cetera. To produce these goods and services, millions of different inputs or "factors of production" (different materials and forms of energy, different types of labor, different sorts of capital goods, etc.) are needed. All the transactions in the American economy, including both final goods and the inputs to produce them, amount to $26 trillion a year (data for 2008).[3] These goods and services must be available when and where the consumers want them, and when and where the producers need them to produce other goods. Something produced but not available to consumers is as good as if it had never been produced, which is why the economic concept of production (as used in this book) includes marketing, transportation, and distribution.

What economists call a "good" has physical features that allow it to be resold. A "service"—a haircut or a doctor's examination, for example—can be exchanged only once. Apart from this, there is no distinction between a good and a service, and the first term is often used generically to include the second.

Every good requires for its production a long series of inputs and processes. Journalist Leonard Read told the story of a simple pencil, as it was made circa 1958.[4] It apparently started with Northern California or Oregon cedar fell by loggers armed with chain saws, and transported to the railroad siding. In fact, the story began much earlier than this: hemp, ore, steel, food, and many other goods and services had to be produced before the logging camps could operate. A train transported the logs—imagine what had been necessary to build the train—to a mill in San Leandro, California. There, the logs were cut into small slats, tinted, waxed, and dried. Picture what had been required in all these production processes, from the machines to the electric power. The pencil factory itself was even more complicated. Graphite mined in Ceylon and shipped to the United States was mixed with Mississippi clay, treated with Mexico wax, and run through several chemical processes before being inserted into each small slat. Six coats of lacquer were applied to each pencil. Produced with castor oil among other ingredients, lacquer had an industrial history of its own, too long to tell here. The pencil was marked, and received a metal ferrule and a tiny eraser. The manufacturing of the ferrule with brass and black nickel was an engineering and economic adventure in itself. The eraser required rapeseed oil from the West Indies.

Countless individuals cooperated in these production processes, most of them not knowing the child in a New Hampshire school who would owe them his pencil. As Read says, talking on behalf of the pencil, "not a single person on the face of this earth knows how to make me." A related and remarkable fact is that nobody had planned the production of this pencil and its uncountable inputs, and nobody would know how to plan it. It would be very difficult for a "pencil czar" to produce pencils or, at least, quality pencils.

How the wood pencil has nearly disappeared, replaced by automatic pencils and computer keyboards, is barely more extraordinary. Yet, the traditional pencil has not completely disappeared, as there still exists some demand for it: such is the diversity of individual circumstances and preferences.

Producing a laptop is incredibly more complex than the already complex production of a pencil. Imagine that some event—say, a nuclear war—has destroyed all factories, and we need to build laptops anew. This would first require manufacturing plastic, transistors, silicon wafers, and microprocessors, and everything that enters into these inputs and everything necessary to produce the latter, and so forth. Try to follow the chain of all the machines necessary to manufacture the machines necessary to manufacture the machines, and so forth. Producing laptops also requires finance, that is, finding individuals willing to forego satisfying their wants in order that machines may be produced and labor hired to manufacture computer components, and putting the savers in touch with the investors. And all these operations have to be coordinated through time and space. Moreover, trade-offs have to be made between using plastic for Bach CDs or for laptop components, that is, consumption too has to be coordinated across different goods.

The situation would be even worse if all libraries and bookstores had been destroyed, and all the theories necessary to understand and build computers needed to be reformulated. No single individual knows how to build a laptop, and thinking about the industrial and financial infrastructure necessary to do it is mind-boggling. No wonder that centrally planned communist economies were not able to produce personal computers. In China, entrepreneurs had to be given some free rein and Western technology imported before it could be done; Lenovo had to buy the PC division of IBM before they could manufacture computers that would appeal to world consumers. Producing complex industrial goods is a great social adventure.

Coordination and information are keywords in the story of the pencil and the laptop. The main problem of an economy and of the whole society is how the actions of numerous individuals can be coordinated. This requires that the information dispersed among all of them be used in the decisions of what to do and what to produce. Without this information, coordination is blind, mismatches will occur between what is wanted and what is produced, and individual opportunities will not be maximized in any meaningful sense. Friedrich Hayek, winner of the 1974 Nobel Prize in economics, developed the idea that social complexity is based on an efficient use of information in coordinating individual actions. Imagine, he said, that a new use for tin has increased this metal's demand somewhere; alternatively, you may imagine that tin supply has been reduced. Efficient coordination of tin consumers and producers requires that the new scarcity be somehow communicated to all so that they take the new fact into account, each one in his own decisions. Free market prices play this role. The price of tin will increase. Most users ignore the cause of the price increase, but consumers get the signal that they should consume less tin and producers are informed that they should produce more. Local information has spread to the whole system.[5] All acts of consumption (or of nonconsumption) and all costs are thus signaled to everybody, so that individuals coordinate their actions given other people's actions. And like in the production of a pencil, nobody has been in charge.

Complex Finance

Finance illustrates social complexity and the issues related to information and coordination. Some individuals in society prefer to postpone their consumption to the future and others to consume now; in other words, at any given time, some prefer to save, others to borrow. Finance is the process whereby savers transfer control over resources to borrowers—and everybody tries to protect himself against the risks involved in this sort of transactions. The resources that don't serve to produce (say) wine now will serve to build a winery (or whatever the saver will want to consume later). Some consumer may also choose to borrow from other consumers, who want to save. Finance is thus tied to the "real" economy, to people making consumption and production choices.

The financial sector is made of institutions that intermediate between lenders and borrowers (or manage the risk of this intermediation). Banks were, for a long time, the main intermediaries. You would save $100 and lend it to—deposit it in—a bank, which would lend it to somebody else. A bank's balance sheet is simple: its liabilities are its depositors' money plus its other borrowings (the bonds it issues to investors) and shareholders' equity; its assets are composed of its loans and other investments. If savers change their way of doing things and lend their $100 directly to a final borrower or invest it in shares of stock, the process is called "disintermediation"—bypassing the (banking) intermediaries. The development of capital markets where firms can borrow more directly from savers has been part of the disintermediation process. What often happened, though, was a change of intermediaries. Other vehicles for pooling savers' money have replaced banks and formed the "shadow banking system," where "near banks" started doing what banks had traditionally done: borrowing money short term and relending it long term. The nearly $1 trillion in residential mortgages issued during 2006, for example, essentially came from the shadow banking system, which financed it with short-term debt, including ABCP. During that same year, businesses increased their net financial liabilities by $185 billion, which they raised from many corners of the financial markets.[6] These numbers are not important except to start getting an impression of the complexity of modern finance.

Financial markets are huge. They are also difficult to measure. A loan to you increases your liabilities and the assets of your lender; if you are both in the "household sector," these cancel out when the sector's assets and liabilities are netted out. The total size of the financial sector thus depends on how you define the sectors and what is netted out. The broader the sectors' definitions, the more netting out and the more the measure of the financial sector shrinks. By whatever measure, however, the financial sector is huge. By a standard measure, all financial liabilities (and all financial assets) in the United States exceed $60 trillion, of which about $10 trillion are residential mortgages and $4 trillion government debt (data for 2006).[7] In normal times, about $2 trillion of new assets and liabilities are created every year.[8] The estimates are for the United States only, and do not take into account most financial assets and liabilities in the rest of the world.

These estimates do not include derivatives (options, futures, swaps, etc.), whose price depends on the price of the underlying securities. Derivatives are valued at close to $600 trillion in the world, if you measure them by the value of the underlying securities or commodities, or at some $15 trillion using the market prices at which the derivatives themselves are traded.[9]

These huge financial markets limit Authority's power. There is no question that government agencies like the Fed have much power. They can impose and enforce regulations, and contraveners are liable to heavy fines or jail terms, so people generally abide by the rules. Government is a major player in financial markets, with $200-$300 billion of annual borrowing before 2008, or 10 percent of total borrowing. In 2008, with reduced private borrowing and humongous federal deficits, the amount of government borrowing exceeded $1 trillion and amounted to more than two-thirds of all borrowing.[10] It remains that in normal times, that is, before the recent crisis, government financing still amounted to only a portion of U.S. financial markets, not to mention global financial markets. The authorities are not omnipotent on financial markets.

The power of the Fed to move interest rates with its standard monetary intervention tools is easily exaggerated. Even after the more than doubling of its assets to slightly over $2 trillion in mid-2009, the Fed's weight in the U.S. financial markets (conservatively measured without the derivatives markets) is less than 5 percent. A firm with a market share of 5 percent probably has some influence on prices, but it does not literally control them. Influenced by the media and the misleading name of "federal funds," many people think that the Fed sets the so-called federal funds rate, which is the interbank rate at which banks lend to each other on a very short-term basis (usually one day) in order to cover the reserves they maintain on their deposits. Even financial reporters fall into the trap: "The central bank steers the economy," wrote a *Wall Street Journal* reporter, "by setting short-term interest rates."[11] The Fed does not set short-term interest rates. It only set targets for the federal funds rate, and tries to reach them through open market operations. Open market operations mean that the Fed sells to banks government securities that it owns, exerting downward pressure on their prices and therefore upward pressure on their yields or interest rates, or that alternatively it buys government securities from banks, exerting upward pressure on their prices and therefore downward pressure on their yields or interest rates. When one short-term interest rate is influenced, other short-term interest rates follow, because all lenders will try to lend where the rates are higher, and all borrowers to borrow where they are cheaper, which tends to equalize rates.

It is important to understand one simple technical point: the yield or interest rate of a bond varies inversely with its price. If a bond worth $100 carries a $4 interest coupon per year, its yield (or actual interest rate) is 4 percent. If its price on the market rises to $133, the $4 coupon implies a yield of 3 percent.

The Fed's influence is limited because it can normally buy or sell only a relatively small proportion of existing government securities—at most a quarter of them before the crisis. (During the crisis it assumed new powers that increased its influence on interest rates.) This means a sizeable influence on short-term rates (the ones that are targeted), but not omnipotence. Indeed, the actual or "effective" federal funds rate stayed stubbornly higher than the target rate for two months after the latter was cut at the beginning of the crisis.[12]

Although the Fed succeeded in pushing down short-term interest rates starting in mid-2007, long-term rates did not follow. Nobody could purchase a 30-year mortgage at the federal fund rates of less than 1 percent. In fact, high-rated corporate bond yields even increased slightly in late 2008 while, at the same time, junk-bond rates (rates on low-rated corporate bonds) went through the roof.[13] This observation is related to what determines the term structure of interest rates, also called "the yield curve": long-term interest rates are usually higher than short-term rates, because they carry more risk of default or inflation (but the curve sometimes gets inverted). In October 2009, for example, the federal funds rate was 0.15 percent (nearly zero), the bank prime rate (the lowest rate the banks charge on short-term business loans) 3.25 percent, the 30-year mortgage rate 5.06 percent, and the yield on long-term corporate bonds 5.13 percent. If the Fed can influence short-term rates, is it able to influence long-term rates? To a certain extent, yes, because the spread between rates of different maturities cannot be too large, due to arbitrage: if investors think that long-term interest rates are too high compared with short-term rates, they will contract short-term loans, increasing short-term rates, and use these loans to relend long, bringing long-term interest rates down. Financial institutions will, for example, issue commercial paper (short-term loans on capital markets) and offer long-term mortgages, which is exactly what happened in the years running up to the crisis. The Fed can use "quantitative easing" to try and influence long-term interest rates, but this tool is also of limited influence. The point is that even if the Fed can influence interest rates, its power is indirect and far from unlimited.

A form of private money creation also limits or dilutes Authority's power. The way central banks like the Fed try to stimulate economic activity is by increasing the money supply—which is called an expansive monetary policy. Conversely, a restrictive monetary policy means reducing the money supply. These policies are (or were) mainly carried out through open market operations. The Fed increases the money supply by buying government securities from banks, and crediting its purchase to the accounts the banks keep with it. Inversely, the Fed decreases the money supply by selling government securities to banks, and debiting their accounts. In a "fractional" banking system, like all contemporary banking systems, banks don't keep 100 percent reserves: they lend some of the money depositors have lent them. It is because banks lend part of their deposits that they can pay interest on them. Banks are obliged by law to keep some reserves to cover their deposits and be able to redeem them when depositors make withdrawals. Of course, they would also keep some reserves in the absence of any legal obligation: in early nineteenth-century Scotland, where banking was unregulated, banks kept about 2–3 percent of their deposits in reserves.[14] Now, the compulsory reserve ratio in the United States is about 10 percent. When the Fed buys or sells securities, the banks expand or reduce credit to private borrowers as they end up with, respectively, more or less money to lend. This process leads to a (positive or negative) multiplication of credit and thus money through the whole banking system. The process is known as the "money multiplier."

To visualize what happens, suppose the Fed buys $100 worth of government securities from Bank A. (Bank A is not obliged to sell but the Fed bids up the price of the securities it wants to buy.) Bank A now has $100 more in reserve. With a required reserve ratio of 10 percent, it will lend $90 more (because it wants to earn interest income). Whoever gets this loan will spend it, increasing the deposit of somebody else by $90 at Bank B. Bank B, which also faces a reserve ratio of 10 percent, will lend 90 percent of the $90, that is, $81. Deposits at Bank C are increased by $81, which will give rise to $72.90 in new loans, and so forth. Adding $100 + $90 + $81 + $72.90 + ... to infinity, it can be calculated that the result will be $1,000. More generally, the money multiplier is equal to the inverse of the required reserve ratio: if the ratio is 10 percent, the multiplier is ten; if it were 20 percent, the multiplier would be five; and so forth.

An increase in the bank reserves generates credit by a multiple of the original increase. Inversely, a decrease in bank reserves leads to a multiple contraction of credit. Through this credit process, the supply of money is increased or decreased in the economy. The central bank—the Fed in the United States—must always take into account the money multiplier when it plays with the money supply. It must always take into account the repercussions of its actions on the banks' decisions, and their cascading effect.

Moreover, the banks can always decide to keep more reserves, and to limit credit more, than what the mechanical operation of the money multiplier would dictate. If the Fed buys government securities (or private securities, as it did during the recent recession) but the capacity of private borrowers to honor their commitments is in doubt, the banks may decide to hold to their money instead of lending it. Inversely, if the central bank moves to restrict credit, banks can restrict it even more by keeping more money in their reserves. The power of the Fed on private banks is limited—at least as long as the banks are private and make independent decisions. The Fed must always take into account the expectations and incentives of participants in financial markets. The Fed can try to "pump money into the economy" but it will not work if banks hoard the money because they have no confidence that economic conditions will allow borrowers to honor their commitments. In a complex monetary economy, managing around incentives and expectations is not an easy task.

Finance constrains Authority in other, more direct ways. It creates an incentive for governments to maintain good ratings with credit rating agencies, because the interest rate at which they will be able to borrow depends on their lenders' confidence. The holders of government securities are the domestic public, banks, and foreign governments. A government with a lower credit rating will have to pay a higher interest. As a consequence, governments have an incentive not only to pay the agreed interest and to reimburse the capital at maturity, but also to manage their budgets in a way that does not scare their lenders.

It is a well-known economic fact that well-functioning financial markets further economic growth. For example, the World Bank estimates that if financial markets double the amount of private capital available to businesses in a developing country, the rate of economic growth will be two percentage points higher. This implies that GDP will double in 35 years compared with what it would otherwise have been. Of two countries that start with a difference of two percentage points in annual economic growth, one will end up, after 35 years, with a standard of living double that of the other.[15]

A last point must be noted about how finance constrains Authority. Modern financial markets not only allow entrepreneurial individuals to raise capital more easily for their projects, they also allow people to move their financial capital across national borders. Note that the term "capital" can mean either real assets (like machines and building), which produce other goods, or financial capital, the claims on real capital and the goods it produces. When we say that financial capital is mobile, we mean that people can obtain claims on real assets in foreign countries, and thus move their claims from one country to another by selling in one and buying in another. One advantage of this international mobility of capital is diversification, as people can hold assets in different countries. Another advantage is to make confiscation of assets by national governments more difficult. Either directly or through intermediaries (pension plans, mutual funds, etc.), people can invest their savings all over the world. As Professor Reuven Brenner of McGill University argues, finance is a democratizing force.[16]

The Impossibility of Planning

One objection to the difficulty of Authority in dealing with incentives and expectations is that it needs only to use force to be obeyed even if it is democratic. Democratic governments do use force when necessary. Authority can coordinate by force. After all, it has all the guns—or, if the right to keep and bear arms is entrenched in the Constitution, most of the firepower any-way. In other words, Authority can coordinate the economy by planning it. Planning ultimately requires the use of force in order to enforce planning laws and decrees. It is not without reason that "force" is a part of "enforcement." Authority can decide, directly or indirectly, what will be produced, how, and for whom. This, however, is more difficult than appears at first sight.

Authority must strike a compromise between force and consent: the more force it uses, the less consent (even if only tacit) it can marshal. To remain in power and to govern on a day-to-day basis, Authority needs the consent (at least passive) of a large portion of the population. Obtaining consent is a big part of the art of politics, and a big part of Authority's chores, as a rich tradition of economics and political science discourse has pointed out.[17] In a regime based on brute, unmediated force, the rulers continuously fear for their power and their lives. Lest the people conspire, freedom of speech is curtailed. This removes the only reliable feedback on the people's real situa-tion, their complaints and wishes, for the rulers cannot rely on information from their subordinates, who fear for their jobs or their lives if they have failed to attain the objectives of the Plan. As force becomes less predictable and more arbitrary, the incentives of the subjects to produce and save dimin-ish, and less tax can be extracted from them. The least consent Authority obtains, the most difficult and costly it is to rule, and the fewer benefits the rulers get for themselves. From the rulers' own viewpoint, it is better to rule mildly over a wealthy country than to rule by brute force over a des-titute people. In its own interest, Authority will try to increase consent and eschew arbitrary force. University of Maryland economist Mancur Olson has shown how an enlightened ruler, whether democratic or not, will maximize his tax revenues by moderating the tax rate he levies on his subjects.[18] No regime can avoid the necessity of managing around people's incentives and expectations.

Planning, it will be objected, does not necessarily imply brute and arbi-trary force. It can work through incentives like "indicative planning," French style.[19] Yet, economic planning implies that Authority—even if, in some sense, it represents the wishes of a majority—replaces the market's alloca-tion of resources and distribution of income by its own decisions. Authority assumes part of the market's coordination rule—that part which is not the black market. Controlling prices directly or through manipulation of supply or demand is inseparable from economic planning. This, however, distorts prices, and the planner deprives himself of the only medium that carries extensive information about the scarcity of resources compared with people's preferences. Remember Hayek's example of tin. The limited knowledge of the planner—which in practice is a planning commissariat and a structure of planning bureaus—replaces the dispersed knowledge about local circumstances and diversified individual preferences that prices conveyed. The problems of central planning, its incapacity to deliver the goods, are inherent in its mission, which requires replacing decentralized decision making and coordination by Authority's limited information and blind diktats.

Communism was as good a laboratory experiment about socialism as one could hope for, and it lasted during most of the twentieth century. Starting in the 1920s, Ludwig von Mises and Friedrich Hayek led a debate on what they believed was the impossibility of socialism because of the impossibility of making meaningful economic calculation under central planning.[20] Economist Ludwig von Mises was a major participant on Hayek's side in the debate. Their thesis was vindicated by the fall of communism half a century later, and the general recognition of the terrible inefficiency of central planning. Professor Bryan Caplan of George Mason University points out that perhaps more than the calculation problem, what fell communism was an incentives problem: in a socialized and bureaucratized society, nobody has any incentive to be efficient.[21] If socialism is not literally impossible, it is certainly impossible as an efficient system. Coordination by Authority is incapable of providing a decent level of opportunities to the people.

The indictment of planning does not only doom the most centralized and totalitarian forms of planning. It's all a question of degree: much planning creates many problems; a little planning creates fewer problems. In all cases, planning is a simplifying process that limits social complexity and efficiency. Mussolini declared: "We were the first to assert that the more complicated the forms assumed by civilization, the more restricted the freedom of the individual must become."[22] Hayek's argument is the exact opposite of Mussolini's claim: it is when Authority leaves individuals more or less alone that civilization can become complex and the economy efficient. Freedom does not impede social complexity, it generates it.

When, in our freer societies, Authority tries to be in charge of complex economic processes, we observe some aspects of the impossibility of planning. The authorities were as much unable to forecast the economic crisis as private agents were. Most people, including regulators and politicians, did not see red flags in the explosion of the mortgage market; as I will document in Chapter 5, government actors actually welcomed the most dangerous developments and threw oil on the fire. Economist Arnold Kling correctly notes that "[i]t is difficult to have confidence that regulators will be able to distinguish ex ante the dangerous innovations from the benign ones."[23]

Consider how the federal government responded to the crisis that developed in the summer of 2007. Investment bank Bear Stearns was bailed out in March 2008 but another investment bank, Lehman Brothers, was allowed to fail six months later. A few weeks later, the government shifted gears again and rescued American International Group (AIG), an insurance company heavily involved in financial markets.[24] The Emergency Economic Stabilization Act (EESA) of October 3, 2008, empowered the Treasury to spend up to $699 billion on the TARP, which aimed at purchasing troubled assets from banks but soon changed its mission.[25] In February 2009, Congress passed the American Recovery and Reinvestment Act, which contained $787 billion of stimulus money, of which about 60 percent was in new expenditures targeting a wide range of politically attractive projects that the *Wall Street Journal* described as a "40-Year Wish List."[26] Spending rapidly such a huge amount of money is impossible: the government expected it would take more than a year and a half to expend (in expenditures or tax cuts) three-quarters of the money.[27] Barth et al. politely refer to "a series of flip-flops that have exacerbated the uncertainty gripping the marketplace"[28] and the "zigzagging from one approach to another."[29]

Despite all its computers and surveillance apparatus, the contemporary state knows relatively little on what's happening in the economy. It has to rely on global, aggregate statistics. Consider GDP, a measure of all production within a given country. Even without considering the theoretical shortcomings of the measure, its statistical measurement is so fraught with difficulty that published data are regularly revised. Jeffrey Hummel, a professor of economics at San Jose State University, noted in August 2009 that the BEA (Bureau of Economic Analysis, the Department of Commerce agency responsible for measuring GDP) had just revised the (annualized) rate of decline of (real) GDP for the first quarter of the year to 6.4 percent from the previous figure of 6.1 percent. This previously published figure was itself revising a preliminary estimate of 5.7 percent and a first final revision of 5.5 percent. Hummel explains that these revisions are routine, and often consequential. In the fourth quarter of 2007, the cyclical peak before the recession, according to the National Bureau of Economic Research (NBER), a private organization that dates U.S. recessions, the BEA first calculated that real GDP had dropped by 0.2 percent but later revised the figure to a 2.1 percent increase. Moreover, Professor Hummel continues, the BEA (like other national statistical agencies) regularly publishes comprehensive revisions of the whole series going back to 1929. These revisions sometimes require some reinterpretation of economic history. For example, the 1990 revision found a major recession just after World War II, of which nobody had been aware; but then, the severity of this recession was attenuated by a more recent revision that changed the way inflation is taken out of nominal GDP to get the constant-dollar or real estimates.[30] These incorrect estimates and revisions do not point to bad statistical work, but to the simple fact that GDP is a complex concept whose measure is, even with the best statisticians, fraught with problems.

Research shows that errors in estimates that are corrected when more comprehensive census data become available are now relatively small, that is, of the order of 1 percent of GDP levels on average. Similarly, initial quarterly estimates are correct (compared with posterior revisions) 98 percent of the times as pertains to the direction of GDP change, and 75 percent of the times as to whether the change is accelerating or decelerating.[31] Yet, urgent decisions of fiscal and monetary policy rely on these figures.

The Great Depression can be viewed as a humongous illustration of economic complexity and the difficulty for Authority to forecast, prevent, or cure recessions. The depression lasted from 1929 to 1933, by which time real GDP had dropped by 27 percent and prices by 26 percent, which means that nominal GDP lost about 53 percent. In 1933, per capita real income had nearly reverted to its level of 1908, a recession year.[32] One major problem during the Great Depression was that some 20 percent (of the roughly 25,000[33]) banks failed. The cooperation between private banks that, before the 1930s, had limited the impact of bank panics did not work this time, "possibly because self-regulation was pre-empted by the control of the Federal Reserve System,"[34] says Columbia University professor Charles Calomiris. After the establishment of the Federal Reserve System in 1914, there was no incentive for banks to cooperate as they had done, under the leadership of banker J.P. Morgan, to counter the banking crisis of 2007. The Fed was now in charge.[35]

The Great Depression deepened not only despite the creation of the Federal Reserve System 15 years before, but also despite the economic activism of Herbert Hoover, who was U.S. president from early 1929 to March 1933. Contrary to conventional wisdom, Hoover did not follow laissez-faire policies to counter the crisis—although he was in some ways less interventionist than his successor, Franklin D. Roosevelt. During his four years in office, Hoover increased annual federal expenditures by 48 percent (from $3.1 billion in 1929 to $4.6 billion in 1933), and transformed a surplus of $734 million into a deficit of $2.6 billion. If you take into account the 26 percent price drop, Hoover's expenditure record is comparable to Roosevelt's increase of 65 percent during his first term (from $4.6 billion in 1933 to $7.6 billion in 1937), a time when prices stopped decreasing. On the deficit front, Hoover can be considered looser than Roosevelt: the latter brought the Hoover deficit down to $2.2 billion in 1937, after a peak to $4.3 billion in 1936; even at this peak, Roosevelt increased the deficit by less ($1.7 billion) than what Hoover had done.[36] Note again that Hoover's dollars were worth more than Roosevelt's. Hoover later wrote about his policies during the Great Depression:

> We might have done nothing. That would have been utter ruin. Instead we met the situation with proposals to private business and to Congress of the most gigantic program of economic defense and counterattack ever evolved in the history of the Republic. . . .
>
> Some of the reactionary economists urged that we should allow the liquidation to take its course until we had found bottom. . . . We determined that we would not follow the advice of the bitter-end liquidationists . . . [37]

A good case can be made that the Great Depression was caused or at least worsened by mistaken government policies.[38] The standard interpretation has been proposed by Milton Friedman, laureate of the 1976 Nobel Prize in economics: the Fed allowed the money stock to decrease until 1933, transforming into a deep depression what would otherwise have been an ordinary recession like the preceding ones.[39] The Smoot-Hawley Act, signed by President Hoover on June 17, 1930, increased tariffs on dutiable imports by 17–20 percent, provoking retaliation from other countries, and further reducing trade and production. More than a thousand economists had unsuccessfully petitioned Hoover to veto the bill: although they were deeply divided on the monetary and fiscal policy, economists were nearly unanimous against protectionism.[40] Economist Thomas Rustici argues that the Smoot-Hawley Act, which had been debated in Congress several months before the stock exchange crash of October 1929, was a major factor in starting the Great Depression.[41] Many other policies of Roosevelt quite certainly worsened the contraction, including tax increases (in 1932) and the anticompetitive legislation that mandated business cartels and encouraged trade union power. Not only rich men were arbitrarily prosecuted by the Roosevelt administration, but also little businessmen, guilty of violating the absurd anticompetitive codes of the National Recovery Act of 1933.[42] All this scared businessmen and investors.

Roosevelt gave many examples of the ignorance and irrationality of the central planner. In many ways, economic planning is voodoo. Amity Shlaes relates this episode among others:

> One morning, FDR told his group he was thinking of raising the gold price by twenty-one cents. Why that figure? his entourage asked. "It's a lucky number," Roosevelt said, "because it's three time seven."[43]

Although Roosevelt is widely credited with ending the Great Depression, unemployment remained over 20 percent during the first 21 consecutive months of the Roosevelt Administration, and never fell below double digits during its first seven years. A second recession hit in 1936–1937. Unemployment was still 14.6 percent in 1940. In fact, a real recovery did not show up until 1941, when the United States entered the war.[44] Thomas Sowell, a well-known Hoover Institution economist, writes:

> In short, the war ended the New Deal—and the end of the New Deal saw the economy recover, as it had recovered from depressions on its own throughout the history of the country prior to the 1930s.[45]

For a long time, many economists believed that the Great Depression was an "outlier," a one-time statistical event that would never be repeated. Thanks to macroeconomic theories developed after economist John Maynard Keynes, serious economic recessions were thought to be a thing of the past. The Employment Act of 1946 had declared that "it is the continuing policy and responsibility of the Federal Government . . . to promote maximum employment, production, and purchasing power."[46] The 1966 Report of the Council of Economic Advisers (CEA) concluded:

> Twenty years of experience have demonstrated our ability to avoid ruinous inflations and severe depressions. It is now within our capabilities to set more ambitious goals. We strive to avoid recurrent recessions, to keep unemployment far below the rates of the past decade, to maintain essential price stability at full employment, to move towards the Great Society, and, indeed, to make full prosperity the normal state of the American economy. It is a tribute to our success under the Employment Act that we now have not only the economic understanding but also the will and determination to use economic policy as an effective tool of progress.[47]

The recession of 2007–2009 was to prove that "we," including Authority, did not have either the economic understanding or the will or both.

Entrepreneurship and Innovation

Another sort of obstacle on the shining path of Authority is the entrepreneur and the innovator. The entrepreneur is the one who finds new, more efficient ways to satisfy consumer demand. Although he may become rich, he often starts as a marginal who competes against the economic establishment. The entrepreneur is an innovator in the sense that he invents new ways to do things, but he may not be an innovator in the usual sense of product innovation. Entrepreneurial innovation need not be technological—it can also improve marketing, distribution, or finance. The entrepreneur is necessarily an innovator, but the innovator is not necessarily an entrepreneur. Innovation necessarily involves risk: the innovator is never sure to succeed. The explanation of American prosperity probably lies in the complex of entrepreneurship, innovation, and risk that is so typical of the American economy. Just think that virtually all of the innovations of the last century have come from America. And these innovations could only materialize into new products by waging what the great economist Joseph Schumpeter called "creative destruction," the replacement of old industries or production processes by new ones. The car industry all but eliminated the buggy industry. The slide rule industry has been totally destroyed by the manufacturers of pocket calculators. Personal computers have more or less eliminated the job of typist. Polaroid photography was destroyed by electronic cameras. Junk bonds allowed medium businesses to access the capital market for loans. Online retailers are shaking the retail industry. And so forth.

Innovators and entrepreneurs bring new financial products on the market. Take the credit default swap (CDS), a financial instrument invented in the late 1990s that insures the holder of a security against default of the security's issuer.[48] In 2008, CDSs on the market had a value of about $62 trillion.[49] Although CDSs were designed to protect investors against risk, it turned out that they did not provide perfect protection when AIG, a seller of such protection, appeared unable to honor its commitments in March 2008. The company was rescued and nationalized by the federal government. Reducing risk to zero is impossible, and some risk takers will necessarily see their risk turn sour. Risk has costs and benefits, and individuals establish their own tradeoffs between risk and reward. Indeed, the CDS market has survived the crisis because it obviously meets a demand for reducing risk.

The idea that Authority can reduce risk to zero is a mirage as much in financial matters as in life in general. The illusion of zero financial risk partakes in the general mirage of a riskless society. Prohibiting or otherwise stopping people from smoking, eating fat, driving as they please, engaging in risky sports, et cetera, may very well save some lives but at the cost of a big increase in the risk that Authority will create a regimented society. Reducing the risk for some people often increases the danger to others. A down-to-earth (no pun intended) example of this sort of risk shifting was provided by an accident that happened in Scotland in July 2008: a woman who had fallen into a 60-feet deep abandoned mine shaft was not rescued for six hours because the senior fire officer on the scene prevented his men from using ropes to rescue the victim; she died shortly after being finally brought to the surface by a mountain rescue team.[50] Her life was sacrificed in order to protect the safety of the professionals who were supposed to save her.

IF CDSs were a decade old and computer models of risk also quite recent, many financial innovations blamed for the 2007–2009 crisis were much older. Options and futures—trading securities or commodities by setting a future date and price for the actual transaction—have existed for centuries. Short selling—the sale of a borrowed security with the hope of purchasing it at a lower price when the borrowed share needs to be returned—dates back to at least 1609, when the Dutch East India Company complained about shorts to the Amsterdam stock exchange.[51] Commercial paper is two centuries old. Money market funds (mutual funds made of money market instruments) appeared in the 1970s. Securitization of debt obligations is several decades old. Innovation, whether in finance or other fields of human endeavor, is a necessary consequence of entrepreneurship, and is inseparable from modern prosperity.

Entrepreneurs and innovators often constrain Authority because they change the way things are done and the way Authority wants things to be done. But there is another way in which entrepreneurs and innovators limit Authority's power: they constantly try (often legally) to dodge the constraints and regulations Authority wants to impose them. It is impossible to have a nation of "economic" entrepreneurs without also having entrepreneurs in regulatory avoidance. Authority's intervention is always limited by the inventiveness of the entrepreneurs and the innovators. We will see that some of the factors that played in the economic crisis were of that sort: shadow banks developing to compete with overregulated banks, MBSs used to satisfy government-imposed capital requirements, et cetera.

Because a prosperous economy is so complex and so incredibly difficult to coordinate, effective economic planning is impossible, not only in practice but also in theory. The planner cannot know what he would need to know in order to plan efficiently. Authority is constantly outwitted by the entrepreneurs and the innovators. The only way out is to build such a bureaucratic society that all incentives for efficiency and progress are strangled. And if Authority cannot plan, cannot impose structured and coherent policies, it cannot really be in charge.

The Inconvenient Individual

In late August and September 2009, the U.S. Mint noticed a sharp surge in "large repetitive orders" for its $1 coin. In order to put more of these coins in circulation, the Mint was selling boxes of 250 coins at par—that is for $250—and shipping them for free. Small businesses depending on coin machines were among those interested. It was soon discovered that one could buy the coins with a frequent-flyer-miles credit card, deposit the coins in the bank when they were received, pay the credit card purchase with the money, and earn free frequent-flyer miles in the process. Richard Baum, as software consultant, bought 150,000 coins and did not even open the boxes before bringing them to his bank. He was not alone. Banks, who are tied to the government by a thick web of surveillance, started alerting the Mint. More than $1 million in coins were bought by mileage lovers before the Mint put an end to the scheme. "Is this illegal? No. Is it the right thing to do? No," said a Mint spokesman, apparently oblivious to the idea that the rule of law allows the state to stop illegal acts, not acts that it feels are not "the right thing to do."[52]

How do you "run a society" with individuals like these enterprising lovers of frequent-flyer miles? When Authority wants to be in charge, the most serious obstacle it faces, the one that perhaps subsumes all constraints on its power, is the individual, the inconvenient individual. The individual has a way to look for his own interest and undermine Authority's plans.

The existence of the inconvenient individual explains why all attempts to build a new man have ended in concentration camps. Greed is only one manifestation of this self-interest; it is the name given to self-interest in market transactions. Whether he is buying or selling a car, negotiating his salary, or participating in an IPO, the individual tries to buy low and sell high. Greed is certainly not the only sentiment that moves man. In closer forms of interactions, like the family or other small groups, the individual often does things "for free." In one of his two great books, *The Theory of Moral Sentiments*, Adam Smith, one of the founders of economics, the so-called dismal science, identified such behaviors as sympathy or "fellow-feeling" for others.[53] Yet, even in close relationships like friendship or love, there is a sort of barter trade going on, for who would continue loving and giving if it were never reciprocated? In a sense, then, greed underlies anything man does—in fact, everything a living creature does.

In his other masterpiece, *The Wealth of Nations*, Adam Smith wrote: "I have never known much good done by those who affected to trade for the public good."[54] Mankind has not changed since, and much fake altruism lies around. Dan Gifford, a journalist and film director, reports that while top corporate salaries are 411 times the salary of the lowest-paid worker, star actors are often paid 1,000 times more than the lowest-paid person on the set. But, he adds, "[k]eeping in mind that members of the said chattering class do not consider themselves to be part of 'private enterprise,' its members in good standing undoubtedly see their multimillion dollar incomes as exempt [of] the limitations that the pay czar imposes on others."[55] Try and find the logic in the populist sentiments that attack the greed of corporate executives but leave unscathed greedy artists and sport stars.

The idea that recessions are caused by greedy capitalists is untenable. If the claim were true, capitalist countries would always be in recession. If it is argued that recessions are caused by spikes in greed, why these spikes happen at certain times and not at other times would need to be carefully explained. Moreover, as we will see, some of the presumably least greedy people, those "who [affect] to trade for the public good" in public housing agencies and government-sponsored enterprises, were closely associated with the causes of the recent economic turmoil. On the other hand, some people generally portrayed as the worst greedy capitalists did not have anything to do with the crisis. Many consider hedge funds as the incarnation of greed. Hedge funds are pools of money from institutional investors (like pension funds or investment banks) and very wealthy individuals that trade in more risky financial instruments. Despite the bankruptcies of two Bear Stearns hedge funds on July 31, 2007, the crisis did not originate from hedge funds, as many had been expecting. The two Bear Stearns funds had heavily invested in MBSs—a market that, as we will see later, was much promoted by government. And despite several silent and nonsubsidized failures, the total losses of the hedge funds industry were probably more limited than the general losses on stock exchanges. In 2008, the typical hedge fund lost 20 percent,[56] while the Dow Jones Industrial Average dropped by 49 percent and the S&P 500 by 38 percent. Domestic hedge funds were not invested in MBSs more than commercial banks.[57] Some hedge funds actually bet against MBSs, like John Paulson's fund, as we learned from the strange suit that the Securities and Exchange Commission later slammed on investment bank Goldman Sachs.[58]

The problem that many investors, corporations, and families met during this recession was that they were highly leveraged, that is, indebted. Among corporations, leverage can be measured as the ratio between total assets and equity or capital. (It can also be measured as the ratio of debt to equity). A leverage ratio of 33 (roughly Bear Stearn's situation in 2007) means that the organization has purchased assets for an amount equal to 33 times what its shareholders own in equity.[59] Suppose a hedge fund used $3 in capital to borrow $97. With its total cash of $100, the hedge fund purchases an MBS worth $100. It now has $100 in assets, $97 in debt, and $3 in capital. Its leverage ratio is 33, that is 100/3. It's easy to see that the higher the leverage, the higher the profit made by the hedge fund owner. Suppose that the $97 is borrowed at 5 percent interest (by issuing commercial paper) and that the MBS pays 6 percent in interest. The hedge fund pays $4.85 a year for its borrowing and gets $6 in interest revenue. The profit of $1.15 amounts to a return on equity (ROE) of 38 percent ($1.15 over $3). The higher the leverage, the more "free" profits to be made. However, the slightest decline in the value of the assets (the MBS in this case) wipes out the capital and renders the entity unable to reimburse its creditors. For example, if the value of the MBS falls by only 4 percent to $96 (say, because the annual revenues from the underlying mortgages are expected to decline by 4 percent due to a 4 percent rate of delinquency by the mortgage borrowers), the hedge fund's assets are reduced to $96, but creditors are still owned $97. The hedge fund is insolvent. The creditors realize that they will never be paid in full and stop lending by refusing to roll over the commercial paper when it comes due. Without an infusion of capital, the entity declares bankruptcy.

The only way Authority can prevent this is by forcing taxpayers to foot the bill or by prohibiting something. It could theoretically forbid organizations from borrowing or buying MBSs or forbid the securitization of mortgage loans or prohibit individuals from buying mortgages. One way or another, there is some coercive intervention involved, and it undermines the support of some people. It also stifles financial innovation and compromises economic growth.

"Saying that 'greed' caused today's problems," wrote Don Boudreaux, an economist at George Mason University, "is like saying that gravity caused the death of someone pushed from the top floor of the Empire State building. Some things are sufficiently constant in human affairs—and self-interest, even greed, is among them—that they explain nothing."[60] If egoism is part of human nature, repressing private greed will just make it bulge into the public sector. Powerful public officials will start seeing their jobs as easy ways to enrichment and become corrupt. Politicians and bureaucrats may start selling the right to open hedge funds or to build houses. Greed and ambition are more dangerous when they are exerted by the authorities than when they are channeled toward private enterprise satisfying consumer demand. Despite promoting government intervention to prevent depressions, Keynes understood this to a certain extent. In his famous *General Theory of Employment, Interest and Money,* he wrote:

> There are valuable human activities which require the motive of money-making and the environment of private wealth-ownership for their full fruition. Moreover, dangerous human proclivities can be canalised into comparatively harmless channels by the existence of opportunities for money-making and private wealth, which, if they cannot be satisfied in this way, may find their outlet in cruelty, the reckless pursuit of personal power and authority, and other forms of self-aggrandisement. It is better that a man should tyrannise over his bank balance than over his fellow-citizens; and whilst the former is sometimes denounced as being but a means to the latter, sometimes at least it is an alternative.[61]

Not only can greed and ambition be substitutes for tyranny, but they can also constrain Authority and prevent it from becoming tyrannical. The "disobedient psychology of the business world,"[62] which Keynes blamed, may sometimes be useful. Disobedience is related to entrepreneurship: the entrepreneur doesn't just repeat what he has learned. Shorting a stock is a way for investors to express their opinion on its poor prospects, whatever Authority thinks. Napoleon called short sellers "enemies of the state."[63] But there may be more to the usefulness of businessmen's greed and ambition: they may help build intermediate powers between the state and the individual. Greedy men will constitute great corporations with enough clout to counterbalance state power. Wal-Mart is much smaller than the federal government but is still too big to push around; so is Harvard University. The most dangerous situation is for individuals to be isolated and dispersed under the state, to have no intermediary bodies between the state and them. These intermediary bodies can be private associations and local governments, but they can also be large corporations. There is always the danger that large corporations will use the state for their own purposes instead of constituting a counterpower, so the recipe is not foolproof. The point remains that private greed has the potential to provide a barrier to Authority's arbitrary power.

Entrepreneurial and innovative individuals—inconvenient individuals—will undermine Authority's plan by trying to circumvent any regulation or constraint imposed on their private activities. The phenomenon, when involving only legal actions, is called "regulatory arbitrage," of which we will see a few examples. You can't have a nation of entrepreneurs and innovators without also having one of regulatory minimizers.

A Rational Animal

Who is this individual I have been talking about? Is he the rational maximizer of standard economic theory, who maximizes his profits or his "utility" (satisfaction)? (Utility is a concept broader than satisfaction, but the difference does not matter for our present purpose.) Or is he, at the other extreme, a creature moved by irrational optimism or pessimism, by "animal spirits," as Keynes seemed to argue?[64] And does it matter for our present purpose anyway?

Economists have traditionally assumed that the individual is rational in the sense that he has preferences and tries, usually successfully, to maximize his utility, reach his most preferred position, given these preferences and the constraints he is confronted with. In other words, every individual tries to reach his maximum happiness given what is accessible for him. This assumption has been a defining characteristic of economics as a discipline. One advantage is methodological: the rationality assumption allows one to say something but not anything. We can try and predict individual behavior over large numbers. If the individual behaved irrationally, like if he were throwing a dice before making choices, little could be said except in a purely probabilistic sense. An irrational individual could increase as well as decrease his quantity demanded of a good whose price has gone up. He could commit more crimes just because his expected punishment has increased. It makes more sense to assume that the individual will respond to incentives: other things being equal, he will want more of what costs less, and he will engage less in actions that impose higher costs on him. Another advantage of the rationality assumption is that it corresponds to what we generally observe in the real world.

Note that rationality is not a property of the contents of an individual's preferences. It is no more "rational" to prefer dark or white chocolate. As the Latin proverb says, *De gustibus non est disputandum*—tastes are not debatable. The only thing *The Economist* assumes about the contents of an individual's preferences is that they are consistent: if he prefers wine to Coke and Coke to milk, he will prefer wine to milk. Rationality pertains mainly to the relation between an individual's preferences and what he does. It is an instrumental concept: whatever his preferences—and whether you or I believe that his preferences are mistaken—the individual will act on them.

Greed is inconsistent with extreme irrationality. If individuals are moved by irrational animal spirits, they will sometimes be absolutely greedy, sometimes infinitely altruistic, and sometimes anywhere in between. Greed is the manifestation of rationality in the market sphere. It can be more or less open, more or less dampened by other preferences (notably for leisure), but it appears to be inseparable from rationality. One cannot blame the capitalists for being both greedy and irrational, except if one arbitrarily defines "greedy" and "irrational" as synonyms.

A rational individual will form "rational expectations." As one of the pioneers of the theory of rational expectations explains, "outcomes do not differ systematically (i.e., regularly or predictably) from what people expect them to be."[65] In the contrary case, people will change their expectations, so that any remaining divergence between their expectations and what happens is random. For example, if people expect the level of consumer prices to remain constant but it continuously increases, they will change their expectations and adapt their behavior to their new expectations—they will ask higher wages. If people expect the domestic currency to keep its value but the state continuously depreciates it, they will change their expectations and take measures to protect themselves like by spending their money as soon as possible (before prices increase) or exchanging it for a more stable currency. The consequences of rational expectations are major: the state cannot fool all the people all the time; people will adapt their behavior given their revised expectations.

The "efficient-market hypothesis," first formulated by economist Eugene Fama in 1970, is a special case of rational behavior and expectations. Although the theory comes in weaker and stronger forms, its essential claim is that the price of a security reflects all available information about the security's value. If this not the case, it means that some people have information that they think justifies a (say) higher price; they will therefore buy the security as long as the price has not been pushed up to a level consistent with their expectations. Once this process has run its course, nobody can "beat the market." If a stock is priced at $100 on the market, it means that the expected present value of its future returns (the future returns discounted by the market rate of interest) and, thus, the profits expected from the real underlying asset (say, a factory) are equal to $100. There is no existing information that can change this market valuation because all existing information has already contributed to the formation of this price, which comes from a consolidation of all demand and supply on the market. The price of a security tends to its "fundamental" value with only random noise around it. Since all factors that can be known in advance have been incorporated in the price, the only factors that can move it are random factors. Short-run variations in stock prices must thus be random. Starting with the work of French mathematician Louis Bachelier in 1900, much statistical information has been gathered showing that stock prices do follow a random walk around an average return equivalent to the rate of interest plus a risk premium. The best you can do on the market, barring good or bad luck, is to put your money in an indexed fund (a fund that moves with a diversified basket representative of all securities).

Yale professor Robert Shiller and Berkeley professor George Akerlof (a Nobel Prize winner) are Keynes followers—"our hero, John Maynard Keynes," they write in their recent book[66]—who argue that people are often "guided by noneconomic motivation,"[67] that they follow their animal spirits instead of being rational. Although they never define "rational," they try to give some content to the animal spirits, which would include four elements: confidence and trust, immoral behavior and corruption, a sense of fairness, and money illusion.[68] Money illusion describes a situation where people only focus on nominal values without taking inflation into account. Workers under money illusion would fight a reduction in their nominal wages even if their real wages were unchanged or have increased because of a simultaneous drop in the general level of prices. If all prices have dropped by 20 percent and their wages by 10 percent, workers would not realize that they earn more in real terms. Thus, when prices drop during a depression, workers would refuse a reduction in their nominal wages, which means that their real wages would increase, fuelling unemployment, which worsens the depression, leads to other price decreases, and so forth in a vicious circle. Moreover, suggest Shiller and Akerlof, people think it is unfair to reduce nominal wages.[69]

Shiller and Akerlof's book tries to explain the current recession with Keynes's animal spirits. The two authors are right to stress the importance of trust and confidence, especially in an economy with credit and debt. The rest of their theory, however, relies on vague animal spirits that serve to plug their own moral preferences and their elitist belief that ordinary people fall victim to illusions while they are themselves immune to any.

The two approaches—animal spirits versus rational choice—are not as contradictory as they may look, provided one admits two points. First, information is never perfect and rationality is necessarily bounded by imperfect information and by cognitive limitations inseparable from the human condition. Individuals often make decisions by following the herd, which is rational given their imperfect information.[70] People make mistakes when evaluating the outside world and choosing the means to maximize their utility. We can learn something from the "behavioral economists" who stress these facts.[71] Second, as I explained, rationality comes after preferences. People's sentiments and personalities—their optimism or pessimism, for example—are part of their preferences. It is on the basis of these preferences that people make rational choices. A "Big Mac attack" is neither rational nor irrational; what is rational is to go to McDonald to fight it, provided that one's budget constraint, health concerns, et cetera, don't justify another course of action. The first point qualifies the rational-choice approach. The second destroys the straw man built by some theorists of animal spirits. In this perspective, I would suggest that financial markets are relatively efficient given available information, even if temporary herd behavior and bubbles are not impossible.

We can further attenuate the standard economic concept of rationality by invoking Hayek's theory of rules. According to Hayek, individuals are more rule followers than utility maximizers, precisely because information is imperfect. For example, most people get married not because this maximizes their utility in any immediate and clear sense, but because the social rule that has developed and survived is that one gets married. "Get married and stay married" is one of the rules of thumb given as advice to become rich.[72] Social rules are adaptations to our ignorance, just as rules of thumb are often used in business and ordinary life. If you build a house, you won't normally hire an engineer to figure out the distance between the 2×4 studs in the frame: you will use the usual rule of thumb (assuming building regulations don't impose a norm). When raising a child, you will rely on multiple rules of thumb that have proven efficient: make the child have good night sleep, don't baby talk to him, et cetera. You don't need to be a psychologist to know this.

The Hayekian concept of rationality is thus much fuzzier than the traditional economic concept, and perhaps reconcilable with Keynes's animal spirits.

In the general debate on the role of reason in knowledge and action, philosopher Nassim Nicholas Taleb sides with Hayek against pretentious reason and the efficient-market hypothesis. Taleb argues that one cause of the recent recession is the trust put in the financial models that tried to estimate the likelihood of improbable events, like a major recession, and hugely underestimated expected losses. Expected losses, Taleb reminds us, must be calculated as the probability of the losses times the amount of the losses should they occur; even if the probability is small, the cost of a crash can be enormous, so that its expected cost can be huge. Thus, he argues, we should mistrust the rationality of investors and beware of misused statistical knowledge.[73]

Hayek's and Taleb's warning against pretentious rationalist claims should be heeded. Yet, I would argue that the Hayekian approach is not inconsistent with financial markets being relatively efficient—for two reasons. First, entrepreneurial investors will, through their trading, make sure that the prices of securities reflect all information available. This information may be imperfect, but it is the only, and all, information available. Indeed, entrepreneurs will hunt for information. For markets to be efficient, you need entrepreneurs to make them efficient and keep them so. Some prescient entrepreneurs may even make nonrandom fortunes doing so. Second, in a business context, it is easy to see why irrational behavior is selected out. Irrational investors will lose money and leave the market either through bankruptcy or by realizing that they should let intermediaries (their pension funds, their banks, etc.) manage their money.

This whole debate may be a bit overrated. Ultimately, everything is based on opinions and preferences, including opinions about what the future holds. The value of a security depends on opinions about the future performance of the underlying assets. These opinions, based on the information available to participants, are aggregated by the market. The performance of the asset itself—say, a factory—depends on consumers' preferences for the goods it will produce and the price of these goods. These prices are influenced by the cost of the resources used, which depends on the valuation consumers put on the other goods and services the resources can produce. In this reverse causal chain, we go from the price of a security, to the price of the goods produced by the underlying assets, to the preferences of consumers, to the cost of satisfying their preferences, and to how consumers value other goods and services. In short, the price of a security is related to the opinions of investors and, ultimately, to consumers' preferences. The economy can be viewed as an enormous and complex system of equations, where everything depends on everything, but where individual valuation of goods and services—preferences and opinions—is the ultimate reason.

The hiatus between the market price and the "fundamentals" of a security is a false dichotomy. All fundamentals depend on opinions and preferences as aggregated by the market. Even when people make mistakes—for example, by overevaluating houses—these opinions and preferences become part of the fundamentals. It is true that, when people change their minds, prices will change, and so will, *ex post*, the fundamentals. But there is no *a priori* way to tell if today's price will be maintained in the future, if today's fundamentals will change. Prices change because people change their minds. Financial markets are efficient in one crucial sense: they aggregate the information contained in people's opinions, preferences, and choices. We can't ask more, but it's already quite a feat.

Errors can be made. Although individuals don't act randomly but try to reach preferred positions in life, they may occasionally choose means that, with hindsight, were not appropriate. But certainly, they learn something from their errors. Individuals have an incentive to try and detect errors, fads, and bubbles, and bet against them, so that they are not eliminated from financial markets or, more generally, from the ranks of the nonpoor. In short, there is some incentive to be a contrarian, to go against the crowd, when the crowd is going where the future cannot be. It is partly because some people are contrarians that economic recessions eventually stop. It is also because contrarians exist that false fads are not more numerous and recessions don't happen more often. Contrarians are part of the reasons why markets are ultimately efficient.

The are many good stories about the incentives for being a contrarian. Investor and philanthropist John Templeton (1912–2008) started building his fortune in 1939 when, betting against a wave of pessimism, he borrowed $10,000 and bought 100 shares of everything trading at less than $1 on the New York Stock Exchange. In early 2000, he sold all his technology stocks before the market crashed. His principle was "to buy when others are despondently selling and to sell when others are greedily buying." Over his investing career, he did beat the market: between 1954 and 1992, his Templeton Growth Fund grew by 14.5 percent per year, some 60 percent more than the long-term growth in stocks.[74]

In the dark days of October 2008, Warren Buffett, the second wealthiest man in the world, explained his contrarian principle: "A simple rule dictates my buying: Be fearful when others are greedy, and be greedy when others are fearful." Announcing that he was investing heavily in stocks of American companies, he explained, "In short, bad news is an investor's best friend." He turned a quote from former hockey player Wayne Gretzky into a piece of investment advice: "I skate to where the puck is going to be, not to where it has been."[75]

David Tepper, the principal of Appaloosa Management, now one of the largest hedge funds in the world, earned a fortune in 2009 by betting on the idea that America would avoid another great depression. Among other contrarian investments, he bought shares in banks when most investors were trying to get out. True, Mr. Tepper's optimism was in large part due to his trust in government supporting but not nationalizing the banks, so he could be thought of as more of a political follower than an economic contrarian. However, he may have done the same if the government had not been in the picture. Tepper, writes the *Wall Street Journal,* "explains his investment philosophy with a line from Allan Meltzer, a professor at his alma mater [Carnegie Mellon University]: 'Trees grow.' In other words, growth is the natural state of economies, so optimism is usually rewarded."[76] Tepper pulled the same trick by investing heavily in Asian markets after they had tumbled in 1997, making much money when they rebounded two years later.

DuPont and Procter & Gamble invested heavily and built their future successes during the 1930s. Several companies took off during the Great Depression, including Revlon, Hewlett-Packard (now HP), Polaroid, and Pepperidge Farm. Similarly, corporations like McDonald's, PepsiCo, and Cisco took advantage of the 2007–2009 recession to invest or make acquisitions. A study by the Kauffman Foundation concluded that about half of the *Fortune* 500 and *Inc.* 500 companies, including FedEx, CNN, and Microsoft, were created during recessions or bear markets.[77]

In the banking sector, JPMorgan Chase provides an example of contrarian prudence that paid off. The large commercial and investment bank was prudent with CDOs and SIVs even though it had contributed to the development of both products. *The Economist* notes that the bank "jettissoned an SIV and $60 billion of CDO-related risks" and "closed 60 credit lines for other SIVs and corporate clients" before others realized the looming danger.[78]

Many unknown banks were prudent and have been rewarded for this. Take Hudson City Bancorp, a conservative New Jersey savings bank that chose not to relax its mortgage standards and not to participate in the subprime market. The bank was able to increase its profits in both 2008 and 2009,[79] and its share price is about the same as in early 2007.[80]

Contrarians are, by definition, less numerous than those who follow the herd. They run high risk, but get high rewards when they are right. They also help bring securities prices to their correct level. Their very actions contribute to incorporating all the available information in the prices. They bring other market participants to wonder whether the herd is mistaken. John Paulson's hedge fund made billions betting against MBSs when, before the crisis appeared, most investors were bullish on them.[81] Mark Hart III, a Texas hedge fund manager, reportedly made a fortune in late 2007 by betting against subprime mortgages. His hedge fund European Divergence Fund LP later made much money by buying CDSs on sovereign debt of European countries like Greece: as the risk of default increased, the fund was able to resell these CDSs at higher prices.[82] Buying CDSs on sovereign bonds exerts upward pressure on their prices, signaling to the market that some participants have reasons to believe that the emperor is naked. Napoleon was right: speculators are enemies of the naked emperor.

The individual is very inconvenient for Authority, because he can think individually. Whether he is a cold rational calculator or whether he is motivated by animal spirits, the individual will always try to sidestep Authority's plans when they don't correspond to what he wants to do.

Authority's Dilemma

The reader may think that there is something wrong with the foregoing argument on the limits of Authority. Can't Authority run society like managers run an organization? There exist efficient organizations—some large corporations, for example. Perhaps Authority can run society like Ford was run as opposed to GM?

Much of Friedrich Hayek's work was meant to address this intuition, which is closely related to the idea that somebody must be in charge in society.[83] Hayek explained that an organization and a society are two very different kinds of entities. An organization—think of a club, a firm, or a political party—has a few precise goals for the attainment of which its members have joined. An organization's activity is the means by which it reaches its goals. Society, on the other hand, has not been created by anybody to attain a particular goal; it is an evolved network of individuals and organizations with their own goals and means to attain them. Society exists because it has proved useful for the attainment of individual ends. As different sort or orders, organizations and societies are governed by different types of rules. The rules of organization are commands and specific directives designed to oblige individuals to contribute to the goals they have agreed to further when they joined the organization. Organizations are essentially governed by control and command. The rules governing society must by necessity be more general, abstract, negative, since there is no single goal (except the maintenance of a general context of liberty) that could justify imposing diktats on all individuals. Consider the rules of the common law: they define property rights and determine what makes contracts valid, leaving a wide field for individuals to pursue their own objectives. Hayek spoke about the "Great Society" to describe a society where this distinction is maintained. It has little to do with Lyndon B. Johnson's "Great Society" and what his CEA referred to.

President Barack Obama recently gave a practical example of the difference between what Authority does in an organization and in a Great Society. After receiving the Nobel Peace Prize, he said: "I am the commander in chief of a country that's responsible for ending a war."[84] Perhaps a slip of tongue made him elide the crucial words "the Army and Navy" before "of a country." Article II, Section II of the Constitution states: "The President shall be Commander in Chief of the Army and Navy of the United States, and of the Militia of the several States, when called into the actual Service of the United States." But he later repeated himself in his Nobel Prize acceptance speech: "I am the Commander-in-Chief of a nation in the midst of two wars."[85] Obama was echoing Roosevelt's March 5, 1933, inaugural speech: "I assume unhesitatingly the leadership of this great army of our people dedicated to a disciplined attack upon our common problems."[86] There is a huge difference between, on the one hand, being the commander in chief of a particular organization called "the Army" or "the Navy" or "the Militia of the several States, when called into the actual Service of the United States," and, on the other hand, being the commander in chief of the country. The first formulation is consistent with a Great Society; the second one implies that America is an army-like organization.

In a historical perspective, only the Great Society allows for economic growth and general opportunities for personal development. It is when the great, impersonal, market-based society started appearing in the eighteenth century that life expectancy and material conditions began to improve for the masses. During the first millennium of our era, it is estimated that real GDP per capita did not exceed $450 per year anywhere in the word. In fact, in Western Europe, the standard of living decreased slightly over this period. The Industrial Revolution started in the eighteenth century and, by the early nineteenth century, GDP had tripled in Western countries. Between 1820 and 1998, GDP per capita was multiplied by 19, from $1,130 to $21,470.[87] As Nobel Prize-winning economist Edward Prescott puts it, "standards of living were more or less constant from the beginning of civilization until the industrial revolution; then something changed."[88] As a consequence, population itself started exploding.[89] World population at the beginning of the eighteenth century was not much more than 600 million people, at most three times what it had been 2,000 years ago; by the end of the nineteenth century, in less than two centuries, it had more than doubled.[90] Life expectancy increased dramatically. So did the quality of life by virtually any measure.

The two Koreas have provided as close a controlled social experiment as could be devised on the consequences of trying to run society as an organization in the North, compared with letting society develop more spontaneously like in the South. In 1950, real GDP per capita in both North and South Korea was $770. By 1998, it had barely increased to $1,183 in the North, while it had jumped to $12,152 in the South. Nobel Prize winner Paul Krugman notes: "In 1975 the average hourly wage in South Korea was only 5 percent of that in the United States; by 2006 it had risen to 62 percent."[91] Similar experiments have given similar results in East and West Germany, Hungary and Austria, Cambodia and Thailand.[92]

University of Maryland's economist Mancur Olson wrote that "[a]n economy with free markets and no government or cartel intervention is like a teen-aged growth; it makes a lot of mistakes but nevertheless grows rapidly without special effort or encouragement."[93] Two centuries and half before, Adam Smith said about the same:

> Little else is requisite to carry a state to the highest degree of opulence from the lowest barbarianism but peace, easy taxes, and tolerable administration of justice: all the rest being brought by the natural course of things.[94]

Authority is limited by its necessarily imperfect comprehension of the complexity of the world, the impossibility of obtaining the information necessary to plan in any "rational" way, and the inconvenient individual. The impotence of Authority is most obvious in a Great Society offering large and growing opportunities to all. Authority can certainly try to be in charge by flexing its coercive muscles, but it will be at the cost of liberty and prosperity. As Adam Smith explained, if public policy and individual liberty coincide, "the game of human society will go on easily and harmoniously, and is very likely to be happy and successful. If they are opposite or different, the game will go on miserably, and the society must be at all times in the highest degree of disorder."[95] If we concentrate on two extremes points of the spectrum, disregarding what is of course a question of degree, we see clearly what the dilemma of Authority is: it can mildly govern a prosperous Great Society or rule over a destitute people.

CHAPTER 2

Keynes's Old Clothes

In the nurseries, the Elementary Class Consciousness lesson was over, the voices were adapting future demand to future industrial supply. . . . "But old clothes are beastly," continued the untiring whisper. "We always throw away old clothes. Ending is better than mending, ending is better than mending . . . the more stitches the less riches . . . "

—Aldous Huxley[1]

The conventional wisdom of our times suggests that the state must intervene to prevent economic crises. This conclusion depends on two hypotheses: first, that economic crises would occur without the authorities' guiding hand; second, that these authorities know how to manage the economic cycle. Should we take these two hypotheses for granted?

We call "business cycle" the succession of booms and busts, periods of growth and recessions. Why is there a business cycle? Why do recessions and, *a fortiori,* depressions occur? How can we explain such economic crises? Do they happen spontaneously, out of the blue? The truth is that it is much more difficult to understand why recessions happen than why they would not occur. In the depth of the Great Depression, Irving Fisher, a famous economist who taught at Yale University, raised the question:

A depression seems, indeed, to fall upon mankind out of a clear sky. It scorns to choose a moment when the earth is impoverished. For, in times of depression, is the soil less fertile? Not at all. Does it lack rain? Not at all? Are the mines exhausted? No: they can perhaps pour out ever more than the old volume of ore, if anyone will buy. Are the factories, then, lamed in some way—down at heel? No: machinery and invention may be at the very peak. But perhaps the men have suddenly become unable or unwilling to work. The idea is belied by the spectacle of hordes of workmen, besieging every available employment office.[2]

A recession can be defined as a general, unwanted, self-perpetuating but temporary, mutual reduction in exchange. It is general because it affects many industries. It is unwanted because everybody affected would like to work, earn, and consume more, but they can't. It is mutual because many people are paradoxically in the same situation: A cannot exchange with B for apparently the same reason that B cannot exchange with A. It is self-perpetuating as opposed to a disturbance that would be immediately and automatically self-correcting: the more people have problems selling and buying, the more it seems difficult to find somebody who wants to buy or has something to sell. It is temporary: secular stagnation and long-term poverty are different problems. Booms and busts occur around the long-run growth trend of an economy. The "reduction in exchange" conveys the idea that people who were previously exchanging goods and services with others cannot do so anymore, or cannot do it as much as they did before. A depression, as I mentioned before, is simply a deeper and longer recession.

In a recession, the unemployed would be willing to produce something, a good like lumber or a service like technical support; his potential employer would like to hire him but thinks that no buyer would be found. The missing buyers are people who would like to consume what our unemployed individual would be producing, but are prevented to consume because they themselves can't produce enough and get enough income to buy. You have people who would like to produce and exchange but don't because they each think that others won't produce something to exchange. And there is not only the unemployed, but also the underemployed, those who can't work as many hours as they would like, who have been subjected to furloughs: underemployment is another form of unemployment. The babysitter would like to work more to buy wine, the wine producer wants to produce and sell more in order to buy a new car, the car factory worker would love to work more hours to produce one more car in order to hire the babysitter. All these people are unable to hook up and exchange. What's the problem?

Generations of economists have labored on this puzzle, "the mystery of a depression" as Irving Fisher called it. What prevents individuals from continuing to engage in what Adam Smith identified as "a certain propensity in human nature . . . to truck, barter, and exchange one thing for another"?[3]

Classical Economic Theory

Classical economists believed that, in a free-market economy, recessions could only be short-lived. The great names associated with classical economics include Adam Smith, David Hume, John Stuart Mill, Jean-Baptiste Say, and

David Ricardo. At the end of the nineteenth century, the school merged into neoclassical economics, which, at least until the Great Depression, continued to believe in the impossibility of anything but short recessions. The great names in neoclassical economics include Alfred Marshall, Vilfredo Pareto, Léon Walras, and Irving Fisher. Classical and neoclassical economists believed that economic disequilibriums are rapidly self-correcting as prices change and individuals adapt their production and consumption accordingly. They based this belief on two theories: Say's law and the quantity theory of money.

As its name implies, the proposition called "Say's law" is attributed to the eighteenth-century French economist Jean-Baptiste Say, although it appears to have been formulated first by economist James Mill, the father of the better known classical economist and philosopher John Stuart Mill.[4] Mill junior explains Say's law in a few luminous sentences:

> [I]s it, in that case, possible that there should be a deficiency of demand for all commodities for want of the means of payment? Those who think so cannot have considered what it is which constitutes the means of payment for commodities. It is simply commodities. Each person's means of paying for the productions of other people consists of those which he himself possesses. All sellers are inevitably and *ex vi termini* [by force of the term] buyers. Could we suddenly double the productive powers of the country, we should double the supply of commodities in every market; but we should, by the same stroke, double the purchasing power. Everybody would bring a double demand as well as supply: everybody would be able to buy twice as much, because every one would have twice as much to offer in exchange.[5]

Supply creates its own demand. Every supplier who comes to the market with something to sell, be it something he has produced, some service he is offering, or simply his labor, does it precisely because he wants to consume an equivalent value. If you produce something worth $100 on the market, it is because you want to consume (today or tomorrow) $100 worth of something else. If somebody had not wanted to consume the equivalent of what he produced, "he would not have troubled himself to produce" as Mill puts it. One does not work and produce for the pleasure of working and producing—if one does, he is engaging in leisure, not work. Work is what we do in order to consume. Thus, the equivalent of everything that is produced is necessarily consumed.

Mill understood that there can be a *temporary* oversupply of *certain* goods on *certain* markets. Consumers demand changes, new goods appear, new processes of production are developed, suppliers don't make perfect forecasts. Certain markets will be temporarily oversupplied while others are temporarily undersupplied. The price of unsold inventories will fall, the mistaken suppliers will sustain a loss, and less of the surplus good will be produced in the next round. Conversely, the price of undersupplied goods will rise, leading to increased production. "Because this phenomenon of over-supply, and consequent inconvenience or loss to the producer or dealer, may exist in the case of any one commodity whatever," Mill explains, "many persons, including some distinguished political economists, have thought that it may exist with regard to all commodities; that there may be . . . a supply of commodities in the aggregate, surpassing the demand; and a consequent depressed condition of all classes of producers." But there can't be general overproduction or underconsumption. "[P]roduction is not excessive, but merely ill assorted," Mill notes.[6] At the aggregate level, the producers' output is their income, which is thus necessarily sufficient to purchase everything they have produced.

This conclusion remains valid when people save part of their incomes. What individuals save and don't directly invest in shares of stock or in their own businesses, they put in savings instruments paying interest—savings deposits, for example. The higher the rate of interest, the more would-be savers will want to save. Savings represent a sacrifice of current consumption for future consumption, a sacrifice rewarded by interest. Other things being equal, people prefer consuming now rather than later. The bank is able to pay interest because it lends the money to investing firms (or to other consumers, but in that case there is no problem of saving leaking out of the flow of income). Investing firms, on their side, want to borrow and invest more the lower the rate of interest. We thus have a demand and a supply of loanable funds, and the interest rate is the price that adjusts to clear this market. In practice, of course, there are many different interest rates on different submarkets, but we can abstract from this complication here. If people want to save more than others want to invest, the latter will be able to get their funds at a lower interest rate; conversely, if savers save less than borrowers want to borrow, the interest rate will be bid up. Once the rate of interest has adjusted, loanable funds demanded will be equal to loanable funds supplied, which is the same as saying that investment will be equal to saving.

Everything consumers do not consume will be invested by borrowers in capital goods: machines, equipment, and inventories to supply future demand. Nothing leaks out of the flow of income between production and total demand. On the supply side of the equation, producers (everybody who works in the economy) get their incomes from the production of consumer goods and capital goods. On the demand side, consumers spend their money on consumption goods and on savings instruments. Since, as we just saw, investment is equal to saving, total demand is equal to total supply. Everything produced is paid in incomes that serve to purchase total production through either consumption or investment. Our previous conclusion remains valid: supply creates its own demand.

If supply creates its own demand, it follows that anybody who wants to work will be able to. John Stuart Mill gives the example of a newcomer to the country who brings a new demand, which corresponds exactly to what he offers in exchange. If the newcomer gets a salaried job instead of working as an independent craftsman, we know that the salary he earns is equal to the value of what he produces; he will then spend it on consumer goods or, through savings, on capital goods. If a salaried worker were not paid the value of what he produces, other employers, precisely because they are greedy, would bid up his salary until it is brought up to equality with his marginal productivity (the value of what he produces at the margin, i.e., what would not be produced if he were not there).

Imagine that some workers in a given industry are unemployed because the demand for their labor services has dropped. A number of causes could account for this disturbance—perhaps consumer demand for the output of this industry has decreased or technological progress is substituting labor for capital (machines) or an external shock has hit supply. Wages are determined by supply of labor (the relative preferences of people for work and leisure) and demand for labor (from firms). When we say that the supply of labor depends on the relative preferences of individuals for work and leisure, we are simply referring to the fact that an individual may prefer to have either more leisure or more of the goods that working allows him to purchase. Some workers who want a job at the going rate but cannot find one will offer their services at lower wages. Some people prefer to earn less to earning nothing, just as businesses prefer lower profits to no profit at all. The wage rate will go down, increasing the quantity of labor demanded by firms and decreasing the quantity supplied by workers. The movement will continue until the wage rate is down to a new equilibrium level, where everybody who wants to work at the lower going wage gets a job. At this equilibrium, there can be frictional unemployment because some people are between jobs until they find a suitable one. But there can't be *involuntary* unemployment, that is, there will not be anybody who wants to work at the going wage rate but cannot find a job. With free labor markets, unemployment is impossible—except perhaps for a short period of adjustment. Wages adjust to clear the market and automatically bring full employment, just as interest rates adjust to insure that investment equals saving. Although temporary disturbances are possible, they will be rapidly self-corrected.

The quantity theory of money is the second building block of classical economics. It shows that the previous conclusion also applies in a monetary economy. What is money? Simply defined, money is anything that people use as a medium of exchange when they purchase or sell goods and services. Money is very useful; it is indispensable for a prosperous economy. Without money, exchange would be complicated. You would always have to find the exchange partner who wants what you have and is offering what you want. The babysitter who wants wine would have to find a wine producer who needs babysitting services. The wine producer who wants a car would have to find a car manufacturer who happens to be looking for wine. The car manufacturer who wants babysitting services would have to find a babysitter who is shopping for a car. With money, this double coincidence of wants in exchange is not required. The babysitter earns her money by working for the car manufacturer and uses the money to purchase wine, or whatever else she wants. The wine producer uses the money he earns to buy a car, or whatever else he chooses. The car manufacturer can spend his money on babysitting services, or whatever he fancies. When thousands of goods and services are available to large numbers of consumers from uncountable producers, money becomes indispensable to efficient exchange.

Money is also a unit of account. A unit of account is what prices are expressed in, and is needed in anything but the simplest economy. If there are two goods, bread and beer, only two price ratios need to be considered: the price of bread in terms of beer (one baguette costs half a bottle of beer, for example) and the price of beer in terms of bread, which is the inverse of the other one (one bottle of beer costs two baguettes). But with three goods—bread, beer, and babysitting services—six price ratios will be in usage: the price of bread in terms of beer and in terms of babysitting time, the price of beer in terms of bread and in terms of babysitting time, and the price of babysitting time in terms of beer and in terms of bread. If 1,000 goods are for sale, 999,000 different prices will need to be posted. With money, each good can carry only one price, its money price, and anybody can easily convert it into the relative price he is interested in.

A unit of account could be purely abstract, corresponding to no actually traded "physical" medium of exchange, and serve only to quote prices. The ancient French *livre tournois* and the guinea in England were examples. At least one actual case persists under our own contemporary eyes. The French franc was abolished as legal tender (legal money) in 2002 and replaced by the euro. Yet, in France, prices are still occasionally quoted in francs, at the conversion rate of February 17, 2002, which is 0.14245 euro. Société Générale, one of the main French banks, provides the franc equivalent of all entries on bank statements. The same may be observable in other European countries. One of the main currency converter websites, oanda.com, publishes the "irrevocable conversion rate" of all the former currencies of euro-zone countries at the date the transition was made (usually in February 2002).[7] Yet, it is convenient to use the circulating currency as the unit of account, which is why this second function of money can be considered ancillary to its first function as medium of exchange.

Note that any good can serve as *numéraire,* which is a French equivalent for "unit of account." The original meaning of *numéraire* is "which serves to count" or measure.[8] The price of beer can be expressed in terms of any "numéraire good." I have expressed it in baguettes, but any other good would do. Indeed, classical economics (and much of neoclassical economics) tries to dispense with money and view all economic phenomena in real terms, in terms of real goods and services. In everyday exchange, though, the medium-of-exchange money is the most convenient *numéraire,* which is why the latter term has become, in ordinary parlance, synonymous with money.

The third function of money is that of a "store of value." In the context of classical monetary theory, this means that money keeps its value between two transactions, that it remains a medium of exchange over time. It is easy to see how exchange would be impaired if money had to be used quickly before it deteriorated and ceased to be exchangeable. Hence, what was historically accepted as money tended to evolve toward precious metals (like gold and silver) or other nonperishable commodities.

A medium of exchange needs to be liquid, that is, accepted by exchange partners and rapidly negotiable. It can take many forms: coins, Federal Reserve notes (dollar bills), or bank deposits from which money can be withdrawn and on which checks can be drawn and electronic transfers made. Liquidity is the name of the game: money has to be easily exchangeable for any good or service. The condition for something to be liquid is that everybody trusts it as such. Liquidity is another name for trust. When convenient coins, banknotes, or scriptural money (transferable entries in entries in physical or electronic ledgers, like bank accounts) are not available, people will use other things as money: tobacco in colonial Virginia, cigarettes in World War II prison camps, cognac in Germany after the war, et cetera. "The only thing that all these items used as money have in common," writes Milton Friedman, who modernized the quantity theory of money, "is their acceptance."[9] A more precise definition of money is thus: "a liquid medium of exchange"; in practice, it amounts to what people trust and accept as money.

Because money is defined in terms of liquidity, it is not as easy to measure as one might imagine. Some forms of money are slightly more liquid than others. At the end of 2008, U.S. currency (coins and notes) amounted to $812 billion. Adding the nearly equally liquid money in bank deposits that can be tapped immediately when needed (plus the now insignificant value of traveler's checks), we obtain a measure of the money stock called M1, which comes up to $1.6 trillion. Other forms of money are thought to be nearly as liquid: bank deposits that could take some time to draw upon but usually don't (like savings accounts) and deposits in money market funds (which, until August of 2007, were thought to be always very liquid). Including these other forms of money, we obtain M2, which totals at $8.1 trillion. Other measures of the stock of money exist. Since 1971, all the money stock has been made of "fiat money," that is, money not backed by gold or any other guarantee.

The classical theory of money can be summarized in a famous equation called "Fisher's equation," in honor of the same Irving Fisher we met before. Fisher's equation simply says that the money supply times the velocity of money is equal to the nominal value of total production (or GDP), that is, real output times prices. Since there are many goods and services, each one of them is multiplied by its price and added to the others to give total nominal GDP. The velocity of money is the number of times the average dollar turns around in the economy. If nominal GDP is $14 trillion per year (roughly what it was in 2008) and if one dollar is, on average, spent 1.8 times a year (i.e., spent by one person and respent by the recipient during roughly the same year), a money supply (calculated as M2) of $8 trillion is what is needed. (Note that velocity is different if we use other measures of the stock of money.)

The quantity theory of money is built on this equation. It says that what adjusts to a change in the supply of money can only be the price level. Velocity is believed to be determined by institutional factors and habits and thus relatively constant over long periods of time. According to Say's law, output is always at its full-employment level, and thus determined exogenously. So if money supply increases, all prices must rise proportionately. If there is more money chasing the same quantity of goods, the prices of all the goods will increase in terms of money. Imagine that helicopters drop dollars bills on each house such that everybody's income increases by 10 percent. Consumption and investment expenditures will increase by 10 percent, but since no additional output can be produced, all prices and costs will go up by 10 percent. At the end of the process, everything will cost 10 percent more, and real output—the real standard of living—will be unchanged. An increase in the money supply causes only a rise in prices. Nothing else happens. Conversely, a reduction in the money supply will only generate deflation.

Milton Friedman said that "[i]inflation is a monetary phenomenon arising from a more rapid increase in the quantity of money than in output."[10] A continuous increase in the money supply leads to continuing inflation. Large increases in the money supply cause hyperinflation. Historical evidence of the relationship between increases in the money supply and inflation is overwhelming. It includes hyperinflation in France following the 1789 revolution,[11] inflation in the South during the Civil War, the German hyperinflation after World War I, the Brazilian hyperinflation of the 1950s, inflation in the United States during the 1970s,[12] and the recent hyperinflation in Zimbabwe. During the two world wars and their immediate aftermath (1914–1920 and 1939–1948), the U.S. money supply more than doubled and prices also more than doubled.[13] Indeed, this is how the government succeeded diverting to war uses the resources that would otherwise have been allocated to producing consumer goods. If the state, through the central bank, prints money or increases the money supply in more subtle ways, inflation unmistakably results, and the steeper the increase in the money supply, the higher the jump in the price level. When the Reserve Bank of Zimbabwe was issuing single notes worth 100 trillion Zimbabwe dollars in mid-2008, the monthly inflation rate was 3,740 percent and soon to reach 79,600,000,000 percent.[14] A loaf of bread was priced at several million Zimbabwe dollars.[15] In late 2009, 100-trillion-dollar bills from the Reserve Bank of Zimbabwe could be purchased on eBay for 3.35 U.S. dollars.

The classical and neoclassical economists were not blind to the possibility of mild recessions, which were observed several times during the nineteenth century. During the first two-thirds of that century, there was a recession about every ten years; during the last third, and indeed until the 1929–1933 Great Depression, they were much less frequent.[16] In his 1920 *Principles of Economics,* the great neoclassical economist Alfred Marshall argued that "reckless inflations of credit" was "the chief cause of all economic malaise."[17] The "chief cause" of why an economic malaise (a recession) was not immediately self-corrected was "a want of confidence."[18] But the "economic malaise," Marshall believed, was limited by the operation of Say's law, and was mild and temporary.

Writing during the Great Depression, Irving Fisher was less optimistic. He stressed overindebtedness and deflation as the "two dominant factors" in "the great booms and depressions."[19] He believed that "[e]asy money is the great cause of over-borrowing,"[20] thus generating a boom that will end in a bust. Overindebtedness means that a localized disturbance will be transmitted by cascading defaults throughout the economy, credit and money supply will drop, deflation will set in. The deflation factor is important. With deflation, debtors get into more trouble as they have to reimburse their debt with more expensive money; they sell assets, which leads to further deflation; and so on. Fisher argued that "it would be as silly and immoral" for government "to 'let nature take her course' as for a physician to neglect a case of pneumonia." Economic science, he claimed, "has its therapeutics as truly as medical science,"[21] and "scientific medication (reflation)," that is, an increase in the money supply by the central bank, is to be preferred to laissez-faire.[22] We are already moving out of the classical perspective.

It remains difficult to understand how a recession could last a long time or degenerate into a depression. For after losses have been incurred and indebtedness has started decreasing, confidence should come back. And since everybody knows this, confidence should never remain far below the surface. Although a mild business cycle is possible, a depression is unlikely to happen, because disruptions in output and employment are normally self-correcting. Milton Friedman and other economists argue that mistaken economic policies after 1929 changed what would have been an ordinary recession into the Great Depression. It is not self-evident that somebody should be in charge. This is the first lesson of classical economics.

A second, more general, lesson lies in the benefits of exchange. The reason why people fear recessions is that these events force them to reduce their market transactions, to exchange less. It is a serious but common error to think that only one party benefits from an exchange, an error that recessions eloquently put into focus. All parties benefit from a voluntary exchange. If exchange benefited only one party, why would the other one consent? Even the least favored party—assuming we can find a standard to compare the benefits obtained by the two parties—benefits from the exchange compared with the situation where no exchange would have been possible. If market exchanges always harmed one party, lots of people would welcome recessions, and depressions even more. People fear recessions because they mean a reduction in exchange. The advantages of market exchanges and the "consumption society" are demonstrated *a contrario* by the costs that accompany their reduction.

The Old Idea of Underconsumption

A Cambridge University economist and sometime civil servant in Her Majesty's government, John Maynard Keynes was made a Lord in 1942. His famous 1936 book, *The General Theory of Employment, Interest and Money,* argued that the classical theory was wrong and that recessions and depressions were normal features of the market economy. Lord Keynes was to wield a heavy influence on economic policy up to the 1970s. President Richard Nixon's 1971 statement that "we are all Keynesians now"[23] was widely shared among economists and policymakers. Then, for a few decades, there was an eclipse of the Keynesian influence. After the 2007–2009 recession, a Keynesian revival may be under way.

We saw how the old idea according to which a recession is caused by underconsumption or, what amounts to the same, overproduction was debunked by the classical economists. In 1932, Irving Fisher brilliantly repeated the demonstration. If there is overproduction, he pointed out, it must be because there are more goods than the public will buy. And why could that be? Because people don't earn enough money. This, in turn, means that they are not producing enough. How, asked Fisher, can overproduction be explained by underproduction?[24] If there were overproduction, overconsumption would follow—not underconsumption—because people consume with what they earn in production.

Yet, as Keynes admitted in the *General Theory*, the old idea of underconsumption was still lingering in popular imagery. "Since the war," he wrote, "there has been a spate of heretical theories of underconsumption, of which those of Major Douglas are the most famous."[25] Clifford Hugh Douglas was a British engineer, an economic quack, and the founder of the Social Credit movement, which claimed that the state should give a free "national dividend" to every individual in order to allow him to purchase the equivalent of what he produces—a nice recipe for inflation! The idea that it is necessary to consume more in order to prevent underconsumption was widespread enough to bleed into science fiction. In Aldous Huxley's *Brave New Word*, published four years before Keynes's *General Theory*, people are fed slogans like "old clothes are beastly," "ending is better than mending," "the more stitches, the less riches." Don't repair your old clothes, buy new ones. Boost consumption. "Otherwise the wheels stop turning."[26] The more we consume, the richer we are. Keynes's *General Theory* gave a theoretical basis to these old ideas, mending the old clothes of popular economics.

Keynes's Theory

Keynes's central argument is that a recession is caused by the deficiency of aggregate demand. Aggregate demand is the total of all goods and services that people buy. The deficiency is relative to the total of all final goods and services produced—output or GDP. (The "final" means that we are neglecting intermediate inputs, in order not to double count, say, the flour that went into making the bread.) A deficiency of aggregate demand is just another way to say "underconsumption" (or, equivalently, overproduction). Say's law, Keynes argued, is false. People consume only a part of the revenue they earn from their production, and save the rest. Therefore, total consumption is lower than total production. Faced with overproduction, businesses cut production and employment, GDP drops, and the economy enters into recession.

Unemployment is the other side of the drop in output: actual output is below potential output because some workers are unemployed. Economists refer to this relation as "Okun's Law," in honor of *The Economist* who formulated it in the 1960s. Potential output is the maximum output obtainable if everybody who wants to work is employed. If the involuntary unemployed are put to work, output will increase to its potential, and the recession will end. The question is why involuntary unemployment is not self-correcting, and the reaching of potential output automatic. Why don't the unemployed workers offer to work for less, bidding down wages until everybody is employed? This is what would happen under Say's law. Keynes, however, argued that this self-correcting mechanism will not work. First, the nominal wage rate—as it is paid in nominal dollars, without correcting for deflation—is inflexible downward as workers will not accept a wage reduction. Second, even if workers did accept a reduction in their nominal wages, real wages (nominal wages with inflation deducted) would not follow because general deflation would lead prices to drop by at least as much as nominal wages. Even if workers can influence their nominal wage rate, they are unable to control their real wage rate.

For Keynes, glitches affect not only the real side as we just saw, but also the monetary side of the economy. During a recession, where interest rates are low, people will want to hold their assets in more liquid form, that is, as money instead of bonds or other financial instruments. One reason is that bond prices are expected to drop as interest rate will rise in the future—so better hoard money now and buy bonds later. This speculative demand for money implies that all savings don't get translated into investments. This tendency is exacerbated by deflation as people will keep their money to take advantage of lower consumer prices in the future. A sort of liquidity trap may even develop where an increase in money supply will not lead banks to lend more nor people to spend more, as everybody will want to stick to liquid money; however, Keynes thought this was a "limiting case" of which he knew of no example.[27] Another implication of the existence of a speculative demand for money is thus that the authorities will not be able to use monetary policy to restart the economy.

Not only is there no self-correcting mechanism to bring aggregate demand at the level of full-employment output, but the businessmen's behavior will constantly create shocks that will disturb any passing equilibrium. Businessmen act erratically, on the basis of "animal spirits," and "individual initiative will only be adequate when reasonable calculation is supplemented and supported by animal spirits."[28] Investment, which is part of aggregate demand (the other part is consumption and government expenditure—disregarding foreign trade), will change unexpectedly. When it drops, it will bring down demand with it and spark a recession.

Like Fischer and most of today's economists and central bankers, Keynesian economists especially fear deflation, which takes hold as the tightening of credit reduces the money supply. When the general price level starts declining, a deflationary spiral and a deepening recession will set in. Business will fear for their profits and reduce investments and employment further. Similarly, consumers will postpone their purchases, waiting for lower prices, worsening the reduction in aggregate demand. Debtors will have to reimburse their creditors with scarcer money, so that defaults will increase, generating cascading defaults, higher credit risk, and reduced lending by banks. Another way to see the plight of debtors is to realize that deflation increases the real rate of interest: assume the nominal rate of interest is 3 percent per year and that deflation proceeds at an annual rate of 5 percent; the real rate of interest is thus 8 percent because the 3 percent interest of next year will have to be paid with dollars worth 5 percent more. The real interest rate being higher, businesses will invest less, further dampening aggregate demand. The magazine *The Economist,* Keynesian as usual, argues that between deflation and inflation, the former is "the greater of two evils."[29]

In a recession, Keynes argued, the role of the state is to stop the downward spiral. It must boost aggregate demand by increasing government expenditures, even if this generates a deficit. More generally, the state should dampen the business cycle by fine-tuning its fiscal policy, running deficits during recessions and surpluses during the expansionary phase of the business cycle. In this way, full employment will be maintained without inflation. In the brave new world, the wheels of the economy will continue turning.

The Trees and the Forest

One implication of Keynesian theory is a permanent, long-run inverse relation between inflation and unemployment. Unemployment characterizes recessions; booms are plagued by inflation as aggregate demand hits the limit of potential output. Keynesian theory is often reformulated in terms of aggregate supply and aggregate demand, just as individual markets are modeled as the interaction of suppliers and demanders. If aggregate demand is higher than aggregate supply and there is no slack in the economy, the price level will increase, that is, inflation will appear. If aggregate demand is lower than aggregate supply, deflation will occur and unemployment will develop. The policy prescriptions were summarized in the so-called Phillips curve, which described a trade-off between inflation and unemployment: the authorities could run fiscal and (in certain cases) monetary policy so as to target full-employment at the cost of some inflation, or fight inflation at the cost of some unemployment. This theory was shattered in the late 1970s and early 1980s when both unemployment and inflation increased simultaneously. The unemployment rate jumped from 5.5 percent in 1974 to 8.3 percent in 1975 and to nearly 10 percent in 1982 and 1983. Consumer prices simultaneously increased, by 11 percent in 1974 and up to a peak of 13.5 percent annual inflation in 1980.[30]

Besides the contradictory empirical evidence, there are many theoretical reasons to doubt the claim that deficiencies of aggregate demand will naturally generate recessions.

Wage rigidity is a complex issue. Many empirical studies seem to confirm that nominal wages are sticky downward, that they are much more easily increased than cut.[31] Even during the first two years of the Great Depression, real wages increased instead of falling. Casual observation of the milder recent recessions points to the same direction.[32] During the 2001 recession (March-November 2001), for example, average hourly earnings in the United States increased by 2.1 percent, which, given the CPI (consumer price index, an index of prices in a typical consumer's expenditures) increase of 0.8 percent, translates into an estimated increase in the real wage rate of 1.3 percent. Similarly, over the whole 2007–2009 recession, average weekly earnings increased by 5.5 percent while the CPI gained 1.9 percent, for an estimated increase of 3.6 percent in the real wage rate.[33]

So wages do seem to be sticky downward, even in periods of unemployment. Why? One set of explanations revolves around the concept of "efficiency wages": to get better workers, goes the theory, each employer pays wages slightly above the minimum he has to pay, so that the general level of wages is always a bit above what would otherwise be its equilibrium. And when a recession strikes, firms don't cut money wages rapidly: even if they are legally allowed to, they prefer to fire less productive workers and make sure that the ones retained are happy and motivated.[34] Another reason why money wages may not adjust rapidly is that they are often fixed by long-term or implicit arrangements between employers and employees.[35]

It is indeed because wages are sticky downward that we observe unemployment during a recession. When prices (wages in this case) don't adjust, quantities (employment) adjust instead. On this, Keynes was partly right.

Wage inflexibilities should not be exaggerated, though, especially in the American economy, where the labor market is more flexible than in other economies. The oft-cited evidence from other countries[36] should be partly discounted. And as time passes and the unemployed put pressure on wages, the latter must drop at some point. The longer the recession, the more pressure will be exerted on wages, just as happens with prices of goods and services. Indeed, real wages did drop in 1932 and 1933,[37] and they showed a tendency to fall in the middle of 2008. The question is how much time it takes, but it should be remembered that, historically, most recessions do not turn into depressions.

Note that, when nominal wages start decreasing, prices should not drop as much proportionally, so that real wages will go down and the quantity demanded of labor will increase. We can think of at least two reasons for this. First, wages are only one component of cost, so that a 10 percent drop in wages should not automatically translate into a 10 percent price drop. Second, even assuming that workers get lower wage incomes in total (because the elasticity of the demand for labor is such that employment increases less than wages have decreased), it does not follow that aggregate demand will be deficient, pushing prices down further, as Keynes argued. For whatever production the laborers don't buy, other owners of factors of production (owners of capital and land) will buy, for somebody must have received the income from the increased production that accompanies higher employment.[38]

Moreover, the inflexibility of nominal wages often come from institutional or policy constraints. Both Hoover's encouragements to businesses to maintain wages and Roosevelt's National Industry Recovery Act exerted upward pressures on wages, thereby deepening the depression.[39] In today's world, wage inflexibility is increased by the legal powers of trade unions to impose inflexible collective agreements—although these powers have recently been on a downward trend in the private sector of the United States and other countries. If wage inflexibility creates unemployment and causes trouble during recessions, the solution would be to change the institutions and policies that generate such inflexibility. Perhaps the problem of inflexible wages, unemployment, and long recessions would largely disappear as the classical economists would have predicted?

A second broad condition under which aggregate demand falls short of full-employment output, argues Keynesian theory, is that not all savings are necessarily invested. Another price, the rate of interest, is presumed not to adjust to equalize supply and demand. This is because, for Keynes, the rate of interest is, in the short run, not only the price of loanable funds but also the price of money balances: the lower the rate of interest, the lower the price of keeping money idled, and the more money people will want to hold as opposed to investing it. We can admit this, but it is a short-run phenomenon. Except if one expects the rate of interest to go up, or equivalently the price of bonds to go down, in the very near future, there is no reason not to put money in short-term, money-market, interest-bearing instruments. If the short run lasts too long, people will put their money to work. Except for short-term disturbances, the interest rate does equalize saving and investment. We always come back to Say's law—at least after a not too long short run. Except if the authorities compound short-run troubles, like they did in the Great Depression, supply tends to create its own demand, following individuals' propensity "to truck, barter, and exchange one thing for another."

Not everything is wrong with Keynes. He emphasized short-run adjustment problems. He stressed the importance of uncertainty and the limits of rationality in much the same way as Hayek or Taleb. His reminders on the role of confidence, although not absent from neoclassical analysis, are also welcome. Yet, his obscure "animal spirits" and his fixation on the short-run risk hides the deep equilibrating forces at work in the economy. On the market, prices guide behavior and prevent people from acting foolishly. These prices can be expected to equalize supply and demand simply because individuals always try to improve their situations by exchanging on markets. If not forbidden to do so, the unemployed will offer to work at lower wages instead of earning nothing. Interest rates on the credit market will be bid up or down so as to eliminate any discrepancy between saving and investment. Nothing is perfect, and discrepancies can certainly appear in the short run. Yet, it is difficult to believe that prices will not adjust before a deep recession sets in. Again, most recessions, even before Keynes, do not turn into depressions.

Keynes's theory has more serious theoretical problems, related to its basic methodology. Keynesian macroeconomics is built on broad, holistic, very abstract constructs that often have only tiny relations with what happens in the real world of economic actions and interactions. Of course, it is not surprising that Keynesian theory hides things: every theory does. But a theory must not ignore crucial features of reality. Keynesian theory constructs big aggregates whose meaning is obscure and that blur relative prices and coordination mechanisms. It conceals particular markets—the microeconomy—behind a broad macroeconomic vision that shows the forest but hides the trees. Keynes invented the whole field of macroeconomics. "Macro" comes from the Greek *makros,* which means "big," as opposed to "micro," from *mikros,* which refers to the small. Words like "macrocosm" and the "microcosm" have the same roots. For sure, getting the broad picture is useful, but the big picture must still be made of small pieces. For sure, we must guard against the "fallacy of composition," that is, against comprehending the whole as a simple addition of its parts, and admit the possibility that the aggregated consequences of the actions of a large number of interacting individuals may be different from the consequences of one individual's actions. Indeed, this is what economics does all the time: build social and economic phenomena as complex consequences of individual actions. But seeing the forest must not make us forget that it is made of trees and that the forest growth is grounded in the growth of the trees. The more so if the basic elements, instead of trees, are separate individuals with individual minds.

GDP is one of those broad constructs far removed from acting individuals and social interaction. It is not totally useless, but it is much overrated. To add all outputs in the economy literally requires adding apples and oranges. Weights are needed, and prices fill this purpose. Using prices when they are market determined is a good idea for they represent the value[40] that individuals give to things; but when they are distorted by government intervention, their normative value becomes questionable. Even disregarding this issue, comparing GDP between two periods of time (quarters or years) raises a special problem: it must be decided if the prices used as weights will be those of the first or the second period, or a mix of them. Every alternative has advantages and drawbacks, and creates its own biases. Moreover, several conventions are used in constructing GDP, like which transactions and activities to include and which ones to exclude (like nonmarket and black market transactions). The BEA announced that considering research and development expenditures as investment instead of an intermediary input would, on average, add nearly 3 percent to GDP, and change its annual rate of growth.[41] A small variation in GDP can be due as much to the multiple conventions used in its calculation or statistical difficulties as to a significant change in the economy—although big changes over a reasonable time horizon mean something. Other global concept like "investment," which try to capture millions of individual investment decisions and actions, suffer from similar problems.

The "price level" is an even more ethereal and perilous concept. If all—literally all—prices increase by 10 percent, it is unobjectionable to say that "prices have increased by 10 percent " or that "the price level has increased by 10 percent." But if different prices increase in different proportions, or if some prices fall while others rise, the different changes have to be weighed in order to calculate an average. We get into problems similar to when we compare GDP between two years. In fact, the problems are worse because the average price of an apple and an orange is a fuzzier notion than their total production. As we saw in Chapter 1, an individual price conveys much information and transmits incentives to many individuals. But what is the meaning of the price level and what signal does it transmit? If it can be unambiguously interpreted as inflation or deflation—all prices move more or less in parallel because of a changing money supply—the price level does convey some information. As prices increase, Zimbabweans will try to get rid of their Zimbabwean dollars, and hold other forms of money. But if an increase in the "price level" reflects the weighing of some prices that rise and others that fall, what does it imply for individual choices? Friedrich Hayek rightly criticized such holistic concepts as the price level as meaningless for understanding the economy.[42]

The problems are compounded when we throw in other obscure constructs like "aggregate supply" and "aggregate demand," which are supposed to be related to the "price level." Perhaps we can make sense of consumers demanding fewer goods if the price level is higher, because—money supply being constant—they have less money to buy goods and services. It is more difficult to make sense of all businesses increasing activity because the "price level" increases. If businessmen expect high inflation, they are as likely to decrease production in order to guard against uncertainly and disruptions. A business bases its decisions on the price of the goods it produces, not on some "general price level." The owner of the business is interested in the relative price of what he sells compared to the prices of the inputs he uses and to the prices of what he wants to buy and consume, not in some average of those prices. The idea that the general price level establishes an equilibrium between aggregate supply and aggregate demand belongs to the domain of fairy tales. How can an average price be bid up or down to equalize the demand and supply of millions of goods demanded and offered by millions of individuals? Says Paul Romer, an economist famous for his work on economic growth, "it is finally clear that you can't think about the aggregate economy using a big supply curve and a big demand curve."[43]

Because it hides relative prices and their coordination role, it is easy for Keynesian theory to draw the conclusion that markets naturally fail.

Although it enjoyed the prestige of a modernist intellectual fad for four decades (from the 1940s to the 1970s), Keynesian theory is, in many ways, a primitive way of looking at society and the economy. The Keynesian approach is often referred to as a "hydraulic model." It shows a "circular flow of income" as a network of pipes, where aggregate demand flows into output, output into income, and income back to aggregate demand with savings (and imports) leaking into another circuit. To compensate for the leaks, government's fiscal policy must "prime the pump." In 1949, economist A.W.H. Phillips, the electrical engineer who invented the Phillips curve, built a seven-foot tall machine, called MONIAC, whose plastic pipes, tanks, valves, and other plumbing hardware were supposed to model the Keynesian economy.[44]

The plumbing story is sometimes replaced by a mechanical analogy, which may appear slightly less simplistic. Keynes himself, explaining the Great Depression one year after it started, said: "We have magneto [alternator] trouble." Keynes was arguing, comments Krugman, "that the economic engine would not restart from its own accord, that it needed a jump start from the government."[45] We have to boost the economy's engine. In the *General Theory*, Keynes mentions "the economic machine."[46] Perhaps, *à la* Jouvenel, he imagined government as an immense "power house setting the governed in motion by means of ever more powerful controls."[47] For de Jouvenel, this was a pejorative description; for Keynes, it might have been a compliment.

Substituting a medical or biological analogy to plumbing and mechanical stories appears to be yet another improvement. "Medicine is Working, but U.S. Economy Isn't Healthy Yet," runs the title of a *Wall Street Journal* column.[48] The economy is described as "the patient," credit markets as "the circulatory system of a modern economy," and the private sector as "the heart and lungs of any capitalist economy." There was a "housing virus" in the banking system. *The Economist,* which is not an economic lightweight either, compares Germany to "an outwardly well patient that needs drastic treatment," explaining that "without painful surgery, there is a real danger that the arteries of finance may soon clog."[49] This conception of society as a biological organism is an old error, rightly denounced by several social and political theorists.[50] Italian statistician Corrado Gini, inventor of a widely used measure of income inequality (the "Gini coefficient") and a favorite of Mussolini's regime, rode the "national organism" in his quest for the "scientific basis of fascism."[51]

These analogies are terribly misleading. The only valid analogy for the economy is that of an information network. Millions of individuals consuming and producing thousands of goods are coordinated by information signals called prices, which they themselves generate on decentralized markets. As explained by Hayek, changed circumstances in any part of the system generate new signals and produce a rearrangement of expectations and actions.[52] A disruption in the flow of information causes expectations and actions to be rearranged in often unexpected ways through multiple effects and retroactions. When they interfere in this complex information network, the authorities behave like a would-be programmer who fixes a bug in one of the million lines of code of a complex piece of software and causes other bugs to pop up elsewhere. The authorities tinker with something they don't understand. No single individual or political assembly or bureaucratic committee knows all the code of society. In fact, nobody knows more than a few lines of code. Mussolini, who wanted to restrict individual liberty in the name of a complex civilization, was messing up with the computer of civilization. So was Keynes.

Ex Nihilo

Contrary to what Keynes thought, it is not so obvious that activist government policy can effectively counter a recession. We can never experience a counterfactual and observe what would have happened if government had not intervened, but there are a few well-known instances where government did not intervene in a looming recession and nothing bad happened. Thomas Sewell notes that the stock market crash of 1987 was as close an event as we can find to the crash of 1929. In two weeks in October 1987, the Dow Jones Industrial Average slipped by 28 percent, still less than the 52 percent of a similar period in October 1929, but much more than in the autumn of

2008 when, over the last four months of the year, the index lost 25 percent. The Reagan Administration did not intervene and the economy self-corrected without even a recession, let alone a deflationary spiral.[53] Similarly, when a recession struck in 1921, with a drop of output of 3 percent, the newly elected president, Warren Harding, did not intervene except for lowering taxes. A strong recovery came rapidly after less than one year of recession: in 1922, output grew by 6 percent.[54]

One strange implication of standard Keynesian theory is that something can be created out of nothing, that aggregate demand can be generated by the government at no cost. The idea is expressed in striking terms in the *General Theory*:

> If the Treasury were to fill old bottles with bank-notes, bury them at suitable depths in disused coal-mines which are then filled up to the surface with town rubbish, and leave it to private enterprise on well-tried principles of *laissez-faire* to dig the notes up again (the right to do so being obtained, of course, by tendering for leases of the note-bearing territory), there need be no more unemployment and, with the help of repercussions, the real income of the community, and its capital wealth, would probably become a good deal greater than it actually is. It would, indeed, be more sensible to build houses and the like; but if there are practical difficulties in the way of this, the above would be better than nothing.[55]

The problem is that any expenditure has to be financed either by raising taxes or by borrowing to cover a deficit, that is, it has to be paid for either now or in the future. Money creation is another way for the government to finance a deficit, but it also has future consequences in terms of inflation; and inflation is a hidden tax. Whatever positive impact stimulus expenditures have today—if they have any—must cancelled by a negative impact either now or in the future. The impression that Authority can create production *ex nihilo* is an illusion. This truth became apparent when the deficits of Western governments ballooned after the 2008 and 2009 stimulus expenditures, unnerving government lenders.

Besides financing requirements, government activism has other negative effects. Especially when regulation and control are added to expenditures, government intervention is likely to hurt confidence instead of boosting it. With his massive intervention, Roosevelt created what economic historian Robert Higgs calls "regime uncertainty." Businessmen did not want to hire, produce and invest because they feared that Roosevelt's taxes, labor legislation, planning measures, spending, and general anti-business rhetoric was altering the economic landscape toward some form of socialism. Hence, the depression was prolonged instead of abridged. World War II gave the impression it was over, but not until brisk growth started just after the war did the people's standard of living increased over its pre-depression level.[56]

Economists Gary Becker (the 1992 winner of the Nobel Prize in economics), Steven Davis, and Kevin Murphy make a somewhat similar argument for the slow recovery that followed the 2007–2009 recession. They write:

> So in addition to continuing and extending the Bush-initiated bailout of banks, AIG, General Motors, Chrysler and other companies, Congress and President Obama signaled their intentions to introduce major changes in taxes, government spending and regulations—changes that could radically transform the American economy. . . . Even though some of the proposed antibusiness policies might never be implemented, they generate considerable uncertainty for businesses and households.[57]

These anti-business policies and proposals also included environmental taxes, health insurance mandates, a more activist antitrust approach, and intervention in executive remuneration. The anti-business rhetoric was intensified by regulatory reform and, in the wake of the oil spill, by Obama's attack on BP: "America's justifiable fury with BP is degenerating into a broader attack on business," wrote *The Economist,* adding: "Businessmen are already gloomy, depressed by the economy and nervous of their president's attitude towards them."[58] In a fragile recovery, the U.S. government was playing with the fire of regime uncertainty.

New Macroeconomic Theories

Keynesian theory has been criticized by a number of alternative macroeconomic theories, many of which developed since the 1960s.

Monetarism, a variant the quantity theory of money, returned to the forefront of academic debates with the research of Milton Friedman. Friedman argued that monetary policy could only increase real GDP in times of recession; otherwise, it would generate inflation—or deflation. In this perspective, money matters and monetary policy has an impact for better or for worse. Friedman thought that it was generally for worse, except when necessary to counter a decline of the money supply in a recession. Monetary policy, argued Friedman, has "long and variable lags," and cannot be counted on to fine-tune the economy in ordinary times. The best thing a central bank can do is to increase the money supply at a constant rate corresponding to productivity growth. Later in his life, Friedman proposed instead a sort of zero-tolerance monetary policy: freezing the monetary base (the sum of bank reserves and currency).[59] He believed *à la* Say that GDP normally stands at full employment. Friedman and Schwartz explained the Great Depression by a failure of monetary policy to maintain the money supply.[60] In normal times, increases in the money supply would generate inflation, like in the 1970s.

Friedman argued that monetary policy cannot reliably influence interest rates, except perhaps temporarily for short-term rates. He blamed the Fed, which "has given its heart not to controlling the quantity of money but to controlling interest rates, something it does not have the power to do."[61]

While the Keynesians thought that monetary policy is generally ineffective to fight a recession, Friedman believed that it is fiscal policy that is unreliable. He argued that government could not stimulate the economy through fiscal policy and especially through budget deficits. Interviewed in 1996, he said:

> A deficit is not stimulating because it has to be financed, and the negative effects of financing counterbalance the positive effects, if there are any, on spending. But that may not be the reason because there is another reason: it is much harder to adjust fiscal policy in a sensitive way than it is to adjust monetary policy. So I don't believe that there is any role for fiscal policy in the short term.[62]

The experience of the 2007–2009 recession vindicated Friedman's view on fiscal policy. The American Recovery and Reinvestment Act and its $787 stimulus package were adopted by Congress on February 13, 2009, just a few months before the recovery started in the third quarter of 2009. It is unlikely that the recovery was due to the stimulus if only because only one-third of the money had been expended by the time the recession ended.[63] Even at the time the stimulus package was adopted, the Congressional Budget Office (CBO) expected only three-quarters of the money to be expended by September 2010.[64] So much for the fine-tuning efficiency of fiscal policy.

Another major school of economic thought to take issue with Keynesianism is the so-called New Classical school.[65] Keynesians assumed that individuals were unable to change their expectations when confronted with public policies with known consequences—say, an increase in the money supply that would generate inflation. Starting in the 1970s with the work of economists like Thomas Sargent and Robert Lucas (the 1995 Nobel prizewinner), the new classical school assumed instead that individuals change their expectations when new, relevant information becomes available. They come to anticipate the consequences of public policy and adjust their behavior accordingly. They can make errors, but not with a consistent optimistic or pessimistic bias. Their expectations won't systematically be and remain incorrect. You can't fool all the people all the time. An inflationary policy cannot for long create the illusion of prosperity and reduce unemployment: expected inflation changes behavior, wages catch up with prices, nominal interest rates increase by the amount of expected inflation, and unemployment persists. Both inflation and unemployment can thus coexist—like in the 1970s. Only unexpected inflation can perhaps increase employment temporarily, so there is no real, long-run trade-off between inflation and unemployment. If policy makers think there is, they will end up getting both. New classical economists substituted to the Keynesian representation of the economy a model based on general equilibrium where all markets (including labor markets) automatically clear and full employment is more or less automatic.

The equivalence principle of classical economist David Ricardo, which Harvard University economist Robert Barro brought back into fashion, illustrates how rational expectations work, and allows us to better understand the consequences of government financing. If the government finances its expenditures by borrowing, the results will not be different than if it raises current taxes instead. Knowing that future taxes will have to rise to reimburse the new debt created by the deficit, people will adjust their behavior accordingly. They will save more to pay future taxes, or leave more money to their heirs; one way or another, they will consume less now, exactly what they would have done if current taxes had been raised. Not only the deficit is not transferred to future generations, but it can't stimulate the economy, even in a Keynesian perspective, since it reduces consumption. What the government spends, individuals don't spend. This confirms the vacuity of stimulus expenditures to counter a recession.

A combination of Keynes's aggregate demand apparatus and classical market adjustments, the new classical school seemed incapable of explaining recessions. By the 1980s, a new paradigm was in the works with the Real Business Cycle (RBC) school. RBC theorists include Fynn Kydland, Edward Prescott, Robert Barro, and others. These economists built on the new classical model, but disregarded aggregate demand and focussed on supply shocks caused by technological advances. In their view, the business cycle is an adaptation to real disturbances on the supply side. Money plays no role in pure RBC models. "While recessions are not desired by economic agents," write Brian Snowdon and Howard Vane to explain RBC theory, "they represent the aggregate outcome of responses to unavoidable shifts in the constraints that agents face."[66] The business cycle, which can be seen as a consequence of Schumpeterian creative destruction and the adaptation of individuals to such shocks, is very closely related to long-run growth. In fact, the distinction between the short run and the long run is abandoned. The business cycle comes from frequent and random technological shocks, which leads GDP to fluctuate around its trend. So there is really no regular cycle, but a series of adjustments and equilibriums following supply shocks. Besides technology, other sorts of supply-side shocks can fuel disturbances and adjustments, like natural disasters, war and political upheaval, government regulations, or rapid changes in the price of energy. This suggests that the doubling of the price of oil between 2006 and 2008 might have contributed to the crisis along with the other factors I will analyze later in this book.

Snowdon and Vane note that "real business cycle theorists have challenged the conventional wisdom and forced theorists of all sides to recognize just how deficient our knowledge is of business cycle phenomena."[67] These theories have had a major impact on macroeconomic theorizing. Kydland and Prescott received the 2004 Nobel Prize in economics "for their fundamental contributions to . . . the design of macroeconomic policy . . . [and] how variations in technological development—the main source of long-run economic growth—can lead to short-run fluctuations."[68]

Other schools of economics have contradicted or supported Keynes. The New Keynesian economists, perhaps best represented by Gregory Mankiw, tried to answer some of the challenges raised by Keynes's critics by emphasizing market imperfections and the non-neutrality of money. With the monetarists and against the Keynesians, they argued that money matters. In the process, the new Keynesians incorporated the ideas of many critics of old Keynesian theory. "My own views," says Mankiw, "emerged as much from Milton Friedman as from John Maynard Keynes."[69] The New Political Macroeconomics, another recent school of macroeconomic thought, emphasized the political factors in the choice of fiscal and monetary policies. The older Austrian School, which was partly displaced by the Keynesian steamroller, kept offering a radically different approach (which I will review in Chapter 6).

My rapid overview of macroeconomic theories suggests two conclusions for our purposes. First, it is not totally obvious that serious recessions would occur without government intervention. At any rate, it must not simply be assumed. Second, the diversity of serious macroeconomic theories shows how uncertain is our knowledge of business cycle phenomena. Generations of brilliant economists have tried to understand the business cycle, and still do not agree among themselves. How pretentious it is for parties of politicians or committees of bureaucrats to claim they know how to prevent or dampen recessions!

CHAPTER 3

The Car of Collectivism

But now that we know better, and perceive that the economic forces never have been, never can be, and never should be, left to themselves, and are seeking deliberately to subdue individual action into harmony with collective purposes, the more clearly we can detect the evils which accompany the strength of spontaneous organisation, the more effectively we may hope to check them. . . . The play of individual desires produces many results that outrage the general conscience, and, as we can control the lightning so soon as we understand it, we may hope, as we come better to understand the economic forces, indefinitely to increase our control of them, till we can make the ever-present vigilance of the individual's desire to accomplish his own purposes subject to the control of public aims, and so harness individualism to the car of collectivism . . .

—Philip Wicksteed[1]

The expression "mixed economy" defined economic and social policy during a large part of the twentieth century. It was popular in Europe after World War II, where most states, from France to Italy and the United Kingdom, were keen on increasing intervention in its name. In the glory days of Soviet communism, many economists detected a "convergence" between this regime and the West. A textbook of the 1960s on economic systems was typical, while moderate, in discussing the convergence between Western economies and command-and-control economies of the Soviet type:

But if command is apt to give way to the market mechanism during the process of industrialization, the latter is also likely to yield everywhere more and more social control for the sake of ensuring stability, providing public services, and directing economic development in socially desired ways. In the past, these kinds of planning and steering were instituted too rigidly in the East and perhaps too loosely in the West; some future convergence on this plane is not at all unlikely. . . .

> Another plane on which the systems are likely to move closer is that of the
> welfare state: protection of the individual against various risks, including illness,
> and broad provision of such services as education.[2]

The mixed economy was, on our side, the embodiment of this convergence.

The mixed economy has been growing at least since World War I. It blossomed under Roosevelt's New Deal in the wake of the Great Depression. Paul Samuelson, winner of the 1970 Nobel Prize in economics, admitted that much in the 1976 edition of his famous introductory economics textbook: "After the New Deal, American economic life was never again the same. We had converged with Western Europe to the mixed economy."[3] Harold Vatter, an economic historian critical of capitalism, agrees with the beginning of the New Deal as the date of birth of the mixed economy. In a 1979 article, he celebrated the advent of the mixed economy 46 years earlier, as its title explicitly declared: "Perspectives on the Forty-sixth Anniversary of the U.S. Mixed Economy."[4] The New Deal was just the beginning. Vatter noted that "the Employment Act of 1946 reflected a new, transformed outlook, and did prophetically initiate a lasting public commitment to high employment."[5] He hailed "the decisive and viable character of the transformation from laissez-faire capitalism"[6] and "the demise of laissez-faire."[7] Until very recently, moderate leftists not only advocated the mixed economy, but took for granted that we were living in one. As Vatter wrote, "[t]he mixed economy has of necessity already moved, albeit haphazardly, toward the socialization (government planning) of supply."[8]

The mixed economy is a mix of capitalism and socialism. Capitalism provides the ingredients of nominally private property and limited freedom of contract. Socialism brings the primacy of collective choice, one form or another of economic planning, and public ownership or control of strategic or "systemic" industries. Vatter's lists many features of the mixed economy: "social planning (e.g., French indicative planning), persistent net public budget deficits...jump in government expenditures and transfer payments to persons, the extension of the income tax, a vast socialization of material security for the individual, a distinct drop in the relative importance of 'private' consumption, a dampening of the economic cycle...the federal minimum wage."[9] As expressed by economist Philip Wicksteed at the beginning of the twentieth century, the dream of the mixed economy is to "harness individualism to the car of collectivism."[10] It is noteworthy that both the traditional right (General de Gaulle in France, for example) and the traditional left (the British Labor Party after World War II) have embraced the mixed economy. In the United States, neither the Republican Party nor the Democratic Party questions the basic orientations of the mixed economy—even if they always quibble on the details.

The mixed economy has become so much part of our lives that we don't notice it anymore. Its name has disappeared from the public discourse because it is so obvious. We can't imagine the world differently.

Always suspicious of unregulated capitalism, the hard right also favors a mixed economy. The corporatist ideal envisioned an economy with nominally private property, hierarchical organizations of trades, and strong state control. Mussolini had high hopes for the twentieth century: "it may rather be expected," he wrote, "that this will be a century of authority . . . a century of Fascism. For if the nineteenth century was a century of individualism it may be expected that this will be the century of collectivism and hence the century of the State."[11] Reflecting on the corporatist ideal of Italian fascists, historian Charles Maier writes that "Mussolini looked abroad to find that Franklin Roosevelt was merely seeking to emulate Italy's innovations."[12]

While the left and the right were welcoming the development of the mixed economy, analysts in the classical liberal or libertarian tradition were mourning free markets. They have claimed for decades that we were living in a "mixed economy" and even drifting toward tyranny.

In his 1944 book, *The Road to Serfdom,* Friedrich Hayek argued that the economic policies that were gaining ground in the West were inconsistent with the maintenance of a free society. He attacked delegated legislation— quasi-legislative power delegated to regulatory agencies—and discretionary economic interventions. Discretionary powers, he observed, are necessary if the government is to be in charge of the whole economy, but they are inconsistent with the rule of law. Just as he forecasted the demise of the communist planned economies, Hayek, who was to receive a Nobel Prize in economics 30 years later, saw the slippery slopes in Western countries. It is difficult not to relate *The Road to Serfdom* to current government intervention: the pay "czar" fixing remunerations at nominally private companies, the expansion of financial regulators' discretionary powers, and the entrenchment of the privileges of—and accompanying controls on—companies deemed "too big to fail." Hayek argued that planning is a vicious circle. "Once the free working of the market is impeded beyond a certain degree," he warned, "the planner will be forced to extend his controls until they become all-comprehensive."[13] By the early 1930s, he argued, England and America had moved so far away from laissez-faire "that only those whose memory goes back to the years before the [First World] war know what a liberal world has been like."[14] He was of course using the term "liberal" in its classical, laissez-faire sense.

Lionel Robbins, a well-known London School of Economics professor, was also among the economists who argued that the free market economy had been replaced by another regime since World War I. "The essence of pre-war capitalism," he wrote in 1934, "was the free market . . . in the sense that the buying and selling of goods and the factors of production was not subject to arbitrary interference by the State or strong monopoly controls." Since World War I, he said, the free market "has tended to be more and more restricted"[15] by state intervention. He wrote:

> The cartelisation of industry, the growth of the strength of trade unions, the multiplication of State controls, have created an economic structure which, whatever its ethical or aesthetic superiority, is certainly much less capable of rapid adaptation to change than the older more competitive system. Certainly no one who wishes to understand the persistence of the maladjustments of the great slump can neglect the element of inelasticity and uncertainty introduced by the existence of the various pools and restriction schemes, the rigidities of the labour market and cartel prices which are the characteristic manifestation of these developments. These tendencies are the creation of policy.[16]

He concluded that the Great Depression was not due to the conditions of capitalism but "to their negation":

> It was due to monetary mismanagement and State intervention operating in a *milieu* in which the essential strength of capitalism had already been sapped by war and by policy. Ever since the outbreak of war in 1914, the whole tendency of policy has been away from that system . . . [17]

Despite numerous such warnings, the public debate around the 2007–2009 crisis seemed to assume that we were previously living in a capitalist economy and that, therefore, the causes of the crisis were to be found in capitalism. A good case in point is Richard Posner's book *A Failure of Capitalism*.[18] Posner is a legal theorist and federal judge known as a conservative who, in this recent book, adopts a Keynesian perspective and argues that the crisis was caused by individual rationality producing collective irrationality. Published in early 2009, the book forecasted that the recession would turn into a full-fledged depression, as emphasized by its subtitle: *The Crisis of '08 and the Descent into Depression*. This forecast was exaggerated as a recovery was just about to start. The developing depression, Posner wrote, "is largely a consequence not of the government's overregulating the economy and by doing so fettering free enterprise, but rather of innate limitations of the free market."[19] These limitations are "rooted in individuals' incentives, in irresponsible monetary policy adopted and executed by conservative officials inspired by conservative economists who thought that easy money was no problem if it did not lead to serious inflation, and in excessive, ideologically motivated deregulation of banking and finance compounded by lax enforcement of the remaining regulations."[20] The perverse individual incentives led to "aggressive marketing of mortgages, a widespread appetite for risk, a highly competitive, largely deregulated finance industry, and debt securitization."[21]

Intriguingly for somebody who claims that the recession was as a failure of capitalism, Posner recognizes many government failures that contributed to the crisis, including the Fed's insouciance toward the housing bubble,[22] and the encouragement of home ownership through mortgage rate deductibility and other policies.[23] But for Posner, monetary policy and the other government interventions he blames are all parts of capitalism, so capitalism takes the blame. Capitalism is, in a way, redefined to be the culprit. Since he implicitly identifies "capitalism" and even laissez-faire to the mixed economy, it becomes tautological to claim that the crisis was "a crisis of capitalism."[24] Of course, the crisis must be a failure of the system that existed before. If the system that existed before was capitalism, the crisis shows a failure of capitalism.

Problem is, the system that existed in 2007 was nowhere close to laissez-faire capitalism; it was instead a mixed economy. A very mixed economy.

Government Revenues and Expenditures

The growth of the mixed economy all over the world is easily observable in government expenditures. The standard way to measure the phenomenon is to take the ratio of (total) government expenditures (also called public expenditures) to GDP, which gives an estimate of the size of government relative to the economy. Public expenditures have to be financed by taxes sooner or later, so they represent what government takes from the economy. Government expenditure is made of two parts: expenditures on goods and services government buys for its purposes, and transfers, that is, money redistributed from one part of the population to another. When I talk about "government expenditures" or "public expenditures," I mean the total of all such expenditures, at all levels of government (federal, state, and local).

According to estimates compiled by economists Vito Tanzi (of the International Monetary Fund) and Ludger Schuknecht (of the European Central Bank), the size of government expenditures to GDP in the average industrialized country was 11 percent at the end of the nineteenth century.[25] On the high side figured countries like Australia (18 percent) and Switzerland (17 percent). On the low side, we find the United States at 7 percent and Scandinavian countries at approximately the same level. The United Kingdom's 9 percent was not very far from the U.S. situation. In 1913, just before World War I, these ratios had slightly increased to reach an average of 13 percent, mainly because of the growth of the Welfare State in

Europe—except in Switzerland, where the proportion had decreased. A big jump of 7 percentage points occurred between 1913 and 1920, the ratio reaching 20 percent. Partly because of the Great Depression, the ratio had progressed again in 1937—to 24 percent. Twenty years were then necessary to add another 4 percentage point to the size of public expenditures in the average developed country: government expenditures made up 28 percent of GDP in 1960.

One remarkable fact is that in 1960, countries were quite tightly grouped around the 28 percent average: most were between 25 percent and 31 percent. The United States was now very close to the average, but this was to change during the next 40 years as the variance between countries increased while the growth of public expenditures continued. Most of the growth occurred before 1980, where the ratio of public expenditures to GDP reached 42 percent. By that time, France and several European countries had gone to near 50 percent (Sweden had even reached 60 percent, a doubling in two decades), while the United States, Japan, and Switzerland stayed about 10 percentage points below the average. Until the mid-1990s, government expenditures compared with the size of the economy continued to increase, but more slowly: in 1996, the average country stood at 45 percent.

To summarize the world evolution according to the standard way of measuring government expenditures as a proportion of GDP, the twentieth century saw a fourfold increase, from around 10 percent to more than 40 percent. The growth of government expenditure was especially rapid during and after World War I, and from 1960 to 1980.

During most of American history (except for the Civil War and World War I) up to the Great Depression, total government expenditures stood at less than 10 percent of GDP. It was 7.5 percent on the eve of World War I but had climbed to more than 10 percent in 1920.[26] During the Great Depression, the ratio nearly doubled, because a big drop in GDP and an increase in government expenditures. Until World War II, the ratio stayed around 20 percent as both GDP and government expenditures increased. World War II brought the proportion of government expenditures to 51 percent in 1944. The ratio went down after the war, but not exactly to its former level: it stayed in the range of 22–25 percent. It continued increasing in the 1950s and had reached 30 percent by 1961. It then started a slow but relatively regular ascension to 37 percent at the beginning of the 1980s. Rapid economic growth kept it relatively constant during the rest of the 1980s and, from the early 1990s to the early 2001, reduced it to 33 percent. It then started creeping up again, to 35 percent in 2007. In summary, and excluding World War II, we observe a rapid growth of total government expenditures in the United States from 10 percent of GDP before the Great Depression to 30 percent in 1961, and 35 percent in the early 1990s; from then on, we observe small fluctuations around 33 percent, with an upward trend in the new millennium.[27]

This standard way to measure government expenditures—as a proportion of GDP—facilitates comparison across time and space. But it can be misleading when the denominator (GDP) changes along the business cycle. It exaggerates government expenditures during a recession, like in the Great Depression, and conversely underestimates them in booms, like from the mid-1980s until 2007. On way to avoid this problem is to perform a double operation: (1) measure government expenditures in real terms or "constant dollars," that is, deflate the figure with an index of GDP prices; and (2) put everything on a per capita basis. The first operation takes out the impact of inflation which, even if the inflation is low, ends up vitiating comparisons over long periods of time. The average inflation of 3.0 percent over the whole 1929–2007 period ended up multiplying the price level by ten because of compounding. The second operation excludes the increase in government expenditure that are arguably due to a higher number of taxpayers-citizens. The measure obtained gives us what the government really spends for each inhabitant.

Chart 1 shows total (federal, state, and local) real government expenditures per capita in the United States for the period 1929–2007.[28] All

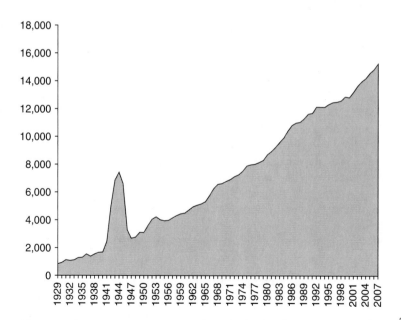

Chart 1   Total government expenditures per capita in the United States (2005 dollars)
Source: BEA and Census Bureau.

data are in dollars of 2005. The growth of government expenditures and the mixed economy is striking. In 1929, the American state (all levels of government) spent $838 per inhabitant. By 1933—that is, roughly over the Hoover presidency—the amount had grown by 33 percent to $1,118. By 1937—Roosevelt's first term—government expenditures per capita had gained another 24 percent and reached $1,383. They continued on the same trend until World War II, climbing to a peak of $7,442 in 1944. After the war, they didn't revert to their 1941 prewar level of $2,469, but decreased to $2,693 per person (in 1947), higher than at any time before the war. They continued on a steeper trend virtually nonstop until 2007. In only five years, 1951, 1954, 1955, 1993, and 2000 did real expenditures per capita show small negative growth—such small blips that they barely show on the graph. It is noteworthy that the growth of government expenditures did not slow down during the 1980s, the "Reagan years." The trend did ease a bit during the 1990s, but became steeper with the new millennium. The result of this virtually uninterrupted growth in government expenditures was that in 2007, American governments were spending $15,266 (which amount to $16,216 in current 2007 dollars) on each man, woman, and child living in the United States—18 times more than in 1929 in constant dollars.

How generous the government has become! Well, not really. What government spends, it takes from the very taxpayers on whom it spends it—albeit sometimes on different groups among the taxpayers. When we say that, in 2007, government spends $16,216 on each U.S. inhabitant, it also means that it takes, in actual or future taxes, $16,216 on average from each one of them.

In 2007, GDP per capita or, what amounts to the same, national income for each man woman and child, was $46,724; and all levels of government spent $16,216 per person. Rounded up, the ratio between the two figures is 35 percent, which is equal to the ratio of government expenditures in the U.S. economy. It is no surprise to find back our previous figure, for calculating the ratio of government expenditures on GDP must give the same answer as calculating the ratios of the two same figures taken per capita. (Dividing the numerator and the denominator of a fraction by the same number does not change the result.) Thus in 2007, on the verge of the recent recession, more than a third of the economy and of people's incomes passed through government coffers, compared with about 7.5 percent before World War I. There is no doubt that America had become very much a mixed economy.

Regulation and Control

Government expenditures provide only part of the picture of the mixed economy. The most important part is the direct and indirect controls that government imposes on transactions and other individual interactions. In a mixed economy, public policy imposes objectives that individuals and businesses must contribute to. For example, the government sets the objective of widespread home ownership, and adopts laws and regulations mandating how mortgage lenders must carry their activities (see Chapter 5). As Hayek suggested, rules of organization are necessary in a mixed economy where the state directs individual activities. The extent of these rules of organization determines whether the mixed economy is closer to the free market or the planned economy end of the spectrum, but a mixed economy and extensive regulation necessarily come together. A mixed economy is more or less authoritarian: only the degree of the authorities' power can vary.

Alexis de Tocqueville had forecasted how regulations would invade democratic societies—of which he thought America was the best example. "I had remarked during my stay in the United States," he wrote in 1840, "that a democratic state of society, similar to that of the Americans, might offer singular facilities for the establishment of despotism." Ancient tyrants like Roman emperors "possessed an immense and unchecked power" which they frequently used "to deprive their subjects of property or of life; their tyranny was extremely onerous to the few, but it did not reach the many; it was confined to some few main objects and neglected the rest; it was violent, but its range was limited." Future democratic tyrannies, Tocqueville continued, will extend "over the whole community," and maintain men "in perpetual childhood": the state "provides for their security, foresees and supplies their necessities, facilitates their pleasures, manages their principal concerns, directs their industry . . . ." The state, as Tocqueville envisioned its future, "covers the surface of society with a network of small complicated rules, minute and uniform, through which the most original minds and the most energetic characters cannot penetrate, to rise above the crowd . . . it does not tyrannize, but it compresses, enervates, extinguishes, and stupefies a people, till each nation is reduced to nothing better than a flock of timid and industrious animals, of which the government is the shepherd."[29] The extent to which people have become "a flock of timid and industrious animals, of which the government is the shepherd" certainly varies across countries, but Tocqueville's view of omnipresent, minute, complicated and uniform regulation can be observed in all Western countries.

Virtually all activities—even those protected by the Bill of Rights—are regulated in some way. Just at the federal level, some 4,000 statutes exist, although it's hard to tell the exact number notes a *Wall Street Journal* reporter "because the statutes aren't listed in one place."[30] The regulations are on top of this. The *Federal Register,* which publishes daily the new and proposed rules of federal agencies and organizations, executive orders, and such, ran its typical

75,000 pages in the year 2007. A quarter of a million federal bureaucrats are employed at writing and enforcing federal regulations.[31] To this must be added the laws, regulations and by-laws at the State and local levels. Since laws and regulations are not pious wishes, it is estimated that 15 percent of all Americans have an arrest record—a truly incredible proportion.[32] An extensive review of all laws and regulations that guide and constrain people's behavior would require several books, but a few impressionistic examples can be given.[33]

Think of the multiple and detailed rules imposed by the Securities and Exchange Commission (SEC) since its creation in 1934, on issuers of securities and listed corporations. In the United States, listed corporations, that is, corporations listed on stock exchanges, are often called "public corporations," dangerously confusing two meanings of "public": available to the public and controlled as public agencies. Under the threat of civil suits and administrative proceedings and orders, the SEC mandates securities registration, regulates brokerage, trading and disclosure of information, and helps enforce the prohibition of insider trading. It often scares large companies into settling suits without trial. The agency imposes fines and work bans. It regulates stock exchanges, which were once private organizations. It files civil suits against violators of the Sarbanes-Oxley Act of 2002. The president of the SEC scolded American CEOs: "You must have an internal code of ethics that goes beyond the letter of the law to also encompass the spirit of the law."[34] A supporter of the rule of law might ask where is the spirit of the law explained in writing so that one knows what is required. The Sarbanes-Oxley Act imposes such wide-ranging requirement for internal controls that corporations now compel their employees to change their computer passwords frequently. The risk of forgetting passwords of course increases, so employees often resort to insecure tricks like writing passwords on sticky notes affixed to their computers![35] Required internal controls may cost the average listed company more than $2.3 million per year.[36]

Detailed financial accounting standards are established by the Financial Accounting Standards Board (FASB), "the designated organization in the private sector for establishing standards of financial accounting." Private sector is somewhat of a misnomer as the FASB's standards "are officially recognized as authoritative by the Securities and Exchange Commission (SEC)." The FASB reminds us that "[t]he SEC has statutory authority to establish financial accounting and reporting standards for publicly held companies under the Securities Exchange Act of 1934."[37]

Columbia University's Amar Bhidé argues that the transparency rules imposed on listed companies since the Great Depression—disclosure requirements, prohibition of insider trading, governance rules, etc.—discouraged the active participation of large and active shareholder, diluted ownership in corporations, and rendered markets more impersonal and therefore more risky.[38] These rules encourage dispersed shareholding and impersonal relations between the firm and its shareholders. Whatever the advantages of impersonal markets, including their contribution to the Great Society, the ideal can be overdone by interfering in the spontaneous mix of personal and impersonal contractual relations that evolve from market interactions. The point here again is the extent and minutiae of government regulation.

Competition—or what is considered competition by laws and regulations—is protected by complex antitrust rules. Some claim that, on that score, the George W. Bush administration was more relax than the Clinton administration, which went after Microsoft. But, as *The Economist* notes, "there was plenty of activity on Mr Bush's watch . . . cartels were pursued enthusiastically, with record convictions, jail terms and fines." A "vitamins cartel" was broken. Google was prevented by the Justice Department from tying up with Yahoo. The Federal Trade Commission (FTC) adopted a sweeping definition of market power and tried to block a merger between organic food retailers Whole Foods Market and Wild Oats. Only the courts saved the acquisition of PeopleSoft by Oracle after the Bush administration tried to block it.[39] The 2007–2009 recession was barely over that the U.S. government announced it was suing Intel.

Money laundering legislation was introduced in 1970 to fight organized crime, which thrived as a consequence of the war on drugs. Gradually tightened from the 1980s on, the legislation now allows the state to monitor all cash transactions over $10,000 and virtually all noncash money transfers. Banks and other financial intermediaries have been drafted in the service of the state for this surveillance purpose. Even after creating costly "compliance departments," financial firms are not immune to the risk of civil or criminal prosecution by the state. William McDavid, general counsel of JP Morgan Chase, used an analogy: "[T]hink if you are running a railroad, and we say to you, 'We want you to monitor everyone who takes your train and see if their trip is legitimate.' " "One unintended consequence," continues the *Wall Street Journal,* "is that banks are simply dropping small money-transfer businesses as clients, a move that could hurt millions of poor immigrants who send cash to relatives overseas."[40] The surveillance of personal finance is so advanced that the government can "freeze the assets" of suspects, and nobody is surprised at its capacity to do so—which, just a few decades ago, would have looked as an impossible mission in a free society.

Control requires surveillance, and surveillance requires that the state be able to monitor individuals. Section 17(f)(2) of the Securities Exchange Act (added to the original 1934 act[41]) reads: "Every member of a national securities exchange, broker, dealer, registered transfer agent, and registered clearing agency, shall require that each of its partners, directors, officers, and employees be fingerprinted and shall submit such fingerprints, or cause the same to be submitted, to the Attorney General of the United States for identification and appropriate processing." This is consistent with a massive but neglected phenomenon of the last half of the twentieth century in America: the introduction of de facto ID papers, generally in the form of the driver's licence with photograph and related database. In the mixed economy, individuals have to be easily identifiable and findable for detailed and intrusive controls to be enforced. The growing accumulation of data on individuals started long before 9/11 and was already raising concerns.[42]

All this, some may object, is only impressionistic discourse. Do we have any hard evidence that regulation has increased? Such evidence is not easy to find because regulation is a multifaceted phenomenon which is difficult to measure. Fortunately, we have some indirect evidence in the data produced by the Mercatus Center at George Mason University and the Weidenbaum Center on the Economy, Government, and Public Policy at Washington University in St. Louis (Missouri).[43] These two think tanks have produced a series on the annual budgets of the federal regulatory agencies from 1960 on. If we assume a direct relation between regulatory budgets and the volume of regulation, that is, if we assume that regulatory budgets are a good proxy for regulatory intensity, which would seem to be a safe assumption, then we can use this series to approximate the evolution of regulation from 1960 until now. This measure is imperfect: it measures only part of the cost of enforcing regulations because the budgets of the courts and ordinary police forces, like the FBI or state and local police forces, are not included; and it does not measure the broader economic costs imposed on regulated firms and individuals. But it is the best measure available.

The Mercatus-Weidenbaum series include about six dozen regulatory bureaus split in two broad categories: "social regulation" and "economic regulation." Although not always meaningful, the distinction is a standard one. Social regulation is defined by its social purpose (whatever that means), in relation with health, safety and the environment. Its subcategories are (1) consumer safety and health, (2) homeland security, (3) transportation, (4) workplace, (5) environment, and (6) energy. I will show separately the homeland security data to avoid the objection that such regulations are of a different sort, and to counter the false claim that they explain the growth of regulation after 9/11. Economic regulation covers all sorts of controls deemed of an economic nature, although again the distinction is often not clear. The economic regulatory bureaus are divided into three subcategories: (1) finance and banking, (2) industry specific regulation (for other industries like

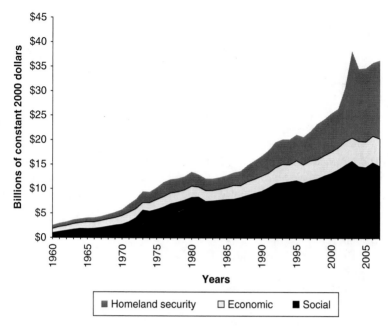

Chart 2 Regulatory expenditures by the U.S. federal government, 1960–2007 (2000 dollars)
Source: Veronique de Rugy and Melinda Warren (2009), including unpublished data.

agriculture, telecommunications, etc.), and (3) general business regulation (patents, antitrust, etc.).

Chart 2 shows the evolution of the regulatory expenditures by broad categories in constant dollars of 2000.[44] Ignore the top area, homeland-security regulations, which have been increasing fast, and not only since 9/11. Social regulations, which already consumed close to $1 billion in 1960, have increased virtually nonstop to $14.7 billion in 2007 (all amounts in constant 2000 dollars): they have been multiplied by fifteen over the period, for an annual (compounded) rate of growth of 5.9 percent. Economic regulatory expenditure, which started at approximately the same level in 1960—$850 million—increased at 4.1 percent per year and reached $5.6 billion in 2007, having been multiplied by seven over the period. Total social and economic regulation expenditures (excluding homeland security) went from $1.4 billion in 1960 to $20.3 billion in 2007, for a 5.2 percent compound growth rate or a multiplication by 11 (the factor is 14 if we include homeland security).

During that period, real GDP increased at a compounded rate of 3.3 percent. Total social and economic regulation (again excluding homeland security) thus grew 66 percent faster (5.2 percent compared with 3.3 percent). Economic regulation grew at a 24 percent higher pace than real GDP (4.1 percent compared with 3.3 percent). Note that homeland-security expenditures, not included in the previous figures, grew at a 6.9 percent annual rate. Although much of the increase was post-9/11, the annual growth rate of national security expenditures was still 6.3 percent up to 2000.

The years 2004 and 2005 were the only consecutive years to show a decline in total regulatory expenditures, contributing to a plateau during the last four years of the series shown on the chart (preliminary data show that the upward trend returned in 2008). The plateau was caused by a temporary recess in social regulation expenditures. Even during these plateau years, economic regulatory expenditures continued their upward movement, by 1.3 percent in 2005, 3.8 percent in 2006, and 3.5 percent in 2007. *The Economist* notes that under George W. Bush, the number of pages of federal regulation increased by 7,000.[45]

It is noteworthy that regulation did not abate during President Ronald Reagan's two terms (FY 1981 to FY 1988). Expenditures on social and even economic regulation did drop at the beginning of his first term, but soon started to rise again, briskly in the case of economic regulations. By FY 1988, annual expenditures (again in constant dollars) were 5.3 percent higher than in FY 1980 for social regulation, and 21.5 percent higher for economic regulation. One could argue that deregulation activity was the source of the increased costs, were it not for the fact that the trend was upward during most of Regan's presidency, and that it was the same trend as before and after.

The Welfare State

Nearly two centuries ago, Alexis de Tocqueville saw the future democratic state as maintaining men "in perpetual childhood": it "provides for their security, foresees and supplies their necessities, facilitates their pleasures, manages their principal concerns, directs their industry." Welcome to the Welfare State which, as its name indicates, takes in charge the welfare of its citizens or subjects. That the Welfare State developed in parallel with the mixed economy is not an accident. On the one hand, the Welfare State requires extensive government power which the mixed economy provides. On the other hand, the powerful state which runs—or tries to run—a mixed economy needs the Welfare State to legitimize its power. It is significant that the legitimization of state power was one motive for the development of the first Welfare State in late nineteenth-century Germany.[46]

Starting at the beginning of the twentieth century, the Welfare State rapidly spread among European countries and, with some lag, to America.

This can be seen in the evolution of social expenditures in this country. In 1929, social benefits (social insurance funds plus transfer payments to persons) accounted for 4 percent of current government expenditures (all levels); in 2007, the proportion was 37 percent.[47] Total social expenditures (which includes social benefits plus all other social expenditures in the fields of housing and community services, health, recreation and culture, and education) make up for 60 percent of government expenditures in 2007, compared with less than 30 percent just half a century ago.[48] Thus, nearly two-thirds of government expenditures in today's United States pay for Welfare State functions.

This galloping growth of welfare expenditures suggests that the Welfare State is concerned not only with redistribution of income for the purpose of poverty alleviation, but also with taking charge of people from the cradle to the grave. Is this a supply or a demand phenomenon—that is, does it respond to some natural growth of power or to the citizenry's demands? I often suggest supply explanations, but the demand side should not be neglected. In a recent article, James Buchanan, winner of the 1986 Nobel Prize in economics, argues for the demand side of state growth: he calls "parentalism" the sort of auto-paternalism whereby the majority of individuals want the state to stand *in loco parentis* (to act like parents) toward them. Buchanan concludes that, for this reason, socialism will continue to progress in the twenty-first century.[49] Whatever the ultimate explanation, the Welfare State, as it developed during the twentieth century aims at protecting individuals against most of the risks and imperfections of life, providing for their health, their education, their security and their pleasures. It is reminiscent of the visions expressed in Aldous Huxley's *Brave New World,* or in George Lucas's 1971 film, *THX-1138.*

Taking people's welfare in charge requires not only providing them with education, health care and income security, but also managing their lifestyles. The first reason is that the inconvenient individual has a way to view his own welfare differently than those who want to manage it for him. The authorities have to intervene to correct their wards' bad choices. The second reason is that redistribution other than straight income is are often more effective for managing people's welfare. The Welfare State tries to take in charge the welfare of the rich as well as the welfare of the poor, and instead of redistributing income from the poor to the rich, which might not be accepted by the masses, it redistributes other benefits of life. For example, the state prevents the poor from living too close to the rich through zoning regulations (minimum size lots, number of housing units, etc.), and prohibits restaurant owners from catering to a smoking clientele (which is more important among poorer people). Inroads in lifestyle control naturally follow the growth of the Welfare State.

When the state appears benevolent toward certain groups, it is at the expense of other groups; there is no such thing as a generally benevolent state. Whatever the powers of authority, it cannot create universal happiness: some people have to be made less happy for some others to be made happier. George W. Bush's saying that "when somebody hurts, government has got to move"[50] is as true when reversed: when government moves, somebody has got to hurt. In the process, state power grows. French political scientist Bertrand de Jouvenel perceptively noted:

> The more one considers the matter, the clearer it becomes that redistribution is in effect far less a redistribution of free income from the richer to the poorer, as we imagined, than a redistribution of power from the individual to the State.[51]

The economic and the social cannot be easily separated: they are simply different dimensions of interindividual relations. The Welfare State can be conceived as the social equivalent of the mixed economy. Just as the Welfare State wants to protect the individual from any "social" risk (illnesses and accidents, ignorance, poverty, inequality), the state presiding over a mixed economy is intent on protecting market participants from "economic" risk, and controlling them for that purpose.

Deposit insurance provides a good case in point. The state protects depositors by guaranteeing their deposits, which removes any incentives for them to worry about their bank's solvability and leads the banks to assume more risk. Consequently, the state has to control the banks' activities. But this is not the whole story. Federal deposit insurance, instituted in 1934, was a response to small local banks prohibited from branching and consequently in need of protection from larger, more solid banks.[52] Deposit insurance was thus both a consequence of former state controls and a reason to impose new ones. When the state takes charge of economic welfare, intervention never ends.

The idea that the state is responsible for the control of the business cycle, that it has some "systemic" economic responsibility, represents a major transposition of the Welfare State in the economic realm. In June 2009, President Barack Obama presented his plan for financial regulatory reform. Transactions in securities "are affected with a national public interest which makes it necessary to provide for regulation and control . . . and to impose requirements necessary to make such regulation and control reasonably complete and effective . . . in order to . . . insure the maintenance of fair and honest markets." The text explains how such intervention is required to face "[n]ational emergencies, which produce widespread unemployment and dislocation of trade . . . and adversely affect the general welfare." Now, these quotes are not taken from Obama's message, but from section 2 of the Securities Exchange

Act of 1934, under Franklin D. Roosevelt's administration. Seventy-five years later, Obama proposes a similar approach with (and here I quote Obama) "a set of reforms that require regulators to look not only at the safety and soundness of individual institutions, but also—for the first time—at the stability of the financial system as a whole."[53] It was not really "the first time." It has started at least with FDR.

The safety net naturally becomes a spider's net. What was officially designed to protect is used to capture. Is this a mere consequence or was the real practical purpose to control? Whatever the answer, the Welfare State is inseparable from the Regulatory State, in the economic as in the social field. A U.S. Treasury spokesman recently used the term "net" in its double meaning: "All financial institutions, including hedge funds, should be covered by the global regulatory net."[54] The safety net catches those who fall, the regulatory net imprisons everybody, and it is the same net.

Domestic Animals

To summarize, capitalism and socialism have converged to produce a system based on the mixed economy and the Welfare State. The convergence was mainly in our own countries: capitalism converged toward communism before the latter collapsed.

John Maynard Keynes was an artisan of this convergence or, at least, provided part of its theoretical justification. He thought that capitalism was unstable under the businessmen's animal spirits, and he wanted the state to continuously fine-tune the economy. He criticized "the arbitrary and inequitable distribution of wealth and incomes."[55] He thought that "the common will" was "embodied in the policy of the State."[56] He believed that the propensity to consume and the rate of investment could be "deliberately controlled in the social interest"[57] by "the State" making calculations "on long views and on the basis of the general social advantage."[58] He promoted a "socially controlled rate of investment"[59] and "communal savings through the agency of the State."[60] "I conceive," he wrote, "that a somewhat comprehensive socialisation of investment will prove the only means of securing an approximation to full employment."[61] He understood that "[t]he central controls necessary to ensure full employment will, of course, involve a large extension of the traditional functions of government."[62]

When discussing the political implications of his theory, interestingly, Keynes is as interested in the long run as in the short run, while his macroeconomic policy prescriptions are supposed to address short-term problems. This comes as no surprise, as the long run is nothing but a succession of short runs. You can't be a socialist in the short run and a capitalist in the long run.

Yet, Keynes often presented himself as a moderate:

> But beyond this no obvious case is made out for a system of State Socialism which would embrace most of the economic life of the community. It is not the ownership of the instruments of production which it is important for the State to assume. If the State is able to determine the aggregate amount of resources devoted to augmenting the instruments and the basic rate of reward to those who own them, it will have accomplished all that is necessary. Moreover, the necessary measures of socialization can be introduced gradually and without a break in the general traditions of society.[63]

"I believe," he also wrote, "that there is social and psychological justification for significant inequalities of incomes and wealth, but not for such large discrepancies as exist to-day."[64] He defended "the decentralization of decisions," "personal liberty," "the variety of life, which emerges precisely from this extended field of choice," against "the homogeneous or totalitarian state."[65] As we saw, he wrote that "[i]t is better that a man should tyrannise over his bank balance than over his fellow-citizens."[66] He warned that public works may be inefficient to control the business cycle: "They are not capable of sufficiently rapid organization (and above all cannot be reversed or undone at a later date)."[67]

At times, Keynes may even seem intent on saving capitalism:

> Whilst, therefore, the enlargement of the functions of government, involved in the task of adjusting to one another the propensity to consume and the inducement to invest, would seem to a nineteenth-century publicist or to a contemporary American financier to be a terrific encroachment on individualism, I defend it, on the contrary, both as the only practicable means of avoiding the destruction of existing economic forms in their entirety and as the condition of the successful functioning of individual initiative.[68]

Analysts still debate whether John Maynard Keynes aimed at saving capitalism or at destroying it. The truth appears closer to the latter when one reads his other works, as shown by Professor Ralph Raico of Buffalo State College.[69] Or perhaps Keynes was just an iconoclast who did not realize the political implications of his theories? Criticizing *The Road to Serfdom*, he blamed Hayek for not realizing that "dangerous acts can be done safely in a community which thinks and feels rightly, which would be the way to hell if they were executed by those who think and feel wrongly."[70] He of course assumed that he was among those who thought rightly. He would be the Prince's adviser, the one exerting "adult supervision."

What did Keynes defend, then, capitalism or socialism? The solution to the enigma is deceptively simple: he defended both. He was a promoter of the mixed economy. He wanted socialism without nationalization. He wanted the state to control businessmen, not to become businessman itself. The businessmen have to be cajoled and co-opted by the state so that they work toward state-defined objectives. In the mixed economy, businessmen are not against the state, they compete for its favors by being nice and obedient. Keynes understood this very well, in a sort of Wicksteedian way. In a letter to President Franklin D. Roosevelt during the Great Depression, he blamed the president for scaring off businessmen (and creating regime uncertainty):

> You could do anything you liked with them, if you would treat them (even the big ones), not as wolves or tigers, but as domestic animals by nature, even though they have been badly brought up and not trained as you would wish.[71]

The story of the mixed economy resulting from capitalism converging to communism before the fall of the latter is not complete. After the fall of the Soviet empire, another surprise was in stock: a second convergence was in process which only became obvious at the turn of the twenty-first century. Not all communist regimes collapsed: one variant, the Chinese regime, survived because it embarked on its own convergence with the mixed economies. Of course, there was no real way to converge to capitalism, which had long dissolved into the mixed economy, but the latter proved to be the savior of Chinese communism. By harnessing the mixed economy to the car of collectivism, the autocrats ruling the Chinese state figured they could both have economic prosperity and retain control. All the vocabulary, the institutions and the tools had been developed in our own mixed economies and *they were not incompatible with an authoritarian regime*. This was a fundamental discovery. Announcing that music sites would require approval for any foreign song they want to distribute, the Chinese Ministry of Culture said the measure was addressing a "lack of supervision and regulation over market behavior." Doesn't this ring a bell? The companies providing music download services would be required to apply for an Internet culture license. When it explained that it was cooperating with the state, Baidu, a Chinese Google-like search engine, used a standard Western formulation, saying that it "complies with local rules and regulations."[72] Google, who had been cooperating with the Chinese state's censorship, found out that the censors are not always cool British types like Keynes. The strength of capitalist companies is that they offer consumers what they want. Their weakness is that they consider the state as just another cost and, at worst, just another customer to satisfy. The former chairman of Alibaba, a Chinese partner of Yahoo, said he will side with the Chinese government in any conflict with a Yahoo China e-mail user. "I'm not a political group," he said, "I'm a businessman."[73] As Keynes knew, businessmen easily become tame domestic animals.

Another manifestation of the same convergence is the so-called hybrid companies, corporations that are, and act as, both state agencies and entrepreneurial organizations roaming international markets. Many are Russian and Chinese, but some come from India, Malaysia, and other countries. They benefit from implicit state guarantees which allow them to raise capital at lower cost on world markets. Some of these hybrid companies, like Norway's Statoil, China's CNOOC, and India's ONGC are even listed on stock exchanges. Fannie Mae and Freddie Mac (to which we will come back in Chapter 5) are the most famous hybrid companies to have been produced by the softer mixed economies.[74] The top twenty-five of Forbes Global 2000 list include four state-controlled companies.[75]

"The line between the bureaucracy and private assets has become increasingly blurred in recent years," writes *The Economist* about Russia.[76] We can say something similar about our mixed economy: the line between politicians and bureaucrats on one hand, and tightly regulated private companies on the other hand, has become blurred. The 2007–2009 recession and the government's bailouts and control of large private companies have just marked another step. We were already deep into the mixed economy when the recession hit.

CHAPTER 4

The Laissez-Faire Scapegoat

Laissez-faire is finished.... The all-powerful market which is always right is finished.

—Nicolas Sarkozy[1]

Richard Posner blamed the economic crisis on "excessive, ideologically motivated deregulation of banking and finance compounded by lax enforcement of the remaining regulations."[2] "The idea of the all-powerful market which wasn't to be impeded by any rules or political intervention was a mad one," observed French President Nicolas Sarkozy, but now "[l]aissez-faire is finished."[3] Sometimes, those repeating the deregulation mantra implicitly admitted it had little substance. "A primary cause of the crisis of 2007–09," wrote the International Monetary Fund (IMF), "was lax financial regulation in the United States."[4] But just two pages later, the IMF editors admit that financial institutions were far from unregulated: "At the heart of the challenge lies a select set of systemically critical financial conglomerates. These groups, straddling the boundary between the heavily regulated, bank-centric core and the more lightly regulated, nonbank periphery of the system...."[5] So, the commercial banks were "heavily regulated" while the investment banks, hedge funds, and other shadow banks were "more lightly regulated," or less heavily regulated. Where is the lax financial regulation?

A Heavy Regulatory Burden

Banks and other financial businesses were, before 2007, subject to a host of general regulations concerning consumer protection, workers' safety and rights, environmental protection, surveillance of financial transactions, and control of employees' immigration status. They were scrutinized by the Securities and Exchange Commission (SEC), a surveillance intensified by the

Sarbanes-Oxley Act of 2002. They had to abide by antitrust laws – and were much more restricted than other corporations in this respect. The general increase in federal regulations, which we overviewed in the last chapter, had not bypassed financial firms. On top of this, a host of state and local laws and regulations had to be obeyed.

Before 2007, anybody who issued or bought or sold securities was regulated by the Securities Act of 1933 and the Securities Exchange Act of 1934, both pieces of legislation having been greatly expanded over the years. The Securities Act of 1933 regulates the issuance of securities and requires their registration with much information about the issuer. It gives large powers to the bureau that enforces it (the Federal Trade Commission before jurisdiction was transferred to the SEC), which, for example, "shall have access to and may demand the production of any books and papers of, and may administer oaths and affirmations to and examine, the issuer, underwriter, or any other person, in respect of any matter relevant to the examination" (s. 7). Violators risk jail sentences.

Interestingly, s. 4(5)(A)(ii) of the Securities Act exempted MBSs "where such securities are originated by a mortgagee approved by the Secretary of Housing and Urban Development ... and are offered or sold ... to ... the Federal Home Loan Mortgage Corporation, the Federal National Mortgage Association, or the Government National Mortgage Association." These three organizations are respectively Freddie Mac, Fannie Mae, and Ginnie Mae, the three government enterprises at the source of the MBSs that (as we'll see in the next chapter) generated the economic crisis. (Although often considered a Government sponsored-enterprise (GSE) like Fannie Mae and Freddie Mac, Ginnie Mae was more a straight government agency.) In other words, the law knowingly exempted risky government-approved securities from certain regulations to which everybody else was subjected.

The Securities Exchange Act of 1934 further regulated the exchange of securities, and created the SEC with vast powers to register and control stock exchanges (which, up to then, had been voluntary private associations), regulate transactions on those exchanges, require regular filings from listed company, compel production of documents with subpoenas, and so forth. The original 30-page law had been expanded to 259 pages by 2007. As it stood before the economic crisis, the law also regulated securities futures (contracts to buy or sell securities at future dates at previously agreed prices), and broker-dealers (persons engaged in the business of effecting transactions in securities for the account of clients or for their own accounts). The SEC had acquired the power of barring or suspending market participants and corporate directors, issuing cease-and-desist orders, and asking courts to impose up to 20 years in jail—compared with two years in the original 1934 law.[6]

The Sarbanes-Oxley Act of 2002 further increased the SEC's powers. This law created the Public Company Accounting Oversight Board to oversee audits of companies regulated by the SEC, mandated more disclosure of corporate information, imposed codes of ethics for financial officers, increased penalties for so-called white-collar crimes (which are often nothing but regulatory violations), and criminalized some accounting mistakes. "Very few start-ups have gone public in recent years, thanks in part to the multimillion-dollar compliance costs imposed by the Sarbanes-Oxley law in 2002," wrote James Freeman in the *Wall Street Journal*.[7] Some argue that Sarbanes-Oxley motivates companies to list in London instead of New York.

The SEC's 2006 Performance and Accountability Report declares: "The US Securities and Exchange Commission serves you by working to secure the trust in our markets."[8] The expression "our markets" stands in opposition to the Hayekian idea of an abstract society with impersonal markets that do not belong to anybody. More directly interesting for our purpose here is the enormous claim that the SEC was securing "trust in our market," just as confidence was about to crash. In 2006, the SEC spent about $900 million, brought procedures in 92 criminal cases, initiated more than 500 civil enforcement actions (most of which have nothing to do with fraud in the traditional sense), and sought orders barring 97 individuals from officer or director positions at listed companies. Ironically, during that same year, the SEC forced AIG to pay an $800-million accounting fine, and imposed a fine of $350 million on Fannie Mae as well as a smaller technical penalty on Bear Stearns, the investment bank that was going to go bust less than two years later. This is how the SEC was "working to secure the trust in our markets."

The SEC has been increasingly involved in controlling what listed corporations must disclose and how they must disclose it. Listed corporations must publish regular quarterly information, plus any new information that can affect the price of their shares. This information must be available to all investors at the same time. Since these controls also apply to the Internet, there is much concern that corporate blogs and tweets "can run afoul of Securities and Exchange Commission regulations on corporate communications."[9] Intel avoids corporate blogs and tweets altogether because of such concerns. A look at the mandated reports on the SEC's website shows how egalitarian disclosure is impossible: understanding the documents disclosed often requires a financial lawyer. Perfect or equal information is a mirage.

Much of the control over corporate speech is meant to enforce the prohibition of insider trading. For several decades now, it has been a crime to buy or sell securities on the basis of material nonpublic information, which is what insider trading is. "Material" means important enough to influence the price of a security. "Non-public information" is simply information that has not been divulged under the forms prescribed by the SEC. Not only does the Justice Department prosecute insider trading as a crime, but the SEC files civil suits. When effective, the prohibition of insider trading simply replaces what would be a slow change in share prices as inside information filters through the market by an abrupt change when the information is officially disclosed. Many economists think that insider trading that does not violate confidentiality agreements or job contracts should not be criminalized, and that civil suits—or perhaps simply job dismissals—by the owner of the stolen information would be sufficient to provide the optimal amount of insider trading.[10] In many cases anyway, the information targeted by the law is not stolen.[11]

The American banks' heavy regulatory burden has a long and tragic history. During most of its history (especially after the Civil War) and in most places, the United States distinguished itself from other countries by legal prohibitions on intrastate and interstate branching—the "unit banking" system. State-chartered banks were forbidden to branch intrastate within most states. Nationally chartered banks were prohibited from interstate branching by federal regulation after the Civil War.[12] Local business and agricultural interests, which wanted a captive local bank unable to lend to anybody else than themselves, were the force behind these strange prohibitions. This system generated a large number of small banks: 26,000 on the eve of the Great Depression.[13] These banks were geographically specialized and undiversified as their loan portfolios were concentrated in local industry or agriculture. They were easily subject to panics and bank runs. A "bank run" occurs when depositors fear that their bank is in danger, and everybody runs to take out his money first. A "banking panic" is when many banks are victims of bank runs. Since banks only keep a small proportion (at most 10 percent in the United States) of their deposits in cash, even a solvent bank cannot immediately honor the withdrawal demands of more than a small proportion of its depositors. In the United States, banks that had been allowed to branch (if only within a state) had much lower rates of failure or "suspensions," that is, periods in which a bank would temporarily halt withdrawals. The incapacity of banks to move capital across the country meant that, at least up to the Great Depression, U.S. financial markets were less integrated than were the East Coast market or the West Coast market with the rest of the world.[14] The numerous bank panics and failures that have characterized the United States are a typically American phenomenon due to the legally fragmented system. The consequences of this system are still visible today in both the large number and relatively small size of American banks compared with other countries.[15]

In Canada, by contrast, branching was always allowed countrywide without restrictions. The consequence was the development of a small number of Canadian banks (ten at the time of the Great Depression) with a large number of branches and very diversified loan portfolios. No banking panic occurred in Canada after the 1830s, and no Canadian bank failed during the Great Depression despite worse economic conditions than in the United States.[16] A central bank was not created in Canada before 1935; until then, a private bank, the Bank of Montréal, generally served as the lender of last resort.[17] Calomiris writes that "the rise of the Bank of Canada as a Depression measure in 1935 was not the result of economic necessity, but of political expediency due to domestic and international political pressures."[18]

Counting all general and specific laws, a banking consultant reckons that banks were subject to more than 80 laws and regulations, including two dozen from the Fed.[19]

Shadow banks were less regulated but far from unregulated. There is no doubt that the shadow banking system had become important. In early 2007, banks had assets of some $10 trillion, and the shadow banking system nearly as much or more depending on how it is defined. The shadow banking system is usually conceived as including investment banks (assets of $4 trillion), asset-backed commercial paper conduits ($2.5 trillion), and hedge funds ($1.8 trillion).[20] Some analysts would add money market funds, private equity funds (which invest in nonlisted companies, or delist companies they purchase, and take an active management role), and mortgage finance companies, but care must be taken not to double count (e.g., a large chunk of the outstanding commercial paper was held by money market funds).[21]

Investment banks were submitted to "voluntary" monitoring of their capital ratios and leverage, instead of strict capital ratios as commercial banks.[22] The SEC had jurisdiction over investment banks. Money market funds were subject to the Investment Advisers Act of 1940 and the Investment Company Act of 1940 and, like all mutual funds, were regulated by the SEC. The regulations covered the maturity, quality, ratings, and diversification of the funds' securities.[23] The funds' leverage was limited by law. They faced extensive disclosure requirements and had to provide multiple reports and prospectuses.[24]

Speaking of hedge funds, Posner repeats the mantra that they "were barely regulated at all."[25] It is true that the investments of institutions and wealthy investors in hedge funds did not need to be registered with the SEC. Hedge funds also faced lower disclosure requirements than mutual funds or other investment vehicles, and they were not restricted in their leverage or short selling (mutual funds were not allowed to short). However, this does not mean that hedge funds were not regulated. They were subject to the general laws applying to business corporations, for example, the prohibition on insider trading. Eighty-six percent of hedge funds were registered with either the SEC or some other regulatory bureau (mainly the Commodity Futures Trading Commission) and, depending on what they traded, may have been required to be. They were also regulated under the Investment Advisers Act as legal fiduciaries. They had to report to the SEC nontrivial holdings in listed companies. They were also regulated under the Employee Retirement Income Security Act if 25 percent of their capital belonged to a qualified employee benefit plan. They faced legal limitations on the loans they could obtain from banks and broker-dealers.[26] Although less regulated than banks, the hedge funds were not involved in the crisis as heavily regulated banks were.

Hedge funds are speculative investors. It is important to understand that there is nothing wrong about speculation. Take shorting. On September 19, 2008, in the wake of the crisis, the SEC prohibited investors from shorting the stocks of 799 listed companies for the next three weeks. The investor who shorts a stock believes that its price will drop and that, when time comes to return the borrowed stock, he can purchase it at a lower price than the price at which he sold it, realizing a profit in the process. It is remarkable that, when the crisis started, the SEC had the power to ban shorting, that is, to prohibit people who think that a stock price will drop to trade on this belief. Only in a very regulated financial system is it conceivable that a regulator would have this power, let alone be able to enforce it. The firms whose stocks were affected by the September 2008 prohibition had lobbied hard to get it, on the belief that preventing investors from acting on their negative beliefs would keep their own share prices from dropping. Like repressed news, the ban probably had the contrary effect as the stock exchange declined in the two following weeks. The prohibition must have hit hedge funds especially hard, as shorting is one of the investment techniques they use, sometimes to hedge against a possible drop in shares they own. The ban was soon discontinued, as everybody knew that it had deleterious consequences.[27]

A company put on the list of non-shortable stocks asked to be removed; its CEO Rod Dillon explained clearly why:

> What is so frequently misunderstood by so many, whether regular investors or C.E.O.'s, is that the goal of the marketplace is to have the stock price be an accurate reflection of fundamentals of your business. They think that the goal is to have the stock price as high as it could be.[28]

Speculators play a stabilizing role as they transmit information to the market as to what they think about the future, contributing to bring security prices to their true value. When a speculator sells there must be an investor who is willing to buy. As famous economist Harry Johnson (1923–1977) pointed out, for every destabilizing speculator, there must be a stabilizing one.[29]

In 2007, banks and shadow banks were constrained in their ownership structure and their activities. Under federal law, a bank could only be a stand-alone company, or be owned or controlled by a bank holding company. As soon as a company became a controlling shareholder in a bank—that is, when it could exert influence on the management—it was deemed a bank holding company. It then fell under the Bank Holding Company Act of 1956, was prohibited from engaging in many nonbanking activities, and was regulated by the Fed.[30] The restrictions imposed on a bank holding company were so stringent that hedge funds and private equity funds were reluctant to invest in banks. A fund that reached 10 percent of voting stocks in a bank was at risk of being deemed a controlling shareholder and thus a bank holding company. If the fund wanted to remain a noncontrolling shareholder, it was prohibited from holding talks with a bank's chief executive or other top officers. In other words, an important bank shareholder could either have no significant influence on the bank's management or else be regulated as a bank holding company.

These restrictions were so inimical to investors that, in September 2008, when the economy seemed to be unraveling, the Fed issued a policy statement interpreting more restrictively the notion of "controlling shareholder," and permitting an investor to hold a larger share and talk to management without falling into the feared category.[31] The policy statement declared:

> The Board believes that a noncontrolling minority investor, like any other shareholder, generally may communicate with banking organization management about, and advocate with banking organization management for changes in, any of the banking organization's policies and operations. For example, an investor may, directly or through a representative on a banking organization's board of directors, advocate for changes in the banking organization's dividend policy; discuss strategies for raising additional debt or equity financing; argue that the banking organization should enter into or avoid a new business line or divest a material subsidiary; or attempt to convince banking organization management to merge the banking organization with another firm or sell the banking organization to a potential acquirer. These communications also generally may include advocacy by minority investors for changes in the banking organization's management and recommendations for new or alternative management.[32]

The fact that the Fed felt necessary to state that shareholders were allowed to talk to bank management (without falling in the dreaded category of bank holding companies) shows how pre-crisis banking regulation was stifling. We were very far from laissez-faire capitalism.

On the eve of the economic crisis, limitations on the activities of different sorts of banks and other institutions distorted the competitive marketplace. Nonconventional banks often met regulatory difficulties in competing against established banks: Wal-Mart was prevented from opening a bank under the form of an industrial loan corporation (a state-chartered form of bank).[33] Add that commercial banks were able to raise cheaper funds because many deposits were protected by deposit insurance, and you get an idea of the distorted regulatory field that banks and other financial firms were facing.

Another aspect of financial regulation relates to securities ratings. In 1975, the SEC gave rating privilege to an oligopoly of three private agencies, Moody's, Standard & Poor's, and Fitch (which have since been joined by a few others). These ratings are often mandated by regulation: certain investors—mutual funds, pension funds, insurance companies—are prohibited from holding low-rated securities. As I will explain later, banks incur special regulatory costs when their balance sheet includes low-rated securities. Thus, ratings were often viewed as just another regulatory requirement. In other cases, good ratings by SEC-approved rating agencies may have fooled securities buyers to understate the risk of what they were buying (MBSs, for example).

After the demise of the MBS market, the rating agencies got a bad press. But it should not be forgotten that they were part of a large financial regulatory complex that was designed, structured, and run by government. Defending his company before the SEC, a Moody's executive made an extraordinary statement:

> Rating agencies are staffed by ordinary people with families to support and bills to meet and mortgages to pay. Government regulators are inadvertently subjecting those people to extraordinary pressure, and share accountability for any scandals that may result.[34]

The statement is extraordinary not by what it says, which is pretty obvious, but by the implication that government bureaucrats would not be, as "government regulators," "ordinary people with families to support and bills to meet and mortgages to pay." More on this in Chapter 7.

For most of American history until the onset of the last economic crisis, banks and other financial institutions had been enmeshed in a tight financial-regulatory complex weaved by the state and the interests it caters to. These interests may be the interests of the bankers themselves, or the interests of important customers as in the case of branching. More than institutions to maximize depositors' value, writes Charles Calomiris, banks often appear "as a tool of the state." They were chartered by government (federal or state) to achieve certain goals, of which the financing of the state itself was often paramount.[35] Still today, one wonders if banking regulations are not partly designed to help finance the public debt. Capital regulation grants preferential treatment to government securities as they are considered riskless and require no capital; banks are thus incited to use a higher proportion of their depositors' money to buy government securities instead of granting private loans. Before the recent economic crisis hit, banks were so tightly regulated that one might be forgiven to wonder if there were still private organizations in the strict sense of the term.

A Phantom Deregulation

When the first signs of an economic crisis appeared in 2007, banking and finance were under the constant surveillance and tight regulation of a host of regulatory bureaus. The Federal Reserve System (Fed), the Federal Deposit Insurance Corporation (FDIC), the Comptroller of the Currency, and the Office of Thrift Supervision (OTS) were the main banking regulators. To these must be added other less important but nonetheless active regulators: the Commodity Futures Trading Commission (CTFC), the National Credit Union Administration, the Federal Housing Finance Board (FHFB), the Farm Credit Administration, and the Financial Crimes Enforcement Network. In 2007, the regulatory budgets of these organizations stood at $2.1 billion (all values in constant 2000 dollars). If we except the FDIC, whose regulatory budget oscillated and declined between 1997 and 2007, from $750 million to $478 million, the trend in virtually all other banking and finance regulatory bureaus has been straight upward. The global picture is a brisk increase from about $200 million per year in 1960 to $2 billion per year starting in the mid-1990s up to 2007. The 12-year plateau from 1995 to 2007 must not hide the fact that over 47 years from 1960 to 2007, the regulatory expenditures in finance and banking had been multiplied by 11 in constant dollars, for an annual rate of growth of 5.2 percent per year.[36] A plateau is not deregulation. This growth factor of 11 over the 1960-2007 period is exactly the same we have calculated for total regulation (excluding homeland security) in the previous chapter. Banking and finance regulation grew in step with other regulations.

Could it be argued that regulation has increased less than the growth of finance and that, in some way, regulatory intensity has decreased? This is not what available data show. From 1960 to 2007, the proportion of finance and insurance in GDP has more than doubled, from 3.6 percent to 7.9

percent;[37] which is far from the 1,000 percent increase (multiplication by 11) in constant-dollar regulatory budgets. Could it be that the growth in the share of finance combined with the growth of GDP account for the expanded regulatory budgets? No more. Using the BEA quantity index of financial services and insurance, we can calculate that the production of real insurance and financial services has grown by seven times from 1960 to 2007,[38] still much less than the factor of 11 for the multiplication of regulation. The only serious argument that could be made is that, during the plateau of total banking and financial regulation between 1995 and 2007, the production of financial services has increased by 58 percent, meaning that, in some sense, regulation per "unit" of financial service has decreased during these ten years. But recall that the plateau occurred after a tripling of constant-dollar regulatory expenditures from the beginning of the 1980s to the mid-1990s.

If there is no smoke without fire, where does the idea come from that American finance had been recently deregulated? There was some modest deregulation, which consisted in opening the banking industry to more competition. This deregulation took four forms.

First, starting in the 1980s, broker-dealers were allowed to compete with commercial banks by offering interest on (non-guaranteed) money-market accounts as well as related banking services like checking. Then, in order to meet this new competition, commercial banks obtained, in the 1980s, the freedom to pay the market rate of interest on deposits. This freedom had been limited since banking legislation in 1933 and 1935, and the Fed's Regulation Q of 1966.[39]

Second, the Glass-Steagal Act of 1933, which prohibited commercial banks from engaging in investment-bank activities like brokering securities, taking equity in firms, and participating in mergers and acquisitions, was gradually abolished. This prohibition was a rather unique American phenomenon. "In other countries," notes Charles Calomiris, "commercial banks financed firms, often owning equity as well as debt and often involving themselves in corporate decision making, as well as finance."[40] The abolition of Glass-Steagall by a series of laws and regulations starting in the 1980s culminated in the Gramm-Leach-Bliley Act of 1999.[41] This was the last step in the process of the process of allowing more competition: not only investment banks were at liberty to offer some commercial-bank services and commercial banks could pay the interest required to attract deposits, but the latter were now allowed to offer investment-banking services.

Third form of deregulation: bank branching was liberalized. Between 1979 and 1991, 39 states relaxed their branch banking laws. The Riegle-Neal Interstate Bank Branching and Branching Efficiency Act of 1994 abolished the federal restrictions on interstate branching.[42] These reforms will take time to achieve their full potential, and the American banking system remained, on the eve of the economic crisis, fragmented and fragile.

A fourth form of real deregulation, which is generally ignored even by supporters of regulation, consisted in the abolition, between 1980 and 1994, of reserve requirements on the components that M2 adds to M1, that is, savings deposits, small time deposits, money market deposit accounts, and retail money market mutual fund shares. David Henderson (a professor at the Naval Postgraduate School and a research fellow at the Hoover Institution) and Jeff Hummel (San Jose State University) argue that this reduction in reserve requirements reduced the Fed's control of the money supply.[43] This was real deregulation but the American banking and financial industry was still very far from laissez-faire at the dawn of the recent crisis.

There has been no other deregulation of banking and finance worth mentioning. The Commodity Futures Modernization Act of 2000, which is often cited as a piece of deregulation, mainly confirmed that transactions in over-the-counter derivative instruments—CDSs, for example—traded by sophisticated investors did not fall under the regulatory purview of the Commodity Futures Trading Commission and the Commodity Exchange Act of 1936.[44] ("Over the counter" means that the derivatives are traded between private parties and not on organized exchanges.)

Those who blame deregulation mostly mean "no new regulation," as if the two situations were equivalent. Leftist political scientist Thomas Ferguson and former Soros manager Robert Johnson ride this theme when they blame Greenspan's supposed deregulation: "Under Greenspan," they write, "the Fed fiercely resisted stronger regulation."[45] Posner similarly invokes the ghost of deregulation when he actually means no new regulation. Speaking of "the movement to reduce the regulation of banking and credit," he mentions that "it was decided not to bring the new financial instruments, in particular credit-default swaps, under regulation."[46]

Pieces of legislation presented as deregulatory often contained new regulations. For example, the Federal Deposit Insurance Corporation Improvement Act of 1991 limited but codified the "too-big-to-fail protection."[47] It was regulation-laden deregulation. Bernard Shull of the City University of New York, who generally favors regulation, points out that "deregulation" has been accompanied by new regulations, including on capital ratios, and by the growth of "supervision" and the bureaus responsible for it. Banks came to be inspected roughly once a year, and new measures of their capital adequacy, assets quality, management, earnings and liquidity were implemented. A bureaucratic acronym, CAMEL, was even created for the capital, assets, management, earnings and liquidity ratings (taking the first letter of each component). In the 1990s, CAMEL ratings were supplemented by evaluations of credit, market, interest rate, liquidity, and reputation risks. "The new approach," writes Shull, "contemplated a more or less continuous monitoring by small groups of technical experts in several different areas, and extensive interaction between supervisors and bank management."[48] The size and power of bank regulatory agencies, especially the Fed, grew. And, notes Shull, all this served as a model for the Sarbanes-Oxley Act, which "derives much of its substance from well accepted banking law."[49] In other words, "deregulation" replaced former regulations by even more formidable regulations. Shull argues that the intensified monitoring of banks before the current crisis was motivated by "regulatory concerns about [their] potential systemic danger."[50] The control of systemic danger appears to be a perpetual mirage.

Banking and financial regulation have grown all over the world during the twentieth century. In many ways, America has been in the forefront of this progression. Deposit insurance started in the United States (at the federal level) in 1934, and no other developed country had a similar explicit scheme as late as 1960; when the recent crisis hit, more than 100 countries had established it.[51] The world hosted 18 full-fledged central banks at the beginning of the twentieth century, 59 by 1950, and 161 by 1990.[52] All over the world, just before the recent crisis unfolded, banks were tightly regulated by central banks and/or other regulatory bureaus with wide powers. An IMF database on banking regulation and supervision in 152 countries provides empirical evidence on the tight controls exerted on banks.[53] In most countries, at the beginning of the 2000s, supervisory authorities had the power to force a bank to alter its internal organization structure; to take legal action for negligence against banks' external auditors, who were legally required to communicate to the supervisory agency any presumed involvement of bank directors or senior managers in illicit activities, fraud, or insider abuse; and to meet with external auditors to discuss their reports without the approval of the bank's management. In most countries, the regulatory bureaus were obliged to report and take action if infractions were found. In most countries, a bank's shareholders could not appeal a bank supervisor's decisions in court, and liquidation could be decreed without a court order. In many countries, banks were submitted to precise guidelines regarding asset diversification, and bank supervisors had the power to supersede shareholder rights, remove and replace managers and directors, and revoke banking licenses. A 1995 survey of 54 countries done by the Center for the Study of Financial Innovation and PricewaterhouseCoopers revealed that, for the first time, the high cost of regulation was perceived to be the greatest threat to the financial sector.[54]

In many ways, banking and finance were more regulated in the United States than in other countries. Consider the United Kingdom. Over the period 1998–2000, financial regulatory expenditures in the United States were 13.7 times what they were in the United Kingdom, and personnel levels 15 times higher.[55] But perhaps the most enlightening comparison is between Canada and the United States, two countries that share a similar culture and similar institutions.

Canadian banks fared much better than American banks during the recent crisis. While the latter were rescued with tax-funded capital, the former required no capital infusion from government. University of Michigan professor Mark Perry notes that between early 2007 and May 2009, the Canadian bank share index dropped by 40 percent compared with 80 percent for the U.S. bank index.[56] During the crisis, returns to bank shareholders decreased by less in Canada than in the United States.[57] More than 100 American banks failed (and even more as the slow recovery dragged on)[58] while no bank failure occurred in Canada—a sort of repeat of the Great Depression on a much smaller scale.

According to conventional wisdom, the resilience of Canadian banks comes from their being more regulated than their American counterparts.[59] In fact, both history and current data suggest the opposite. Canadian banks have never been subject to branching restrictions. As a consequence, the five widely held domestic Canadian banks[60] have branches all over the country and hold an 87 percent share of the deposit market. In the United States, the five largest banks only have a 39 percent share of deposits (as of before the crisis).[61] The Canadian banks' relative size and geographical diversity certainly plays a role in their solidity. Although Canadian banks are small relative to large American banks, the smallest Canadian bank, the National Bank of Canada, is larger than most American banks. The National Bank of Canada shows assets of $129 billion,[62] while 99 percent of FDIC-insured banks have less than $10 billion.[63] The banks that failed during 2009, had typically no more than $1 billion (and sometimes less than $100 million) in assets.[64] The World Bank's database can be used to compare the Canadian and American regulatory regimes as they stood on the eve of the recent economic crisis, and the variables defined by Elijah Brewer, George Kaufman, and Larry Wall of the Federal Reserve Bank of Atlanta over this database are especially useful.[65] All their variables show less regulation in Canada than in the United States.

It is true that the ownership of banks and entry into banking are more restricted in Canada. Yet, 49 foreign banks operate in that country and, like in the United States, no banking license had been denied in the five years preceding the database revision. Total bank assets in the United States are $9,040 billion, about five times the $1,976 billion in Canada (at the end of 2005), so the 49 foreign-owned banks in Canada amount to proportionately much more than the comparative figure of 64 in the United States.

Canadian banks are relatively free. Before the recent crisis, they were allowed to engage in insurance as well as securities brokerage and investment banking. They could freely own voting shares in non financial firms, which was restricted for American banks. Rules were often stricter for personal responsibility of bank directors and audits in America. Supervisors were not allowed to take legal action against auditors in Canada, while they had this power in the United States. In only a few cases did banking rules appear to be tougher in Canada, notably with respect to asset diversification and disclosure of risk management procedures.

Bank regulators generally wielded more power in the United States, which had some of the most powerful banking regulators in the world, while Canada was at the other end of the spectrum.[66] American regulators had the power to, and occasionally did, force banks to change their internal organizational structures, hold bank directors personally responsible for misleading disclosures, order banks to take loan loss provisions, suspend management decisions on dividends, bonuses and management fees, bypass courts to declare bank insolvency, and remove and replace management. These powers were unknown in Canada. And American regulators were often required by law, contrary to their Canadian counterparts, to take public and formal enforcement actions.

Canadian banks were under no requirement to hold liquidity reserves or deposits at the central bank, while it was then required in the United States. Required capital ratios were slightly higher in Canada but, in the more conservative Canadian banking culture, they may have been higher anyway. Moreover, a higher regulatory capital ratio can have perverse effects if it incites the banks to take more risk. There is no evidence in recent world history that higher required capital ratios are associated with more solid banks.[67]

In the United States, there was one banking regulatory agency per state, while banks in Canada (with a few exceptions) were regulated by the federal government only. At the federal level, American banks also faced more regulatory agencies: the Fed, the Comptroller of the Currency, and the FDIC (plus the OTS for thrifts and the National Credit Union Administration for credit unions). In Canada, banks reported essentially to the federal Office of the Superintendent of Financial Institutions (OSFI)—although credit unions were regulated at the provincial level. Were Canadian banks better regulated by their fewer regulators? Difficult to say, but they were certainly not more regulated if we judge by the regulatory budgets. According to the World Bank's data, the budget of U.S. federal banking regulators was 38 times the budget of the single federal regulator's budget in Canada. Considering that banking assets are five times greater in the United States, this translates into U.S. supervision budgets proportionately seven times greater than Canada's.

As for the number of regulatory bureaucrats, they were twice as numerous in the United States as in Canada in proportion of the assets they regulated.

Some observers look for the presence of deregulation in regulatory arbitrage, that is, in the legal avoidance of regulation. A thesis developed by Professor Gary Gorton of Yale University brings grist to their mill. The regulated commercial banks, Gorton notes, saw their market compressed (relatively) by the competition of the less regulated investment banks: between 1990 and 2007, the ratio of investment bank assets to commercial bank assets went from 6 percent to about 30 percent.[68] According to Gorton, commercial banks became unprofitable in the 1980s, and investors started investing in shadow banks instead. "Regulators can make banks do things, like hold more capital, but they cannot prevent exit if banking is not profitable," he writes. "Bank regulation determines the size of the regulated banking sector, and that is all."[69] In other words, the entrepreneurs created a new banking sector to avoid the regulatory burden of traditional banks. When authority dampens a risk somewhere, it pops up elsewhere. I leave it to my reader to decide if avoidance of crippling regulation can be called deregulation.

Gorton argues that this regulatory arbitrage explains the occurrence a banking panic of a new genre. In his opinion, the crisis that appeared in the summer of 2007 was a run on the shadow banking system and especially on investment banks. The panic came from companies and other institutions that had loaned large amounts of money to shadow banks. These deposits of sorts were not covered by deposit insurance but were guaranteed by repurchase agreements, or "repos," whereby the shadow bank transfers collaterals to its "depositors" as a guarantee that they will get back their money whatever happens. In the repo market, many of the collaterals were MBSs, and the spreading doubts about these securities led large depositors to demand more collateral ("haircuts"), which the banks had difficulty providing. If this thesis does raise questions about the susceptibility of less regulated banks to bank panics, it also suggests that more regulation merely shifts risks elsewhere.

Whatever deregulation happened, it was sometimes more timid or slower in the United States than elsewhere. As a matter of fact, note professors Christian Calmès (University of Québec in Outaouais) and Raymond Théoret (University of Quebec in Montréal), Canadian banks were allowed to engage in brokerage activities a decade earlier than their American counterparts.[70]

Necessary Regulation?

Deregulation bypassed one problem area recognized by fans and foes of banking regulation alike: moral hazard. Moral hazard is an insurance term referring to the incentives of an insured person to be less prudent than if he were not insured, thereby increasing the probability of the insured event occurring. Insurance companies are always trying to find ways to reduce moral hazard, with methods that range from deductibles to increasing insurance premiums after claims. If you know that a car accident will still cost you something even if you are insured, you will have some incentive to control the risk—by not lending your car to a risky driver, for example.

As I mentioned before, the moral hazard problem with deposit insurance is that depositors have no incentive to monitor the solidity of their bank which, therefore, has less incentive to be prudent. Depositors' monitoring of their banks is not an idea as strange as it may look like after experimenting deposit insurance for decades. Consumers do get information before they make important financial decisions, like buying a car or a house. Specialized magazines like *Consumer Report* and similar services have developed to assist in this task. And the world does not collapse without deposit insurance: before 1960, the United States was the only developed country with a formal deposit insurance scheme.[71] "Deposit insurance," writes Charles Calomiris, "was the legacy of unit banking."[72] National deposit insurance was mainly promoted by politicians from the states with the most fragmented banking systems. It was because unit banks were so fragile that guaranteeing the depositors' money was thought to be required. But deposit insurance naturally lead to more risk and more bank failures. Once deposits are insured and moral hazard kicks in, government has a reason or an excuse to regulate in order to minimize the problem. Richard Posner admits that "[o]ne reason that hedge funds have not encountered problems of solvency as acute as those of commercial banks may be that no part of their capital is federally insured."[73] Like Posner, Paul Krugman agrees that moral hazard is one of the main problems underlying the recent crisis.[74] But they still argue that more regulation is needed to correct the problems created by previous regulation. Why don't they consider solving the underlying problem by abolishing deposit insurance?

The "too big to fail" principle is another generator of moral hazard. If a company is deemed too big to fail by government, its shareholders, lenders and managers will be tempted to take more risk than they would otherwise do. Although the government did let Lehman Brothers fail, it rescued most of the large companies deemed too big to fail, including Bear Stearns, AIG, Fannie Mae, Freddie Mac, the big banks that needed TARP money, General Motors, and Chrysler.

Any regulation creates some moral hazard. A regulated industry generates a false confidence among consumers and investors. Small investors are less prudent when they believe that risk has been nearly eradicated from financial markets, that these markets are totally transparent, that the same information is instantly made available to all—in short that the market has been made a riskless, equal playing field. Bernard Madoff's fraud provided an extreme illustration when one of the victims claimed that he trusted Madoff because he trusted the government: "We conducted our affairs in good faith in the belief that the SEC would never allow this sort of scheme to be conducted."[75] Some regulations generate more moral hazard and have worst consequences than others, like those with formally guarantee the value of some liabilities (bank deposits) or the survival of some firms ("too big to fail").

Posner recognizes many government failures, including permissive monetary policy, the Bush deficits, "propagandizing for homeownership and pushing banks to make risky mortgage loans,"[76] "fragmentation of regulatory authority, a lack of coordination, turf wars."[77] Strangely enough, he still calls for more government interventions, presumably also subject to failure, to correct previous government failures.

Was all this financial regulation necessary? Regulation in the sense of rules and controls is necessary and inevitable. The question is whether it should be a private and decentralized activity under each firm's jurisdiction, or a public (government) and uniform obligation.

One problem with government regulation is that it often substitutes for, and evicts, private prudential rules. Many instances of this phenomenon can be found in banking and finance. The existence of the Fed evicted the bank coalitions and ad hoc cooperation that, before 1914, helped contain banking panics. Before compulsory capital ratios and deposit insurance, the necessity to maintain the confidence of depositors led banks to keep high capital ratios: in the late nineteenth century, the typical American bank had a core (also called "Tier 1") capital ratio of nearly 25 percent and the typical British bank of more than 15 percent, compared with about 5 percent from the 1980s on.[78] Another example: when American bank regulators ceased to monitor the loan portfolios of individual bank loan officers, the banks themselves started doing it because there was a real need for this monitoring.[79]

There is much evidence that the sort of financial regulations that existed before the current crisis not only did not help prevent it but, on the contrary, fuelled instability. Looking at a large number of countries over the 1988–1999 period, James Barth (Auburn University), Gerard Caprio (Williams College) and Ross Levine (Brown University) identified some 50 banking crises important enough to be classified as "systemic": they involved emergency government assistance to the banking system, nonperforming assets amounting to at least 10 percent of banking assets, and a total cost of rescue operations corresponding to at least 2 percent of GDP. Such banking crisis occurred, for example, in the United States (the Savings and Loans debacle of the late 1980s), Sweden, Norway, Russia, Brazil, Japan, and other Asian countries.[80] Using econometric methods to identify the impact of different factors and separate significant correlation from confounding factors, the economists find that most forms of regulation or supervision had no significant impact on the probability of a crisis, except perversely for restrictions on bank activities and the moral hazard of deposit insurance, both factors which *increased* this probability.[81] The more banks are restricted in the financial activities they can engage in or the more constrained is entry in the banking industry, the more the system is subject to banking crises. The more generous deposit insurance, the more likely the system will face a banking crisis. Note that about one half of countries still did not have government deposit insurance in 2004. The prudently conclude: "Regulatory restrictions on banking activities and generous deposit insurance do not have a stabilizing effect on banks; rather, they tend to increase banking system fragility."[82] Moreover, their research does not support the view that more stringent capital regulations, greater disciplinary powers of supervisory agencies and regulations forcing more information disclosure have any positive impact on the stability of banking systems.

Regulation increased risk in more subtle ways. Amar Bhidé of the Columbia Business School argues that corporate and financial regulations inherited from the New Deal—disclosure, ban on insider trading, and other means of enforcing the elusive "equal playing field"—have artificially promoted anonymous arms-length transactions at the expense of personal relationships and continuous diligence. These regulations have created a false sense of security. Similarly, Bhidé reckons, new financial technologies like securitization and credit scoring have degraded the relations between the borrower and his banker. "Using a credit score produced by feeding a few items of hard data into a mathematical model to assess the likelihood of default assumes that all risks are quantifiable," he writes, contrasting this impersonal system with the old ways of doing business: "Like criminal trials and faculty hiring decisions, the traditional lending process implicitly took into account unquantifiable uncertainties and the uniqueness of individual circumstances."[83] Bhidé believes that the artificial anonymization of financial relations was one of the main factors in the recent recession. This would not be surprising: meddling with the delicate information system of the economy cannot but create bugs.

What made individuals digitizable and continuously monitorable and scorable was not so much the computer per se, as most people believe, but the growing use of "government-issued photo ID" and the universal identifiers created, maintained and strengthened by the state, notably the ubiquitous social security number. The driver's license became the American equivalent here of what ID papers were in other countries. Private vendors naturally jumped on the opportunity, for it promised to reduce their own cost. But note that official ID papers were not a *sine qua non* condition of the electronic age: the old credit card, which is still the main instrument of electronic commerce, did not require them. We are back into Tocqueville's nightmare of the regulated society, continuously watched by Big Brother. Needless to say that this society has nothing to do with laissez-faire.

We need more regulation? We have heard this before. In his inaugural speech of March 4, 1933, Franklin D. Roosevelt was to solve "the evils of the old order" with "a strict supervision of all banking and credits and investments" and "an end to speculation with other people's money."[84] The thirty-second president of the United States set up a complex structure of regulation and controls which expanded virtually nonstop during the following three quarters of a century.

A Light Regulatory Touch in the Spirit of the Times

Financial deregulation is more an urban legend than anything else. Barth et al. write:

> Financial institutions do not answer solely to the market-place; they are also heavily regulated and supervised by numerous federal and state authorities. Indeed, the current crisis cannot be chalked up to a lack of regulators. . . . In addition to regulatory authorities, there are at least 10 U.S. congressional committees that have some jurisdiction over the financial sector.[85]

It is difficult to make sense of what Posner means when he criticizes a "largely deregulated finance industry,"[86] or when he claims that "the depression is the result of normal business activity in a laissez-faire economic regime."[87] Trying to define what he means by "laissez-faire capitalism," he writes: "The depression [he is talking about the recent recession] is a failure of capitalism, or more precisely of a certain kind of capitalism ('laissez-faire' in a loose sense, 'American' versus 'European' in a popular sense)."[88] So "laissez-faire capitalism," we are told, is American capitalism, where real public expenditures per capita have been multiplied by 18 times since the Great Depression, where economic and social regulation measured by constant-dollar regulatory expenditures has grown by a factor of 11 since 1960, and where two-thirds of government revenues are now spent on Welfare State functions. Of course, one can adopt the terminology one prefers, but some terminological twists are misleading. If this regime is "laissez-faire capitalism," perhaps Stalinist central planning can be rechristened "mixed economy."

When pushed to the wall, those who blame deregulation for the 2007–2009 debacle fall back on vague expressions. Ferguson and Johnson blame Greenspan's "nonchalance"[89] and the Fed's "laxity."[90] Paul Krugman writes that "the spirit of the times—and the ideology of the George W. Bush administration—was deeply antiregulation."[91] Richard Posner invokes "a general laissez-faire attitude, 'conservative' in the currently prevailing sense of the word."[92] Speaking about "the kind of officials who tend to be appointed by Republican presidents," he says that they "are heavily invested in the ideology of free markets."[93] He writes about "a doctrinaire, free-market, pro-business, anti-regulatory ideology" dominating "the Bush administration's economic thinking and regulatory enforcement (or nonenforcement)."[94] He blames a "light touch in regulating banking practices"[95] and even "dogmatic libertarianism."[96] For Posner like for Krugman, George W. Bush symbolizes deregulation, while George Bush's two terms was one of the most regulation-heavy periods in American history: during this period, notes Johan Norberg, "new federal regulations were added to the tune of 78,000 pages a year," adding that this was "the highest pace in the history of the United States."[97]

On the eve of the recent economic crisis, the American banking and financial system could certainly not be described as laissez-faire. It was tightly supervised and controlled by the authorities—in the spirit of the times.

CHAPTER 5

The Crime Scene

Do not wait for the Justice Department to come knocking.
                                                    —*Attorney General Janet Reno*[1]

Whatever influence we attach to the many economic circumstances surrounding the 2007–2009 economic crisis, we must not forget where precisely it started, that is, in the market for residential mortgage-backed securities (MBSs). At the very source of the crisis were two interrelated markets: the market for residential houses and the market for mortgage loans on these houses. This is, as it were, the crime scene, and we can't hope to find the culprit if we don't visit it.

MBSs became problematic in the summer of 2007 because defaults on residential mortgages were growing. Investors got the signal: some MBSs would stop paying interest, and their value would tumble. Mortgage defaults were rising because house prices had started to fall. As a result, many homeowners found themselves "under water," that is, with mortgages higher than the value of their homes. Those among them who had to refinance their mortgages were unable to. Many who had variable-rate mortgages faced higher payments. Sometimes, homeowners chose to just walk away from properties that were worth less than what they owed on them. The chain of causation in the housing boom and bust clearly points to the housing and mortgage markets.

The Envy of the World

Since the New Deal, the federal government has been actively promoting home ownership. It made residential mortgage interest deductible, excluded most first residential homes from the capital gain tax, and created agencies and "government-sponsored enterprises" (GSEs) to guarantee and support home mortgages. One of these GSEs, Fannie Mae, was widely seen as a great policy success in encouraging home ownership. "Executives at U.S. mortgage giant Fannie Mae," wrote *Wall Street Journal* reporter James R. Hagerty, "like to tell their critics that the American method of financing home loans is the 'envy of the world.'"[2]

Government spokesmen hailed the role of federal institutions in promoting home ownership. In 1995, President Bill Clinton declared:

> One of the great successes of the United States in this century has been the partnership forged by the national government and the private sector to steadily expand the dream of ownership to Americans. . . . The goal of this strategy, to boost homeownership to 67.5% by the year 2000, would take us to an all time high . . . When we boost the number of homeowners in our country, we strengthen our economy, create jobs, build up the middle class, and build better citizens.[3]

In 2002, President George W. Bush added his intention to "use the mighty muscle of the federal government in combination with state and local governments to encourage owning your own home."[4] In 2004, Senator Christopher Dodd called the two GSEs "one of the great success stories of our time."[5] In 1995, the ownership rate was 65 percent; by 2005, it had reached 69 percent.[6] Mission accomplished! Who said government with its mighty muscles is not efficient?

In February 2010, using a 1921 law dusted off by his predecessor Eliot Spitzer, New York Attorney General Andrew Cuomo sued Bank of America and two former executives fort for their role in the economic crisis. Cuomo had previously been Secretary of the Department of Housing and Urban Development (HUD), whose website proudly reports his achievement in 1999:

> Secretary Cuomo established new Affordable Housing Goals requiring Fannie Mae and Freddie Mac—two government sponsored enterprises involved in housing finance—to buy $2.4 trillion in mortgages in the next 10 years. This will mean new affordable housing for about 28.1 million low- and moderate-income families. The historic action raised the required percentage of mortgage loans for low- and moderate-income families that the companies must buy from the current 42 percent of their total purchases to a new high of 50 percent—a 19 percent increase—in the year 2001.[7]

The *Wall Street Journal* opines that "[e]ven if one believes the allegations hurled by the New York Attorney General, Mr. Cuomo has done far more harm to taxpayers and investors than the defendants, by any reasonable measure."[8]

In a February 4, 2003, lecture, Angelo R. Mozilo, founder, chairman and CEO of Countrywide Financial Corporation, one of the largest private mortgage lenders at the time, used the "best of the word" incantation:

> Our Nation took another important step in 1938—in fact, 65 years ago this week—when Fannie Mae was created to buy those FHA loans, and as a result, the secondary mortgage market was born. We took a few more giant steps in the 1940s with the G.I. Bill in 1944 and the Housing Act of 1949, which stated the goal of "a decent home and a suitable living environment for every American family."
>
> We witnessed the Fair Housing Act in the 60s, the creation of Freddie Mac in 1970, the expansion of Fannie Mae's activities, the Community Reinvestment Act in the 70s, the introduction of adjustable-rate mortgages in the 80s, and more recently, the National Affordable Housing Act of 1990.
>
> We have traveled so far—thanks to a mortgage-finance system that remains the envy of the world; thanks to a constant stream of creative and innovative mortgage products, and efforts directed at encouraging the offering of loans to those who have been previously shut out; and simply put, thanks to housing being an enduring public policy objective and the lasting commitment to that objective symbolized by our partnership.[9]

Encouraging home ownership was "an enduring public policy objective."

A month later, HUD Secretary Mel Martinez, testifying before the House Committee on Small Business repeated in other terms the best-of-the-world mantra:

> The emphasis Americans place on homeownership sets us apart from many other nations of the world. In this country, homeownership provides financial security for families and stability for children. It creates community stake-holders who have a vested interest in what happens in their neighborhoods. It generates economic strength that fuels the entire nation.
>
> The Bush Administration is committed to helping more families achieve the American Dream of homeownership.
>
> To do this, we must eliminate the homeownership gap that exists between the minority and non-minority populations.[10]

Also in 2003, Congressman Barney Frank said:

> I believe that we, as the Federal Government, have probably done too little rather than too much to push them to meet their goals of affordable housing and to set reasonable goals. . . . I would like to get Fannie and Freddie more

deeply into helping low-income housing and possibly moving into something that is more explicitly a subsidy. . . . I want to roll the dice a little bit more in this situation towards subsidizing housing.[11]

The dice were rolling.

The government's encouragement of housing did not respond to a housing problem. American home buyers have never paid more than 25 percent of their incomes on housing.[12] At the beginning of the 2000s, the median house price in the United States was 3.6 times the median income, much less than, say, the 5.5 factor in Great Britain or the 6.3 factor in Australia and New Zealand.[13] In 2002, the 68 percent U.S. home ownership rate was lower than in countries like Spain (81 percent) and Ireland (80 percent), but it was about equal to Britain's (69 percent), and was higher than Germany's (41 percent) and than France's, the Netherlands's, and Denmark's (all around 50 percent). Except for mortgage debt as a percentage of GDP, which was much higher in the United States than nearly all these countries, the American ownership situation seemed exceptional.[14]

Government encouragement of housing in the United States was not a consequence of housing problems—except, that is, if one considers the problems created by government itself. In certain areas of the country, house prices were very high, and this localized phenomenon was often a consequence of zoning regulation that had developed since the 1960s. Consider California. In 1969, the median-priced home in San Jose was 2.2 times the median family income (approximately the same as in San Francisco); in 2005, the factor had jumped to 7.5. The increase in California home prices, argues Thomas Sowell, was not due to increased population. In the 1970s, the population in San Francisco was growing at roughly the same rate as total U.S. population. But laws and regulations restricting land use were spreading rapidly in the Golden Gate state. During that decade, for example, housing prices in Palo Alto nearly quadrupled while population was dropping by 8 percent.[15] "Where the market was more or less left alone—places like Houston and Dallas, for example," writes Sowell, "housing prices took a smaller share of family income than in the past."[16]

Whatever the specific conditions in Silicon Valley, housing prices respond to restrictions on supply. If the supply of houses and apartments is reduced through zoning restrictions and other land use restrictions, prices will increase compared with what they would otherwise have been. Whatever the intentions of their promoters, land use restrictions have the consequence of pushing out less wealthy people. Since 1970, for example, the black population in San Francisco has been cut in half.[17] Young families cannot afford to live in such regulated cities. During the 1970's increase in housing prices, school enrolment in Palo Alto (near Stanford University) dropped by 27 percent.[18] A 2006 Independent Institute study estimated that "smart growth" policies—a now standard justification land use restriction—had added more than $100,000 per home in 50 metropolitan areas.[19] If this argument is correct, high housing prices in certain areas were in large part a consequence of previous government intervention in the residential market. The housing bubble that started in the late 1990s only aggravated the problem.

From 2000 to 2006, the price of the average American home increased by 9 percent per year, compared with less than 3 percent in the 1990s. The ratio of median home price to median household income averaged 3.4 from 1968 to 2007, but was up to 4.7 in 2005. One may look at this phenomenon as a bubble, if one keeps large regional differences in mind: while the annual rate of growth in house prices reached 17.1 percent in Miami, it stood at only 2.6 percent in Dallas.[20] Is it a coincidence that the real estate bubble occurred mainly in a small number of highly regulated states? In California and Florida, home prices jumped by more than 130 percent between 2000 and 2006, while they increased by only 30 percent in Texas and Georgia.[21]

Although an annual price increase of 9 percent may not look very bubble-like, it is much larger than the secular trend. Contrary to conventional wisdom, house prices have not grown fast. From 1890 to 2008, the annual rate of growth of home prices in the United States was 3.4 percent. In real terms, that is, deducting average inflation over this period, this growth rate translates into a real growth of house prices of only 0.6 percent—less than 1 percent—per year. By comparison, over the same period (but excluding the 2008 crash), stock prices increased by 6.3 percent per year in real terms.[22]

A Half-nationalized Mortgage Market

A comprehension of the residential mortgage market is crucial for understanding the housing bubble. Most house purchases are financed by mortgages, and the more easily available these mortgages are, the higher the demand for houses will be. The federal government was active in facilitating the accessibility of mortgage financing for residential homes, and not only with words: it was guaranteeing nearly half of all residential mortgages and imposing loose lending standards.

The American residential mortgage market was haunted by a flock of federal agencies and GSEs. Created in 1934, the Federal Housing Administration (FHA), an agency later attached to the Department of Housing and Urban Development, insures—that is, guarantees—mortgage loans made by approved lenders to borrowers who meet certain criteria, including "borrowers that the conventional market does not adequately provides for including first-time homebuyers, minorities, low-income families and residents of underserved communities."[23] The Federal National Mortgage Association (the official name of Fannie Mae) was created in 1938 with the goal of providing funds to mortgage lenders through purchases of mortgages. It was reorganized as a "government-sponsored private corporation" by the 1968 Charter Act,[24] and has continued to buy mortgages from private lenders, generally packaging them into MBSs. In 1968, Congress also created the Government National Mortgage Association (Ginnie Mae) with the goal of guaranteeing MBSs issued from pools of mortgages guaranteed by other government agencies—like FHA, the Department of Veteran Affairs (VA), the Rural Housing Service (RHS) and the Office of Public and Indian Housing (PIH).[25] As we shall see, the MBS market was in fact created by Ginnie Mae. The Emergency Home Finance Act of 1979 created another GSE, the Federal Home Loan Mortgage Corporation (Freddie Mac), with a mandate similar to that of Fannie Mae. Twelve regional Federal Home Loan banks, created by Herbert Hoover,[26] also count among the GSEs since 1932: thanks to their implicit government guarantees, they borrow cheaply on capital markets, and lend the money to their private-bank members, who use it to make mortgage loans.[27]

To this network of government agencies and enterprises—FHA, HUD, VA, RHS, PIH, Fannie Mae, Freddie Mac, Ginnie Mae, and the Federal Home Loan banks—we must add the regulators overseeing some of them: the Office of Federal Housing Enterprises Oversight (OFHEO) and the Federal Housing Finance Board (FHFB)—which, in 2008, were merged into the Federal Housing Finance Agency. Understanding the activities of these multiple government organizations requires some expertise and some patience.

Before they crashed in September of 2008, Fannie Mae and Freddie Mac were strange animals, with private capital and a legislatively mandated goal of funding affordable housing. They were both listed on the New York Stock Exchange with, at the end of 2006, 22,000 shareholders for Fannie Mae and 2,201 for Freddie Mac.[28] The president of the United States selected about one-third of their directors.[29] The two GESs were able to raise funds on capital markets at lower rates than any private competitor in the market because investors knew that, despite official pronouncements to the contrary, the two GSEs were too close to the state to fail. According to their HUD-set goals, Fannie and Freddie had to provide a high and increasing proportion of their resources to purchase mortgage loans made to low and moderate income borrowers, in underserved areas, or for affordable housing.[30]

Freddie Mac's chairman wrote in the company's 2006 annual report: "The congressional genius in designing the GSEs was to accomplish a public mission not with federal expenditures, but using private capital."[31] In the words of Philip Wicksteed, they were designed to "harness individualism to the car of collectivism,"[32] put the profit motive at the service of state goals. However, profits had not been substantial in recent years and, since at least 2001, the shares of both companies had underperformed the S&P 500 and the S&P Financials.[33] The car of collectivism is heavy to pull. The worst was yet to come.

Of the $9.4 trillion in American mortgages outstanding in 2005, at least 40 percent were financed or guaranteed by the federal government and its GSEs. The market share of government in the residential mortgage market exceeded the 32 percent share of banks and other savings institutions (including life insurance and private pension funds), and the 17 percent share of MBSs guaranteed by private institutions.[34]

The GSEs have been under strong political pressure to increase mortgage lending to the poor and the minorities. A *New York Times* story of 1999 noted:

> In a move that could help increase home ownership rates among minorities and low income consumers, the Fannie Mae Corporation is easing the credit requirements on loans it will purchase from banks and other lenders . . .
>
> Fannie Mae, the nation's biggest underwriter of home mortgages, has been under increasing pressure from the Clinton Administration to expand mortgage loans among low and moderate income people . . .[35]

Fannie Mae and Freddie Mac bought and securitized more and more risky mortgages, thereby transmitting lower lending standards down the chain of lenders.[36] This transmission apparently operated in two ways: the GSEs bought mortgages that were more and more lax regarding the borrowers' financial situations, and the private-label securitizers were pushed to seek more and more risky mortgages as the GSEs had skimmed the best part of it.

Selling more risky mortgages to poorer people implied the relaxation of lending standards. The Community Reinvestment Act (CRA) played an important role in that enterprise. Adopted by Congress in 1977, CRA was meant to force lenders to cater to poor neighborhoods and minority clienteles. The law apparently had little influence until a 1992 study by the Boston Federal Reserve purported to demonstrate discrimination against minorities in the mortgage market. The study compared rates of approval without taking into account other credit factors that weighed in the lenders' decisions.[37] It focused on Blacks and Latinos, neglecting the fact that Asian Americans obtained better loan conditions than whites, a damning fact for the hypothesis that minorities *qua* minorities were discriminated against.[38] In fact, minority individuals of interest to the Fed were more often denied mortgages simply because they presented a higher financial risk. After the Fed study, political pressure started to build up under George Bush Sr. and intensified under the Clinton Administration and Attorney General Janet Reno.

In 1992, the Justice Department charged the Decatur Savings & Loans Association with racial discrimination. While denying the charge, the bank chose to settle out of court as the least expensive and damageable alternative.[39] In 1993, HUD began initiating legal action against mortgage lenders suspected of discrimination. The Justice Department brought a case against the Chevy Chase Federal Savings Bank because it did not have enough branches in minority neighborhoods. The bank settled, committing to open branches and mortgage offices in poor neighborhoods.[40] The threatening advice served by Attorney General Janet Reno dates from the same year: "Do not wait for the Justice Department to come knocking."[41] CRA was reinforced in 1995. Banks received CRA ratings and those with insufficient ratings were not allowed to merge, diversify or open branch offices.[42] The banks got the message.

Around the time of the crisis, the Bank of America's CRA mortgages amounted to 7 percent of its total mortgage lending.[43] CRA and its enforcement increased the number of borrowers who could not afford their mortgages.

The pressure to lend to poorer people naturally contributed to the growth of subprime loans. In 2001, $160 billion of subprime mortgages were issued; four years later, the rate had increased to $625 billion. By 2006, $1.2 trillion in subprime mortgages, or 13 percent of all residential mortgages, were outstanding, after growing at 14 percent per year since 1995.[44] So-called Alt-A mortgages, a compromise between prime mortgages and subprimes, accounted for 13 percent of the mortgages originations in 2006.[45] Between 2005 and 2007, Fannie Mae and Freddie Mac may have acquired as much as $1 trillion worth of subprime and other nontraditional mortgages.[46] Peter Wallison of the American Enterprise Institute suggests that, near the onset of the crisis, the two GSEs held or guaranteed $1.6 trillion in subprime and Alt-A mortgages[47]—which would account for 40 percent of the total mortgages they held or guaranteed and for most of these risky mortgages in the market.

Subprime lending was hailed by government spokesmen. In 2000, HUD declared:

> Subprime mortgage lending provides credit to borrowers with past credit problems, often at a higher cost or less favorable terms than loans available in the conventional prime market. In most cases, these lenders offer credit to borrowers who would not qualify for a loan in the prime market,

thus expanding access to credit and helping more families to own their own homes.[48]

At about the same time, a member of the Board of Governors of the Federal Reserve boasted:

> This should be a time of great satisfaction for the advocates of low-income and minority borrowers. . . . A significant proportion of this expansion of low-income lending appears to be in the so-called subprime lending market. This market has expanded considerably, permitting many low-income and minority borrowers to realize their dreams of owning a home and have a chance for acquiring the capital gains that have so increased the wealth of upper-income households.[49]

In order to the satisfy borrowers' demand and the Nanny State's requirements, innovative mortgage products were introduced. The proportion of adjustable-rate mortgages(ARMs), whose rate were readjusted periodically—as opposed to the traditional 30-year fixed mortgage—made up less than 10 percent of all mortgages in 2001 but their proportion had more than doubled by the end of 2005. Nearly half of subprimes were ARMs. A special sort of ARM, the so-called hybrid mortgages, started with a lower, "teaser" interest rate that reset to the actual market rate after two or three years. In certain cases, the initial monthly payments did not even cover the interest, so the unpaid part was added to the principal when the new rate kicked in.[50]

ARMs are not a problem *per se*. In most countries, they are the rule. The late 1970s and early 1980s faced double-digit inflation that brought mortgage rates to summits. Consider Canada, where most mortgages have adjustable interest rates that reset every five years or earlier. These ARMs carried interest rates of 9 percent at the beginning of the 1970s but, from mid-1979 to mid-1981, they jumped from 11 percent to more than 21 percent.[51] This incredibly rapid and steep increase in mortgage rated did not cause widespread dislocation in the mortgage market nor in the overall economy.

To explain the meltdown of the U.S. mortgage markets in 2007, we have to look at reasons that are related to their being "the envy of the world," and especially at the artificial stimulation of the housing market by the U.S. government. A related reason is the politically dictated relaxing of lending standards, up to the so-called NINJA—"No Income, No Job, no Assets"—loans, where none of these conditions were adequately documented. Down payments were low if not zero. These factors had to lead to a crash at some point in time.

Many analysts saw the danger in the degrading of mortgage lending standards. The 1999 *New York Times* story already quoted about Fannie Mae continued:

> In moving, even tentatively, into this new area of lending, Fannie Mae is taking on significantly more risk, which may not pose any difficulties during flush economic times. But the government-subsidized corporation may run into trouble in an economic downturn, prompting a government rescue similar to that of the savings and loan industry in the 1980's.[52]

At about the same time, economists Theodore Day and Stan Liebowitz wrote:

> We are likely to find, with the adoption of flexible underwriting standards, that we are merely encouraging banks to make unsound loans. If this is the case, current policy will not have helped its intended beneficiaries if in future years they are dispossessed from their homes due to an inability to make their mortgage payments.[53]

Peter Wallison notes that the decline in mortgage standards started with CRA's revised regulations in 1993, and continued with the GSEs responding to their mandates and to political pressure. This created incentives for private lenders to do the same: after all, they were selling most of their mortgages to the GSEs. Public policy was the driving force. The government was engaged in a major operation of mortgaging the poor.

Securitization and the Greedy

Securitization increased the supply of residential mortgages, especially subprime mortgages, and thus made them easier to obtain. Suppliers could offer more mortgages because they could resell them. The buyers, whether GSEs, investment banks or other sponsors, were interested in buying these mortgages because they would turn them into MBSs and resell them to investors. Once a mortgage issuer had sold some mortgages, and once the MBS sponsor had sold his securities to investors, they could all use their revenues to finance a new round of mortgage originations and securitizations. By 2005, 54 percent of the value of all outstanding mortgages, and some two-thirds of the value of subprime mortgages, were securitized.[54]

Securitization of loans, whether mortgages or other loans, has many advantages. Because it pools many loans together, securitization diversifies and thus reduces risk: performing loans offset losses on nonperforming ones. Investors who would not purchase risky loans can be attracted to securities that include them but compensate with safer ones. Securitization allows for the development a secondary market where package loans can easily be resold to investors. It is thus easy to understand why, since the 1990s, consumer loans have been increasingly repackaged in asset-backed securities, whether they were credit card debts, automobile loans, student loans, or mortgages.[55] Securitization is a not a bad thing but, like all innovations, it must survive in the market as opposed to being artificially encouraged or hindered by the government.

The securitization of residential mortgages was not originally a product of greedy Wall Street financiers. It is Ginnie Mae, a government agency, that introduced MBSs in 1970. The agency puts the federal government's formal guarantee—"the full faith and credit guaranty of the United States government"—on MBSs issued by private sponsors from mortgages already guaranteed by other government agencies. On its website, the agency talks about the previous problem of increasing mortgage funding, and boasts that "Ginnie Mae solved this problem and revolutionized the American housing industry in 1970 by pioneering the issuance of mortgage-backed securities."[56] And it is Fannie Mae and Freddie Mac who, in 1983, first divided an MBS into different tranches, "the starting signal for the entire mortgage industry," writes Norberg.[57] This well-known fact is admitted even by Paul Krugman, who writes about securitization that "[i]n fact, it was pioneered by Fannie Mae."[58] The federal government promoted securitization of residential mortgages in order to increase the supply of mortgage loans. Mortgage lenders lend, sell their loans for securitization, and lend again. Of course, there is an ultimate limit: higher supply pushes down prices, that is, interest rate or other loan conditions, up to a dangerous point. But the government did want to go there: remember that Barney Frank was rolling the dice.

As years went by, the GSEs became big securitizers of mortgages and dramatically increased the value of mortgages being securitized.[59] By 2005, 54 percent of all outstanding mortgages in value had been securitized (a value of $5.2 trillion), compared with only 11 percent in 1990. Nearly three-fourths of the securitized mortgages at that time were guaranteed by the government, most of them by Fannie Mae and Freddie Mac.[60] The two GSEs kept many MBSs in their own portfolios,[61] and guaranteed the ones they sold on the secondary market.

Among financial institutions, domestic commercial banks were among the most exposed to subprime mortgages—they held 18 percent of subprime mortgages—and roughly on par with domestic hedge funds.[62] Why did banks keep some MBSs in their own portfolios, and MBSs often made of mortgage loans they had themselves issued? Regulatory constraints are a big part of the answer.

The regulations that encouraged banks to hold MBSs were capital requirements. Banks have been forced to maintain minimum capital ratios since the Basel Committee on Banking Supervision, an international governmental organization based in Basel (Switzerland), decreed them in the late 1980s. The numerator of the regulatory capital ratio is the capital held by the shareholders, the denominator is the bank's assets (loans, securities, and cash). The ratio (of total capital) was 8 percent before the crisis, that is, 8 percent of a bank's assets had to be covered by the capital of its shareholders. In fact, two sorts of capital can be distinguished: core capital ("Tier 1"), for which a lower ratio of 4 percent is required, and supplementary capital ("Tier 2"), which adds another 4 percent; but this distinction is not useful here and we can focus on total capital. Since some sorts of lending are less risky than others—for example, lending to the government by purchasing government securities is deemed riskless—the Basel rules assigned different weights to different sorts of assets in the denominator. The regulatory capital required in the numerator must be compared with these risked-weighted assets in the denominator. Treasury securities carried a zero risk weight, which means that they did not count as (risky) assets against which the 8 percent of capital ratio had to be maintained. Loans to government organizations and securities issued or guaranteed by government organizations like Fannie Mae or Freddie Mac carried a 20 percent risk weight. Mortgages were assigned a 50 percent weight. All other assets, like commercial or consumer loans counted for 100 percent in the risk-adjusted assets. This means that zero capital was needed to cover Treasury securities, that 1.6 percent (8 percent times the risk factor of 20 percent) of the securities of government organizations had be covered by capital, 4 percent (8 percent × 50 percent) of mortgages, and 8 percent (8 percent × 100 percent) of other loans.[63]

The official justification for imposing capital ratios to banks is that shareholder's capital provides a buffer for reimbursing depositors in case the value of the bank's assets is reduced. Many economists have argued that these requirements are superfluous as bank shareholders would want such a buffer anyway in order to attract depositors and bond holders at reasonable cost.[64] I already mentioned that, in the late nineteenth century, long before there was any capital regulation, the typical American bank had a core capital ratio of nearly 25 percent, and the typical British bank of more than 15 percent. When the Basel regulatory capital ratios appeared unrealistic to them, the banks tried to legally dodge them, that is, they engaged in regulatory capital arbitrage.

Securitization of residential mortgages was a preferred means of regulatory capital arbitrage. Suppose you are a bank and have issued a $100,000 mortgage. This loan ties up $4,000 (8 percent × 50 percent × $100,000) of your capital, since this is the capital you need to back it up with according to the Basel rules. If you can find a regulatory-correct way to keep less capital as a buffer against this loan, you will be able use the liberated capital to make a loan to somebody else and make more money. Now—and here is the trick—a mortgage purchased and securitized by one of the GSEs is a government security and requires only a capital coverage of $1,600 (8 percent × 20 percent × $100,000). So what you do is sell your mortgage to a GSE and repurchase it as an MBS—or purchase another MBS for the same amount. You can now lend $2,400 (the difference between $4,000 and $1,600) to somebody else, and earn interest on this new loan.[65]

The banks thus had incentives to sell their mortgages to Fannie Mae or Freddie Mac for securitization, and to rebuy and hold the securitized equivalent, contributing to the growing demand for MBSs. Sometimes, the banks could do even better with the help of structured finance (complex financial products for the specialized needs of large market participants). Banks could take some loans completely off their balance sheets by securitizing them and passing them through to their own off-balance-sheet entities or conduits (SIVs or SPVs[66]), collecting returns without having to set aside any capital. This creative finance was motivated by capital regulations and the special opportunities offered by the GSEs—just like creative accounting is often motivated by the desire to legally minimize taxes.

This form of regulatory arbitrage was known to bank regulators. In 2000, a Fed researcher published an article entitled "Emerging problems with the Basel Capital Accord: Regulatory Capital Arbitrage and Related Issues," where he wrote:

> In recent years, securitization and other financial innovations have provided unprecedented opportunities for banks to reduce substantially their regulatory measures of risk, with little or no corresponding reduction in the overall economic risks—a process termed "regulatory capital arbitrage." (RCA)

> . . . when capital standards are not based on any consistent economic soundness standard (e.g., probability of insolvency), through securitization and other techniques it is often possible to restructure portfolios to have basically similar risks, but much lower regulatory capital requirements.[67]

In other words, when the regulatory capital imposed on banks makes no economic sense, they will manage to hold less capital while complying with the regulation.

Bankers were also well aware of what they were doing. Léon Courville, a former president of the National Bank of Canada (a small private bank), blames the regulatory capital requirements for the flurry of securitization that led to the demise of MBSs. "Securitization became an obsession," he writes, adding that "by reducing the risk to individual institutions, regulation moved that risk to the financial system in general."[68]

The *de facto* lowering of the banks' capital ratios by regulatory capital arbitrage was actually necessary to level the playing field between them and the GSEs, who had lower capital requirements.[69] It is a recurrent problem of intervention in the complex information system of a modern economy: a government intervention creates problems that require another intervention which generate other short-circuits, and so on, until systemic problems explode. GSEs provided unfair competition to private banks, so the latter's capital ratio had to be reduced through regulatory arbitrage, compromising their solidity. The same story can be told about the race to the bottom of lending standards started by the federal government. A complex economy is a delicate information system where brute government intervention easily wreaks havoc.

At the global level, banks (commercial and investment banks) accounted for perhaps as much as half of total financial institutions' exposure to the subprime market.[70] Why didn't the banks foresee what would happen if house prices went down? One big reason was that nearly three-fourths of the MBSs were guaranteed by the GSEs,[71] and thus implicitly by the government of the United States. When they held private-label MBSs, the banks thought that were adequately covered by credit default swaps (CDSs), a form of insurance underwritten by insurance companies and speculators. Their risk management models were also unduly optimistic, vastly underestimating large but unprobably risks: "Hedge funds are better at this than banks," adds *The Economist.*[72]

Another reason is to be found in the perverse effects of deposit insurance. Depositors knew that they would not lose anything however badly their bank was managed. Deposit insurance covered only $100,000 per depositor, but this limit was only formal since wealthy depositors could spread millions of dollars among different banks; there were even organized and inexpensive methods of doing this.[73] Consequently, banks were not monitored by depositors, who rightly thought that they were equally safe from their point of view. The impact of deposit insurance on bank discipline is demonstrated by the fact that the total capital-asset ratio[74] of American commercial banks declined from 10 percent at the time of the Great Depression to around 6 percent after deposit insurance was created—until the Basel rules pushed it back closer to 10 percent.[75] With deposit insurance, banks held less capital because they did not need it to persuade depositors that they were solid.

Consider again the vicious circle of government intervention. The Basel requirements were aimed at correcting what was the effect of a previous government intervention, that is, deposit insurance. The Basel capital requirements in turn incited the banks to engage in regulatory arbitrage by keeping MBSs on (or off) their balance sheets, instead of holding their own mortgage loans. Still another factor in the bank's temptation to hold MBSs was the "too big to fail" doctrine, which had already taken hold of political opinion. Virtually everybody assumed that the authorities would not let a big bank fail. Big banks benefited from this supplementary guarantee. Why would the bankers be overly prudent when profits were private and risk socialized? In July 2010, as I was putting the last hand to this book, the financial reform imposed new regulations to try and correct the effects of the previous ones.

More than 80 percent of securitized subprime mortgages obtained the top debt rating of AAA from the rating agencies, Standard & Poor, Moody's and Fitch.[76] Why were the rating agencies so generous with their ratings. Were they defrauding the securities purchasers while being paid by the issuers? Charles Calomiris persuasively argues that, on the contrary, the rating agencies were responding to the demands of the buyers of the securities who wanted high ratings mainly for regulatory reasons.[77] Even if their clients are the securities issuers, the rating agencies have a reputation to maintain. If the buyers had wanted more severe ratings, the issuers could not have used an agency known for its sloppy ratings. The final buyer always rules. To take an example in another field, a department store has no incentive to obtain loose safety certifications if its customers actually want safe appliances, so nobody can compete with Underwriters Laboratories by issuing false certifications. There can be no race to the bottom excerpt if the "bottom" is what the final customer wants. As final customers, the banks wanted high-rated securities in order to reduce their capital requirements. Other institutional investors (like pension funds or mutual funds) were also looking for loose ratings in order to satisfy the regulations that restrict their purchases of low-rated securities.[78] In other words, ratings had become a simple regulatory requirement, and the ratings agencies were selling the licence.

Issuers of private MBSs—called "private-label MBSs"—came late into the game, but they came with a vengeance. Private-label issuers securitized their own mortgages or purchased mortgages to securitize. They included specialized mortgage lenders such as Countrywide, commercial banks like Bank of America, and investment banks like Goldman Sachs.[79] They obtained guarantees from private insurers—the so-called monoline insurers, who had previously been insuring municipal bonds—instead of government backing. Contrary to the GSEs which normally could not go lower than Alt-A loans, private-label insurers could freely securitize subprime mortgages; indeed, they contributed mightily to the explosion of subprimes.[80] Between 2001 and 2006, the share of private-label MBSs more than doubled in value from 14 percent to 36 percent; by that time, more than half of newly issued MBSs were private-label.[81] Private-label issuers accepted lower lending standards in order not to lose market share to the GSEs, who had already loosened their standards to comply with legal and political demands.[82]

Another factor in the increased popularity of private-label MBSs came from the fact that, after January 1st, 2002, the Basel rules gave them the same low risk weight (20 percent) as GSE-guaranteed securities, provided that they were rated AAA or AA (the two top ratings).[83] Banks could now benefit from lower regulatory capital requirements by holding well-rated private MBSs too. This, of course, applied to the banks of all countries submitted to the Basel rules and, by 2006, private-label MBS were being issued in Europe for hundreds of billions.[84]

The GSEs were not the only culprits in the mortgage crises, but note how the surge in private-label MBSs was a consequence of public policies. The federal government officially encouraged more home ownership and more access to mortgages. The massive presence of GSEs in this market pushed private lenders to look for riskier clienteles. The growth of private-label MBSs responded to a demand for high-rated securities by banks engaged in regulatory arbitrage and by other regulated financial institutions.

Besides regulatory reasons, the attractiveness of MBSs came from their slightly higher returns than other liquid financial instruments, while their underlying assets—the houses financed by the mortgages—were deemed to provide solid guarantees in case of default. MBS provided a return of about 1 percent more than ten-year Treasury bonds.[85] All sorts of "greedy" people were attracted to this higher return. Individuals invested in money market funds, which held commercial paper financing MBSs, instead of putting their money in government securities or savings accounts. State pension funds invested and lost money in MBSs, showing that greed overlaps the private-public frontier.[86] In 2006, CalPERS (California Public Employees' Retirement System) invested more than $1.3 billion in SIVs holding MBSs.[87] Foreigners were greedy too: one fifth of American MBSs were held in other countries.[88] It is estimated that 16 percent of subprime exposure fell on foreign banks and foreign hedge funds.[89]

Subsidization of Risk

With hindsight, too many risks were taken by participants in the housing and mortgage market. Many banks, mortgage lenders, insurers, and fund managers would now agree that their models of risk management were too optimistic. Many private individuals and firms made decisions that they wish they had not made, and are trying to learn how to do better in the future. They have already done much to avoid a future repetition of their past errors. In the meantime, the federal government is trying to put the blame on somebody else.

Lots of companies—and not only the GSEs—as well as individual and families were overleveraged (had too much debt and not enough equity), illustrating the claim of the classical economists that overindebtedness worsens a recession. In 2007, the ratio of assets to shareholder equity was 95 for Fannie Mae, 67 for Freddie Mac, 34 for Bear Stearns, 32 for Merrill Lynch, 31 for Lehman Brothers—all businesses that failed. By comparison, JP Morgan Chase had a leverage ratio of 13 and Goldman Sachs of 32. It is true that Citigroup's low leverage ratio of 19 did not prevent what would quite certainly have been its failure had it not received a large capital infusion from the Treasury.[90] Leverage was only one factor in the crisis. The more general factor was too much risk taking.

Government encouraged and subsidized this risk taking. Government policies diverted resources to the housing market, which contributed to fuelling the bubble that burst in 2006. Deductibility of mortgage interest boosted demand for house ownership. Interest on home equity loans was also deductible, contrary to interest on other consumer loans, inciting individuals to borrow on their home equity to reimburse other debts.[91] The abolition of capital gains tax on up to $500,000 for a couple's house by president Clinton in the late 1990s had the same effect as interest rate deductibility—boosting the demand for houses.[92] There were more direct subsidies to mortgage risks. The federal government provided cheap funding for mortgages through the Federal Home Loan banks. It subsidized Fannie Mae and Freddie Mac through its implicit guarantee, allowing the two GSEs to raise funds at lower cost. It encouraged or mandated lending to individuals with insufficient incomes and the general decline in lending standards.[93] It gave a seal of approval to an oligopoly of rating agencies, whose ratings were required by many of its regulations. It introduced and stimulated mortgage securitization. The capital requirements imposed to banks further fuelled mortgage securitization. Deposit insurance and the too-big-to-fail doctrine encouraged banks to take risks. The signature of government is everywhere.

Blue Watermelons

The bubble that developed was only sustainable as long as house prices increased. When they started receding in 2006, the house of cards was bound to collapse. From August 2007 to August 2008, house prices dropped by 17 percent. This average hid much local variation, from 28 percent in Miami or 27 percent in Los Angeles, to 3 percent in Dallas.[94] But it was only sufficient that house prices crashed in a few big markets for the mistrust toward MBSs to reverberate throughout the whole economy.

Those who had bought mortgages to finance high-priced houses often found that hey were under water. Meanwhile, mortgage interest rates had started climbing in 2004. Those who had purchased ARMs were seeing their rates resetting to higher levels. The transition was especially brutal for those who had been paying interest-only mortgages. Default rates on subprime mortgages, which were typically around 3 percent before 2001, and had increased nearly to 5 percent in 2005, jumped up to 10 percent in 2008.[95] At the end of 2008, 25 percent of subprime mortgages were delinquent.[96] The senior tranches of many MBSs were hit. As the trouble of the housing market spread through the economy, many borrowers of prime mortgages lost their jobs and started skipping payments or defaulting on their mortgages. In the third quarter of 2009, when GDP growth returned, one in seven mortgages were delinquent or in foreclosure.[97]

Default rates on mortgages were worsened by other factors. In most American states, a mortgage lender has no legal recourse on the other assets of a defaulting homeowner—or his recourse is so costly to exert that it amounts to no recourse *de facto*.[98] The governments of these states are in fact prohibiting mortgage borrowers to contractually pledge other assets in order to get (cheaper) mortgages. Consequently, the borrower has an incentive to just "walk away" when get under water. This situation is most likely if the house was bought recently with a low or no down payment, so that the mortgage was already close to the bubbled-up value of the house. A defaulting borrower will temporarily damage his credit score, but it may be worth it if he thereby escapes a net liability of several tens of thousands of dollars. Defaulters included so-called flippers, who had been speculating on house price increases by purchasing houses, sometimes doing light renovations, and reselling them before their mortgage rates resettled; in 2005, perhaps a fourth of homes were bought by flippers.[99]

On September 7, 2008, Fannie Mae and Freddie Mac, on the brink of bankruptcy, were seized, granted guarantees of $200 billion by the federal government, and put in government conservatorship.[100] Just four years earlier, Senator Christopher Dodd had called the two GSEs "one of the great success stories of our time." One year before their demise, he declared that they were "on a sound footing."[101] Fannie Mae and Freddie Mac may end up costing the taxpayer $300 billion or more[102]—$1,000 for each man, woman, and child in the United States.

Although subprime loans accounted for only 13 percent of the value of all residential mortgages, they soon made up half of the foreclosures.[103] Loans done under CRA criteria were hit hard: for example, the Bank of America reported that although these loans represented 7 percent of its mortgage lending, they accounted for 29 percent of its mortgage losses.[104] To say the least, it is not clear that the poor gained in the process. To paraphrase Mencken,[105] the poor deserved affordable houses, and they got them good and hard.

"[T]he subprime crisis," said Barney Frank, in a typical politician's statement, "demonstrates the serious negative economic and social consequences that result from too little regulation."[106] It is difficult to be more wrong. A home market artificially stimulated by government and a residential mortgage market half nationalized had led a large number of people to buy houses they could not afford, contributing to a housing bubble and its unavoidable crash with widening financial consequences. There was somebody in charge: for decades, the government had been the main cheerleader, mover and shaker in the housing market. It regularly bullied private participants into abiding by its regulations, defective research, and whims. Many of the perverse institutions in place had been created by the New Deal, and their effects compounded with other factors in the last decade or two. Former Fannie Mae economist Arnold Kling writes that "the seeds for much of the current crisis were sown in the policy 'solutions' to previous financial and economic crises."[107]

While, as Thomas Sowell puts it, "[l]ending money to American homebuyers had been one of the least risky and most profitable businesses a bank could engage it for nearly a century," government intervention in the housing and mortgage market "changed that disastrously, not only for banks but for the entire economy."[108]

It is true that Fannie, Freddie, and Ginnie did not originate any dangerous loan. They were not in that business. But others did because they knew they could sell them to, or have them guaranteed by, the GSEs. That's what businesses like Countrywide did. A whole private industry developed around the government's promotion and financing of home ownership. Let the state announce that it will buy any blue watermelon for $1,000 a piece, and you will see a whole industry developing to "originate" blue watermelons and sell them to state bureaus. The blue-watermelon bubble will be inflated even more if government spokesmen repeat that ownership of blue watermelons is essential to our society and that the state is committed to increasing the number of blue-watermelon-eating families. "Blue water melons are essential for the welfare of our communities." Let the Attorney General declare, to anybody keeping its distance from the blue-watermelon business, "Do not wait for the Justice Department to come knocking," and you have the recipe for a blue-watermelon bubble. Will you then blame the blue-watermelon industry for causing the bubble?

The consequences have bled far away from the crime scene. The MBSs were owned by a large number of institutions in the United States; one-fifth were owned in foreign countries. Nobody knew exactly where these MBSs and the CDOs containing them were and which institutions were threatened by their demise. These information problems were a consequence of what remains of a free society where economic transactions are generally outside the purview of the authorities. When, in the summer of 2007, it became evident that many subprimes would be in default, that MBS prices would drop, that commercial paper that financed them was risky, the financial crisis had begun.

It was a *financial* crisis only in a derived sense—in the sense that finance is tied to the real economy and reacts to it. It may be, as Gary Gorton argues,[109] that the shadow banks were victims of a bank run—the sort we hadn't seen since the Great Depression—but the problem still originated the real economy. Because of a host of reasons, of which the government's stimulation and control of the residential home and mortgage markets were at the forefront, bad decisions had been made. Individuals had invested in houses they could not afford. Lenders had financed these bad investments. Resources had been allocated to residential housing and wasted, as indicated by the lower value of the houses. A few trillions of dollars of resources had been misallocated. Somebody would have to bear this loss. Would they be the individuals and companies who had made the bad decisions? Partly yes, as shareholders of failed companies took a hit. But the government managed to transfer a large part of the loss to the general taxpayer.

All these problems did not come from a shortage of interventions by public authorities. There was somebody in charge, and that was precisely the problem.

CHAPTER 6

Monetary Meddling

It is clear that monetary policy was accommodative. Rates of 1 per cent were bound to encourage all kinds of risky behaviour.

—Anna Schwartz[1]

S ome readers may be surprised that I have barely mentioned the role of monetary policy in the recent crisis. Anna Schwartz, the NBER economist who wrote the monumental monetary history of the United States with Milton Friedman,[2] agrees with most economists that the Fed's holding down short-run interest rates bears a responsibility in the housing bubble. It is now time to analyze the role of monetary policy in the 2007–2009 recession.

The Austrian Theory of the Business Cycle

Looking explicitly at the role of monetary policy will allow us to bring into the picture a school of economic thought that offers a fundamental critique of, and an alternative to, Keynesian theory. This school of economic thought, the "Austrian school", owes its name to its birth in Vienna with the publication of Carl Menger's 1871 book, *Principles of Economics*.[3] One of the school's main theorists was Ludwig von Mises, whom we have met earlier in this book. Mises's 1912 book, *The Theory of Money and Credit*,[4] was published in English in 1934 but was eclipsed by Keynes's *General Theory*, which appeared two years later. Carl Menger, Eugen Böhm-Bawerk, Ludwig von Mises, Murray Rothbard, and Friedrich Hayek were among the major Austrian economists.

For Austrian economists, the only source of the business cycle lies in expansionary monetary policy. As we have seen, a larger money supply means more money chasing the same quantity of goods, which leads to inflation. However, contrary to the quantitative theory of money examined in Chapter 2, Austrian economists believe that not all prices will increase in the same proportion as the money supply: some will increase more, others less. The new money hits the economy at specific points of entry, as opposed to increasing equally the demand for all goods, services and factors of production. In our economy, money is generally created by the expansion of bank credit: the central bank purchases securities from the banks, which consequently have more money to lend, which translates into higher bank deposits from the borrowers and their suppliers. The money originally lent will go to business investments or the purchase of consumer goods, usually durable goods. The prices of the capital goods (machines, equipment, land) or the durable goods that are hit first will increase. The new money will slowly percolate through the economy, but the process will take time.[5] The differential impact of money creation on prices has major consequences. Relative prices change: the prices of the goods first affected will rise more than other prices. Capital goods and durable consumer goods (houses, for instance) will show higher price increases, while ordinary consumption goods will be less affected. Profits will increase more in the first categories of goods than in the second, leading to a relatively larger increase in the quantity supplied of the former. Thus, inflation changes the *structure* of production, as opposed to simply lifting all prices and all quantities in the same proportion. As inflation distorts relative prices, false information is transmitted to producers. They are led to believe that the production of more capital goods (more investment) and more durable goods, relative to ordinary consumption goods, is needed. Austrian economics brings the coordination function of relative prices to the forefront of the analysis.

One price will be especially distorted and will send the most misleading signals: the interest rate. (Here, I disregard the term structure of interest rates in order to simplify the exposition.) The interest rate is the price of savings and investment, which brings into equilibrium the supply and the demand of loanable funds. The rate of interest is not, as in Keynesian theory, merely the price of money, for the price of money is the goods that are exchanged for money. The rate of interest can certainly influence the demand for money in the short run as people want to hold less of it if the interest they can get on securities is higher, and *mutatis mutandis* in the opposite case; but the first role played by the rate of interest remains to serve as the price of loanable funds in the saving-investment market.[6] In Austrian economic theory, the rate of interest is primarily the price of credit, not the price of money. An increased supply of money translates into a higher supply of credit, which pushes the rate of interest down on the market for loanable funds. While consumers want as many consumer goods as before, cheap interest rates lead to relatively more investment and, thus, fewer consumption goods—or, alternatively, to more goods to be consumed in the future and fewer now.

The misallocation of resources comes from the fact that the time preference rate of consumers (the rate at which they are willing to substitute future to actual consumption) hasn't changed, and that the increased allocation of resources to investment is not in accord with the time preferences of consumers. The increased savings represented by the new credit are artificial. Consumers don't actually want to save more; in fact, they will want to save less after the rate of interest has dropped. But more goods will be produced for the future through the increase in investment. "[A]n interest rate substantially influenced by extra-market forces," writes Garrison, "will lead to an intertemporal misallocation of resources." The focus of Austrian theory, he explains, "is on the misallocation of resources during the period of artificially cheap credit". Alternatively, "[t]he avoidance of such misallocations requires the interest rate to tell the truth about intertemporal preferences".[7]

Contemporary Austrian economist Bob Higgs emphasizes that the problem of money inflation and the accompanying drop in interest rate does not (or does not mainly) lie in overinvestment, but in *malinvestment*.[8] Producers not only invest more in capital goods, they also skew their investment plans toward capital goods more removed from consumer goods in the structure of capital. The "structure of capital" is the network of capital goods necessary to produce, say, a steel hammer—from the iron ore mine to the smelter to the steel-making plant and to the hammer manufacturing plant. In our pencil example of Chapter 1, the structure of capital includes the land, buildings and machines required by the pencil manufacturer, plus the land, buildings and machines required to produce wood and graphite, as well as the land, buildings and machines required to produce these buildings and machines, and up the timeline. A lower rate of interest produces a lengthening of the capital structure: it becomes profitable to invest farther from the steel or the pencil, in order to assure the production of these goods in the more distant future.

O'Driscoll and Shenoy summarize the two contributions of Austrian economics to monetary theory:

> First, it emphasizes the role of money in the pricing process and incorporates money...into the determination of relative prices. Second, it analyzes the effect of such money-induced relative price changes on the time structure of production, that is, the capital structure.[9]

In this perspective, a recession is simply the necessary correction of the misallocation of resources caused by the false price signals that the monetary expansion generated. Monetary expansion creates an artificial economic boom through higher production of capital goods and consumer durables. Because people's preferences for present and future consumption have not changed, consumers reassert their preferences when the increased money supply has percolated down in the form of higher incomes. Prices of ordinary consumption goods will now rise, and producers will rush to satisfy the perceived new demand—which is nothing but the previous demand that consumers are reasserting. The credit-fuelled production of new capital goods (and durable consumer goods) has to be halted, because it is impossible to produce more of everything. Unemployment develops in capital goods and durable goods producing sectors. Lenders restrain credit and interest rates go back up (if the money supply is not continuously inflated). As interest rates increase, more investment projects become unprofitable and are cancelled—especially those with long time horizons. This process will continue as long as resources have not moved back to the consumption sector, or been written off, and the malinvestment has been corrected. At this point, the recession reaches bottom and economic growth resumes. The recession has corrected the artificial boom created by expansionary monetary policy.

Trying to end a recession by further expansion of the money supply will only postpone the necessary correction. Liquidation of bad investments must proceed unimpeded. Similarly, fuelling an economic boom with an expansionary monetary policy only generates the need for a future correction. Roger Garrison writes that "attempts to prolong the boom through continued increases in credit can fuel an asset bubble".[10] Many think that this is precisely what happened between 2000 and 2006.

The state is always tempted to debase the currency, which is a way to levy stealth taxes. Creating and debasing money are the two sides of the same coin. In former times, the Prince reduced the precious metal content of coins, and minted new coins with the recovered metal. In our times, fiat money makes debasing the currency easier: the government runs the printing press; or, more typically, the central bank purchases government securities from banks by crediting their accounts, or by crediting the government's account if it finances government debt directly. In both cases, only accounting entries are necessary. Austrian economists believe that, given the temptation and the danger of such practices, money should not be left in the hands of the state. Preventing states from creating and debasing money requires the abolition of central banking and monetary policy.

We can distinguish at least two strands in what Austrian economists think should replace today's central banks and monetary policy. The first strand, represented by Murray Rothbard, argues for a return to the monetary gold standard, plus a 100 percent reserve requirements for banks or, in other terms, the abolition of fractional banking.[11] The second strand in Austrian monetary theory is the so-called free banking school, which proposes a double freedom for the banks: to issue their own money in the form of bank notes which might or might not be based on a commodity like gold; and to loan out part of their deposits, thereby establishing a free market fractional banking system. Theorists such as Lawrence H. White (George Mason University), George Selgin (University of Georgia) and the late Friedrich Hayek have developed sophisticated arguments supporting the feasibility of such a system of private money.[12] The basic idea is simple: if a bank were free to issue its own currency (the "Wells Fargo Note", the "Bank of America Dollar" . . .), it would have an interest in managing and preserving the value of its money lest customers flee to another one. Such a system of free banking was actually tried in Scotland during the first half of the nineteenth century with very favorable results compared with England, where the Bank of England had a monopoly: Scotland gained large and solid banks with many branches, vibrant competition, high public confidence, and virtually no bank failure.[13]

Whatever the validity of the theoretical arguments for a monetary system completely divorced from the any public monetary authority, from any monetary czar, Austrian economists view the role of monetary policy during the business cycle very differently than the monetarists (and, of course, the Keynesians). Milton Friedman and Anna Schwartz argued that the Great Depression was caused by the Fed reducing the money supply or allowing it to drop, instead of intervening to boost it, in what would otherwise have been a simple recession.[14] In contrast, Murray Rothbard tried to show that the Great Depression was caused by an expansion of the money supply during the 1920s, a somewhat contentious claim as that there was little inflation.[15]

Contrary to the other macroeconomic theories reviewed in Chapter 2, the Austrian theory of the business cycle has been subjected to little empirical research. James Keeler, one of the few empirical Austrian economists, reckons that this is "due to limited ability to express Austrian concepts in operational terms and to methodological opposition to empirical opposition testing".[16] The Austrian school's methodological idiosyncrasies often give it a quasi-religious fervor that has certainly contributed to isolating it from mainstream economics and dimmed its contribution to our understanding of the business cycle. Besides reviewing the (thin) empirical Austrian literature, Keeler submitted the eight American cycles from 1950 to 1991 to econometric analysis. He found that increases in the money supply pushed down short-term interest rates while long-term rates did not move much, thus increasing the slope of the yield curve. This change in relative prices (change in interest rates of different maturities) significantly correlated with a rise in capacity utilization in primary processing industries relative to capacity utilization in advanced processing industries.[17] A higher rate of capacity utilization is taken to imply that more capital (and other resources) moves in.[18] We can interpret Keeler's results as demonstrating that money creation distorts relative prices and brings more capital into industries further removed from consumer goods, a malinvestment that ultimately requires a correction called recession. "The evidence," concludes Keeler, "confirms the Austrian hypothesis that relative price changes, expressed in the structure of interest rates, induce a systematic response in resource utilization and income"[19]—a response consistent with the malinvestment hypothesis of Austrian economics.

Monetary Follies in the 2000s?

Despite its empirical and theoretical shortcomings, despite—or perhaps thanks to—its unorthodox character, Austrian economics offers a useful key for understanding recessions in general and the recent crisis in particular. Austrian economists are at the forefront of those who believe that an expansionary monetary policy fuelled an artificial boom. The Fed pushed the federal funds rate from around 6.5 percent in late 2000 to about 1 percent from mid-2003 to mid-2004. Austrian economists emphasize that, as a consequence of these low interest rates, investment boomed and an asset bubble developed, especially in housing. A correction was inevitable.

This Austrian scenario is not totally waterproof. The correlation between monetary expansion and the housing bubble is not perfect. The rapid increase in house prices started before the loosening of monetary policy began: the Case-Shiller national price index show increases of 6 percent as early as 1998.[20] And the bubble inflated for two more years after interest rates reached their through and started climbing. Moreover, if we measure the growth in the money supply by the evolution of M1,[21] we find that it was at least as rapid in part of the 1980s and in the first half of the 1990s: why didn't we observe an artificial boom and a recession then? There was a recession in 1990–1991, but it was small and lasted only two quarters.

There is another problem. Are we sure that the Fed actually influenced the demand for housing and mortgage financing? Alan Greenspan argues that there was no such influence.[22] House purchases, he claims, are influenced by interest rates on long-term, fixed-rate mortgages, not by short-term rates. His data show a statistically significant correlation between home prices and long-term interest rates, but no correlation with short-term rates. As for long-term interest rates, they were already on a downward trend since the early 1980s, and had been for some time decoupled from the short-term rates that the Fed can influence. Long-term mortgage rates nearly continuously declined from more than 10 percent before the mid-1980s to a 5–7 percent range in the new millennium.[23] This downward trend can be observed for all long-term interest rates.[24] According to Greenspan and other economists, the reason for this trend was a dramatic increase in savings from rapidly developing Asian countries (notably China) and petroleum exporting countries. This hypothesis has become known as the "savings glut": more savings means an increased supply of loanable funds which pushes interest rates down.[25] So, Greenspan's argument goes, the short-term interest rates which the Fed lowered had no impact on the demand for housing and mortgage financing, which was instead fuelled by the decline in long-term rates caused by the savings glut.

The first part of Greenspan's argument—the incapacity of short-term interest rates to influence housing and mortgage demand—has been aptly countered by Gerald O'Driscoll.[26] Many mortgages issued after 2002 were ARMs based on short-term rates. As we saw in the last chapter, the proportion of ARMs, which made up less than 10 percent of all mortgages in 2001, held double that share by the end of 2005 (and some claim it was higher than this[27]), and nearly half of subprimes were ARMs. The Fed's pushing down short-term interest rates led many borrowers to choose ARM mortgages.[28] Greenspan replies that long-term investments are made on the basis of long-term interest rates. This is partly true, but a lower-cost short-term financing still reduces, if only slightly, the total mortgage cost. It is difficult not to conclude that pushing down short-term interest rates had some impact on the demand for houses and mortgage financing.

The second part of Greenspan's argument—that the long-term rates were determined uniquely by the savings glut is not true. The savings glut certainly explains part, and perhaps a large part, of the downward trend. As O'Driscoll notes, however, short-term rates certainly have some impact on long-term rates: when the former drop, investors start borrowing short term to lend long term, which pushes up short rates and pulls down long rates. This arbitrage is easily observable in the run-up to the crisis: bank financed their asset growth with short-term money from depositors, investors financed their purchase of MBSs with ABCP, et cetera. Consequently, the Fed certainly exerted some influence on the downward trend of long-term interest rates. The monetary authorities are not all-powerful, but they are not powerless either.

Neo-Keynesian economist John Taylor supports, with different arguments, the Austrian indictment of the Fed's policy. Taylor is the well-known inventor of the "Taylor rule", which is meant to calculate the level of short-run interest rates that the central bank should target in order to bring the economy to full employment without inflation. Taylor argues that his rule was largely followed between the 1980–1982 recession and the beginning of the new millennium, a period marked by a tamed business cycle and called the

"Great Moderation". According to the Taylor rule, however, the Fed should have started pushing up the federal funds rate just after the recession of 2001 instead of waiting until 2004. Maintaining short-term interest rates too low for too long generated the housing bubble. Taylor concludes that "monetary policy was a key cause of the boom and hence the bust and the crisis".[29] More generally, Taylor writes:

> ...a series of unpredictable government actions and interventions with little or no basis in economic theory or experience threw the economy off track, increased uncertainty, and caused great economic harm...government actions and interventions caused, prolonged, and worsened the financial crisis.[30]

Some economists are more reserved about the Fed's guilt. Although they are themselves close to the Austrian School, David Henderson and Jeff Hummel have argued quite convincingly that the Fed did not increase the money supply, or not by as much as its critics believe. They warn that evaluating monetary policy by looking at interest rates is not satisfactory: interest rates were low when money supply collapsed during the Great Depression, and they were high when the money supply jumped during the 1970s. This is because "interest rates can change as a result of real factors involving supply and demand".[31] The two economists therefore use quantitative measures of the money stock to gauge monetary policy. They admit that M1 and M2 were growing at 10 percent per year in 2002, but note that the growth rate then decreased more or less continuously up to respectively 2–3 percent and 0 percent in 2006.[32] Considering only the monetary base, that is, cash and bank reserves, and excluding the dollars bills that went abroad, they calculate that there was virtually no increase in the money supply between Greenspan's arrival at the Fed and 2005. As I mentioned before, Henderson and Hummel argue that the components that M2 adds to M1 (savings deposits, small time deposits, money market deposit accounts, and retail money market mutual funds shares) were deregulated in the sense that reserve requirements for them were abolished. As a consequence, this part of the money stock was left free to respond to market demand: individuals subtracted or added to the money stock as they wanted to invest more or less in stocks and bonds, and hold less or more money. Thus, argue Henderson and Hummel, Greenspan has a good record: he froze the monetary base (which is what allows government to manipulate the money supply) and let money stock be determined by private demand, which led to a rapid drop in the growth of money stock measures after 2002.

Despite contradicting Austrian economists on Greenspan's monetary policy, Henderson and Hummel are advocates of free banking. They stress that their "preferred ideal would combine abolition of the Fed and unregulated free banking". However, they believe that Greenspan did as well as a central banker can do, and that he is not responsible for the housing bubble or at least for the whole mess. In Henderson and Hummel are correct, Greenspan would have been virtually alone among the people in charge not to have contributed to, or worsened, the crisis.

Yet, the Fed was officially intent on reducing the federal funds rate after 2000, and it appears that it did succeed. It is difficult to believe that the central bank had no influence at all on interest rates and on the housing bubble. The balance of arguments suggests that the Fed did contribute to the low interest rates that made the housing bubble possible, although it was not the only factor. Charles Calomiris suggests that the 2007–2009 crisis has, like all serious economic crisis, been at the confluence of many factors which included accommodative monetary policy magnified by the savings glut.[33] We have seen many of the other crucial factors, notably the heavy regulatory burden on banking and finance and the intense government intervention in the housing and mortgage markets. The authorities in charge messed up in more than one way.

CHAPTER 7

The State's Animal Spirits

Such a world of animal spirits gives the government an opportunity to step in. Its role is to set the conditions in which our animal spirits can be harnessed creatively to serve the greater good.

—George A. Akerlof and Robert J. Shiller[1]

What is perhaps the most surprising in the recent crisis is not the pretensions of the authorities, nor the intricacies of the business cycle, nor the evolution of the mixed economy, nor the myth of deregulation, nor the government jungle in the housing and mortgage markets, nor the mistaken monetary policy; it is why so many analysts ignore the animal spirits of the state. Economists George Akerlof and Robert Shiller are representative of this astonishing neglect when, following Keynes, they blame the market's animal spirits and call on the state to control them. By "animal spirits," Keynes meant "a spontaneous urge to action rather than inaction." He claimed that "individual initiative will only be adequate when reasonable calculation is supplemented and supported by animal spirits." The business cycle depends on the "whim or sentiment or chance," on "the nerves and hysteria and even the digestions and reactions to the weather of those upon whose spontaneous activity [investment] largely depends."[2] We are at the mercy of the businessmen's animal spirits. But why wouldn't the state be affected by similar animal spirits?

As we saw, Keynes generally assumed an efficient state, which would implement enlightened policies recommended by good advisors. He did criticize "the inevitable inefficacy of the legislation to achieve its object,"[3] but his skepticism turned out to be more rhetorical than substantive, and would probably evaporate if the state were run or advised by people like himself. For analysts like Keynes, Akerlof, and Shiller, the state seems impervious to animal spirits.

Even if everything I have said thus far in this book were mistaken, there would still be something to be said before we are in a position to answer our original question: should the authorities be in charge of the business cycle? To answer this question, we have to understand what the state is and how it works. Keynes's intellectual heirs, and the general public, which is unknowingly under the spell of the Cambridge economist, compare the imperfect market with an ideal state manned by angels. This is not a satisfactory approach. As James Madison put it, "If men were angels, no government would be necessary."[4] Since men are not angels and the state is manned by men, we need to compare the market with the state as it is, to look into the state's animal spirits too.

State Greed

During the last half century, economists and political scientists have much enriched our knowledge of the workings of the state through the lens of Public Choice economics. Public Choice economics ("Public Choice" for short) is a body of theories and empirical evidence that analyze how public decisions are made. How are the extent and contents of public education determined? How are foreign affairs and defense policies chosen? How is financial regulation decided? Although other disciplines tried to answer such questions, economists realized half a century ago that the methodology and rigor of economics would bring a much needed contribution. Indeed, since the development of Public Choice theory, which is the economic analysis of politics, political scientists have moved toward the methodology of economics.

Public Choice was born in the 1950s and 1960s, mainly at the Virginia Polytechnic Institute, under the intellectual leadership of economists James Buchanan (for which he was awarded the 1986 Nobel Prize in economics), Gordon Tullock, Richard Wagner, and others. The idea is to study the state as it is, not as some think it should be.[5] The basic assumption is that the state is an organization manned by ordinary individuals who respond to incentives the same way ordinary individuals do—by following their own self-interest, by "maximizing their utility" as economists say. The individuals who man the state are the politicians and the bureaucrats (among whom we include judges). Add to these the individuals who influence the state in their capacity as citizens or members of interest groups. Public Choice analysis tries to understand how these individuals interact to produce public decisions.

Citizens exert less influence on public choices than it is usually assumed, even in democratic regimes. The reason is that a simple citizen whose influence is limited to voting—contrary to, say, a journalist or an academic—exerts on public decisions an influence that is, for all practical purposes, zero.

Whether such a simple citizen votes or not, and whomever he votes for, has not impact on the electoral results: nothing would be different had he not voted. Of course, when a million individuals cast the same vote, they do have an influence, but this would not influence the voting decision of a given voter. If doing action X has no impact on your material interests, you won't decide to do X or not in order to further your material interests. Interestingly, if this is true, if a voter does not vote as if he commanded millions of votes, he will be motivated less by his material self-interest than by ethical concerns, the pleasure of expressing his opinions, or the fun of voting. Those who do not have these motivations will simply not vote. The voter can afford the luxury of taking a moral stance or having fun because it has no consequence whatsoever for the furtherance of his interests. Moreover, because the voter knows that he has no influence, he will not spend much time or money gathering and processing information about the candidates and the issues: he will remain *rationally ignorant.* He will vote blind—perhaps for the nicest or most attractive candidate. It does happen, especially if popular initiative referendums are possible, that citizens impose their majority opinion, that they take over the political machine, but they may vote as much for the fun of it as for expressing a moral stance.

The majority exerts an electoral influence, but who is the majority is not obvious. It can be shown mathematically that the majority is often changing and inconsistent. At other times, it coalesces on a single voter, or class of voters, the so-called median voter, who stands just in the middle of the preference distributions and who, therefore, effectively decides majority votes. When the median voters wins, all other voters are only satisfied with the actual outcome in the sense that it is for them the least bad of all possible outcomes.[6]

Contrary to voters, politicians exercise a direct and continuous influence on public choices. Most influential politicians are professional politicians, who make a living out of politics. What will be a self-interested politician's first goal? To be elected of course, which requires pleasing, or not displeasing too much, half the voters in his district—however rationally ignorant the latter are and whatever short memory they have. The politician is an ordinary individual, and if he has a choice between the good of the country (assuming this concept can be defined unambiguously) and being elected, he will choose the latter. You can't understand the behavior of politicians without starting from that point. The politician who wants to be elected will try to respond to the demands of a coalition of voters that can get him elected. Once elected, the politician will be willing to trade his support for the pet projects of other politicians against their support for the policies that his own critical voters want. Hence, there exists a political market similar to ordinary economic markets. On the political market, politicians sell public policies for votes or—what amounts to the same—they buy votes with public policies. They then trade votes among themselves to deliver what their voters want. The exchange of votes between politicians is called "log rolling." The results of log rolling are not necessarily efficient because voters end up getting lots of things they don't want and don't want to pay for, in order for their representatives to deliver something they want. In the process, the state grows.

Although the incentives they face are structured by a different environment, government bureaucrats are also ordinary individuals. Contrary to what the Moody's executive quoted in Chapter 4 seemed to imply, bureaucrats too have "families to support and bills to meet and mortgages to pay." The bureaucrats' incentives spring from what they want to keep or improve as bureaucrats: their remuneration, their job security, their employment perks, their occasional sense of power, and perhaps an impression of doing good or, at least, of doing something important. The larger and the better financed is a bureaucrat's agency or division, the more likely he will be able to improve his situation in these respects. Bureaucrats in large and prestigious bureaus have more chances of promotion, more travel opportunities, et cetera. As they control a large part of the information the politicians need, the bureaus will often succeed in increasing their funding and maximizing their discretionary expenditures, legally circumventing the wishes of their political sponsors. Thus, the self-interested behavior of bureaucrats creates a bias toward government growth, just like the politicians' behavior does.

Paradoxically, part of the bureaucrats' power and security comes from the rules and procedures they must follow, as these rules partly insulate them from effective political influence. Note that these rules and procedures are necessary to prevent bureaucrats to yield to corruption or to exert arbitrary power. Thus, even an "efficient" bureaucracy remains a bureaucracy. As JP Morgan Chase's CEO James Dimon put it when the House adopted the first regulatory reform bill in December 2009, "[a] new agency is just a whole new bureaucracy."[7] It is a good practice to replace "agency" or "regulator" by "bureau" to emphasize the bureaucratic reality and avoid a misleading beatification of their actors.

Feuds between government agencies are nothing but a reflection of the ordinary self-interest that moves bureaucrats. White House press secretary Robert Gibbs confirmed this theory with the Christmas 2009 attempted bombing of the Northwest Flight to Detroit: "For the last six to eight months," explained Mr. Gibbs, "there's been a feud between the [Director of National Intelligence] and the CIA, and that has to have a negative impact. These agencies are using their skills that should be used against the terrorists against each other."[8] Potentially tragic consequences also follow from bad economic policies, where bureaus feud for their own bureaucrats' interests masquerading as the public interest. The Fed and the FDIC have been warring over who should regulate what in the financial system.[9] Like politicians, bureaucrats defend their own interests more than the public interest. In fact, as we will see later, it is not even clear what "the public interest" means.

Some voters are more equal than others and exert more influence on politicians and thus on public choices. These voters are the individuals who belong to interest groups that have powerful interests to defend and lobby the politicians effectively. When these groups are relatively small, they are easy to organize for the purpose of regulating or despoiling larger groups with more diffuse interests. For example, the small group of farmers obtains large subsidies from the numerous and amorphous groups of taxpayers and consumers. Similarly, trade union or business groups obtain special privileges, subsidies, or protection against (domestic or foreign) competition and thus against consumers. Interest groups exert their influence through political donations, lobbying and media campaigns designed to persuade politicians that they can influence public opinion and deliver large quantities of votes.

Public Choice theory explains many events surrounding economic crises. The fragmented structure of American banking at the eve of the Great Depression was caused by the branching regulations which were largely a response to agricultural and commercial interests wanting to prevent their local banks from investing deposits anywhere else than in loans to themselves. Following the creation of deposit insurance in 1933, FDIC premiums were set as a percentage of all deposits but these were only insured up to $5,000, so the scheme had the effect of redistributing income from large depositors in urban and more solid banks to small and poorer depositors in fragile rural banks.[10] The political entrepreneurship and coalition-building talents of Senator Henry Steagall played a major role in responding to these populist demands.[11] The Smoot-Hawley Act, adopted in June 1930 after more than a year of debates, and which probably played a major role in the Great Depression, was produced by "a series of deals" (to use Senator Robert La Follette's critical description) between Congressmen protecting powerful groups among their constituents. Charles Waterman, a Republican senator from Colorado, declared: "I will not vote for a tariff upon the products of another state if the senators from that state vote against protecting the industries of my state."[12]

Utter disorder is the first impression that emerges from government intervention after the recent economic crisis. The $699-billion TARP created by the Bush Administration in September 2008 was supposed to purchase troubled assets—essentially MBSs. Whether this objective was just a false pretense to cajole Congress into approving the program, or the scheme had simply been badly conceived, or powerful interests wanted a share of the loot, TARP's purpose was modified several times in the months that followed. Less than three weeks after TARP's creation, Treasury Secretary Hank Paulson, who had been given wide discretionary powers, announced that $250 billion would be used to inject capital in banks, instead of purchasing troubled assets as planned. A month later, Paulson announced that the remaining TARP funds would be used for entirely new forms of support, like financing mortgages and guaranteeing student and credit card loans. Then, in mid-December 2008, Paulson's plan underwent its third change by opening the floodgates to all sorts of financial assistance, like for General Motors, Chrysler, and other nonfinancial enterprises.[13]

The Fed purchased a large amount of the troubled assets that TARP was not buying, despite this activity not being part of a central bank's standard policy kit. The "cash for clunkers" program underestimated demand, required a second cash infusion, and had problems processing and paying the dealers' claim on time,[14] all this to displace demand from future car purchase or from the purchase of other goods. In line with the program requirements, nearly half a million old cars were destroyed, many of which would have served poor motorists well (if only by pushing down prices on the used-car market). Destroying cars and bringing consumers to buy new ones was consistent with Keynes and the Brave New World.[15] To paraphrase Huxley, old cars are beastly, we always throw away old cars. In this perspective, a couple of terrorist attacks would have stimulated the economy even better! Many other examples of disorder and inefficiency could be observed, reminiscent of FDR fixing the price of gold as the product of two lucky numbers.[16]

Under the apparent disorder lay a different sort of order: the order of the political market. Citizens did not understand what was what happening and flared against the villains of the day: bankers, speculators, "Wall Street." Bureaucrats argued that they needed more resources to correct the mess they had previously created. Bureaus fought for their turf. Politicians were busy making mileage out of the popular clamor by expanding the powers of government and defending the interests of the better organized among their constituents. When a private business fails its customers, they defect to competitors; when the state fails, as when it provokes or worsens a recession, it obtains more powers from its captive clientele.

Private interests in both the private and the public sector were at work to grab their share of the loot. The gainers were the companies—their shareholders, debt holders, employees and executives—who received bailout money. TARP assisted 685 banks,[17] GM, Chrysler, GMAC, Chrysler Financial, auto parts suppliers, and AIG.[18] Add to this the few hundreds of billions of dollars that Fannie Mae and Freddie Mac will end up getting from the taxpayer. Add to this again the $787 billion of Obama's stimulus package of February 2009—which the *Wall Street Journal* described as a "40-Year Wish List."[19] Private interests well served by the stimulus package included environmental businesses, construction companies, and education providers.[20] Two corporations (Savannah River Nuclear Solutions, LLC, and CH2M Hill Plateau Remediation Company) obtained contracts of more than $1 billion. Several companies got contracts in the hundreds of millions of dollars. State and local governments benefited handsomely, allowing their politicians to spend without apparently raising taxes, and their bureaucrats to expand their turf. The State of California and the State of Texas received billions, closely followed by the State of New York, the State of Florida, and the State of Illinois—plus all the other states that got grants of less than $1 billion.[21] The February 2009 stimulus package will eventually cost (in actual expenditures) more than $1,500 per man, woman, and child in the United States. This is a big amount for an individual family, but much less than many recipients are getting; moreover, it will be paid in future taxes while the recipients get it now. Guess who was more successful at lobbying for or against the stimulus, the taxpayers or the companies and public agencies bound to receive millions or hundreds of millions of dollars each?

The Latin phrase *Cui bono?*—"for whose benefit?"—expresses the idea that you can explain events or actions—government subsidies in this case—by finding who benefits from them. TARP, the stimulus money, and other bailouts were packages for powerful beneficiaries. They were not only investors and executives but also bureaucrats, some employees (like GM's or Chrysler's), trade unions, local governments, and nonprofit organizations.

The same approach explains many interventions that preceded, and played a causal role in, the recent crisis: they benefited some interests in the private or public sector, and were promoted by those interests. Regulation is often tweaked in favor of the regulated: it is conceived for the latter's benefits (notably against competitors), or at least it reduces the burden of existing laws and public policy. Nobel prizewinning economist George Stigler argued that regulation is often captured by the regulated.[22] Sympathy between regulator and regulated is created by their constant interaction. The regulated needs understanding from the regulator, which in turns needs the cooperation of the former for information and data. Spokesmen for regulated companies often speak, nearly fondly, of "our regulator." Before the recent economic crisis, the banks and other financial institutions had probably captured their regulators.[23] "We have an excellent working relationship with our regulator," said the CEO of InterBank, a S&L (savings and loans association), after his bank had been twice hit by an OTS order, in a sort of Stockholm-syndrome reaction.[24] "In accordance with guidance from our regulator," mentioned the Federal Home Loan Bank of Des Moines.[25] "In 1972 we received authority from our regulator to offer full trust services," boasts the website of First National Bank of Hartford.[26] The banks were so tightly regulated that one could think of them as arms of the state; their relationship with government showed some resemblance with the relationship of the Russian tycoons or the hybrid companies elsewhere with their governments. The banks' tight regulation still allowed their executives to earn extraordinary incomes. As the July 2010 financial reform bill was nearing approval, a Wall Street Executive confirmed that regulators are good capture targets: "Frankly," he said, "it's an enormous relief to be dealing with [regulators] again rather than Congress."[27]

Firms in the mortgage industry were among the main beneficiaries of the government's active promotion of home ownership. Mortgage lenders benefited from the reduced lending standards as they were able to sell their shaky mortgages to the GSEs. Fannie Mae and Freddie Mac grew rapidly, and benefited private shareholders or lenders by marshalling an implicit guarantee from the federal government. It is reported that between 1989 and 2008, Fannie Mae and Freddie Mac's employees and political action committees donated $5 million to members of Congress.[28] Not surprisingly, the National Association of Homebuilders was a cheerleader for low mortgage loan standards.[29] Starting in 2002, the mortgage industry increased its campaign donations sharply in districts with high subprime shares. An econometric analysis finds that "both mortgage industry campaign contributions and the share of subprime borrowers in a congressional district increasingly predicted congressional voting behavior on housing-related legislation," and that they "both helped to shape government policies that encouraged the rapid growth of subprime mortgage credit."[30]

The U.S. government was also catering to the median voter, who is a home owner.[31] This does not contradict my claim that electors vote primarily according to their opinions or their feelings instead of their interests, for individuals have a curious tendency to espouse opinions and entertain sentiments that coincide with their interests.

It is not only private parties who benefited from government intervention; the private interest of public sector participants was also at play. All interests are ultimately private anyway. Senator Christopher Dodd received mortgage loans from Countrywide on favorable terms. Several other politicians and some of their staffers obtained preferential mortgages from the same company, who ran a special VIP loan program.[32] In the meantime, bureaucrats in banking, finance and housing bureaus were pushing for regulations and budgets that would enhance the stature of their offices and the perks that come with them. Countrywide's VIP program provided 153 loans to employees of Fannie Mae.[33] More might be discovered.

Standard Public Choice theory explains the behavior of government without resorting to any malevolent intention other than the normal self-interest of citizens, interest groups, politicians and bureaucrats. However, moved by the self-interest of those who control it, the state can be modeled not as a provider of services to the public—or to the majority of the public—but as Leviathan, the sea monster of the Bible whose name was adopted by seventeenth-century philosopher Thomas Hobbes to describe the sovereign state. In this perspective, the state exploits certain groups of individuals for the benefit of other individuals. This vision of the exploitative state is embraced by a minority strand in Public Choice theory. The state is powerful because of its accepted use of force, or threat of force, to enforce its decisions. The majority will be tempted to use this power to exploit the minority, to tax the latter and transfer the money to itself, or to regulate the minority's lifestyles, activities and enterprises.[34] Well-organized minorities—perhaps those individuals who man the state—will also try to exploit the majority.[35] Because any citizen knows that he could find himself among the exploited, he will want a constitution that limits state power.[36] Whenever Leviathan breaks its constitutional chains, it becomes a dangerous wild beast. What the mixed economy has done is to let Leviathan loose.

When we look at the state as Leviathan, some phenomena otherwise puzzling become easily understandable. The growth of surveillance, financial or otherwise, helps Leviathan control its subject. Leviathan likes the "statistization" of society, because information allows for more monitoring and control. As Mussolini observed approvingly, "[s]tatistics has expanded its jurisdiction over all phenomena of life."[37] The growth of ID papers and financial surveillance, before 9/11 or after, is part of this project. It does not appear bizarre that, in January 2009, a troubled S&L was harassed by OTS for not having adequate customer-identification policies in violation of the PATRIOT Act.[38] Nor is it surprising that the British government invoked antiterrorist legislation to seize the assets of an Icelandic bank during the economic crisis.[39]

As we have seen, Leviathan regularly uses the banks to finance its own needs. According to *The Economist,* "one reason why central banks have kept interest rates so low is that it allows the banks to earn more money and rebuild capital by borrowing short term and investing the proceeds in higher-yielding long-dated government bonds."[40] The Basel capital requirements have led banks to load their portfolios with government securities, which are assigned a zero-risk factor and do not require any capital as protection against a possible fall in value. Leviathan indirectly forces the banks to lend him money.

The Leviathan hypothesis nicely explains why the state seems to like crises: it benefits from them as they justify extending its powers. Economic historian Robert Higgs has shown how every crisis, whether a depression or a war, serves as an excuse for increasing state power, and how, once the crisis has passed, power never returns to its pre-crisis level.[41] In November 2008, in the deep of the recent economic crisis, White House Chief of Staff Rahm Emanuel said it quite clearly: "Never let a serious crisis go to waste. What I mean by that is that it's an opportunity to do things you couldn't do before."[42] Such crises, he said, "are opportunities to do big things."[43] According to Thomas Sowell, the federal government has been "*using* a crisis to fundamentally and enduringly change the institutions of American society."[44]

In order to mobilize the citizens, deemed soldiers in the army of the commander in chief as Obama reminded us,[45] the rhetoric of war is useful and often used. Treasury Secretary Timothy Geithner claimed that increasing financial regulation was "a war of necessity" and "a just war."[46] *Nihil novi sub sole:* the state has been fighting a "war on drugs," a "war on poverty," a "war on AIDS," a "war against tobacco," a "war on cancer," and a few others. In his March 4, 1933 inaugural address, President Franklin D. Roosevelt declared a war on the Great Depression. He envisioned the possibility of asking Congress "for the one remaining instrument to meet the crisis—broad Executive power to wage a war against the emergency, as great as the power that would be given to me if we were in fact invaded by a foreign foe."[47] "[W]e must," he declared *à la* Obama, "move as a trained and loyal army willing to sacrifice for the good of a common discipline, because without such discipline no progress is made, no leadership becomes effective."[48] In his first State of the Union address, Obama declared that, in previous crises, "America prevailed because we chose to move forward as one nation, and one people."[49]

This war rhetoric is disturbing. We were forewarned by de Jouvenel[50] and Hayek[51] of the danger of following the way totalitarian regimes planned the economy and mobilized the people. "*Ein Volk, Ein Reich, Ein Führer!*," said a Nazi slogan—"one nation, one land, one leader." Are we really completely immune to this sort of drift? The question should at least be asked.

If my reader does not think that the democratic state can become, or has become, Leviathan, it remains that greed underlies all public choices in the sense that politicians, bureaucrats and interest groups all act in their own interest. What is the essence of greed if not promoting one's own interests either by acquiring money or by getting directly the advantages that money can buy? The term "greed" provides a good metaphorical descriptor of ordinary individual interest. Greed is a major component of the animal spirits of the state, which is manned by ordinary individuals, not by angels. To paraphrase Keynes, the individuals who run the state tyrannize over their fellow citizens instead of tyrannizing over their own bank balances.[52]

Faddish Behavior and State Bubbles

George Akerlof and Robert Shiller note that, in the 1990s, allegations by Martin Luther King III (the son of the civil rights leader) minorities were left out of housing opportunities "led to an almost immediate, and uncritical, government reaction."[53] The government jumped in to fuel the housing bubble. Yet, a few pages later, the same authors propose that government step in to counteract the destructive animal spirits of the private sector.[54] Many analysts—including, strangely, sophisticated economists—rely on the common and unexamined assumption that government can counter bad fads and encourage good ones.

It is an extraordinary idea. We have seen in Chapter 5 how politicians and bureaucrats encouraged the housing bubble with easy mortgage policies. As reported in Chapter 6, the Fed further fuelled house purchases with a loose monetary policy. Not only did government encourage the bubble, but it did not see it coming even when its bursting was imminent. In 2003, Federal Reserve Chairman Alan Greenspan addressed what had "been described by some analysts as possibly symptomatic of an emerging housing bubble." He expressed some concern but added that "any analogy to stock market pricing behavior and bubbles is a rather large stretch."[55] On May 17, 2007, just before subprime securities were to wreck havoc in the economy, his successor, Ben Bernanke, flatly declared that the subprime problems were containable:

> We know from data . . . that a significant share of new loans used to purchase homes in 2005 were nonprime (subprime or near-prime) . . . [and] the share of securitized mortgages that are subprimes climbed in 2005 and the first half or 2006. . . . we believe the effect of the troubles in the subprime sector on the broader market will likely be limited, and we do not expect significant spillovers from the subprime market to the rest of the economy or to the financial system.[56]

The GSEs were at the vanguard of those who, in the public sector, dismissed any cause for concern. In 2002, recent Nobel prizewinner Joseph Stiglitz and two coauthors—one of which, Peter Orszag, was to become director of President Barack Obama's OMB (office of management and budget)—were commissioned to write an article for the *Fannie Mae Papers*. They argued that Fannie Mae's and Freddie Mac's risk-based capital standard made it very unlikely that the two GSEs would ever require a government bailout. The results of their econometric model, they wrote, "suggest that on the basis of historical evidence, the risk to the government from a potential default on GSE debt is effectively zero."[57] The authors underestimated the possible credit losses from a deep recession, besides ignoring the possibility that the quasi-nationalized housing market and the GSEs could themselves generate or precipitate a recession. Serious economists writing for a quasi-government publication just followed the herd. The *Wall Street Journal* uses this gross mistake to argue against a "systemic risk regulator":

> Why should anyone think that regulators—or economists—will predict the next systemic debacle any better? . . . When the next problem erupts, as in 2002, smart people will be on both sides of the argument. And when large, systemically important companies are threatened with curbs on their business, they will pay Nobel laureates to write studies and explain away the dangers, and hire lobbyists to block any reform.[58]

Fannie Mae and presumably the authors are understandably not proud of this paper, which has disappeared from the GSE's site.[59]

The situation of Fannie Mae and Freddy Mac was not quite as bad in 2002 as it would become during the following five years. But even as time passed, the official enthusiasm did not abate. As late as July 13, 2008, a few months before the two GSEs went bankrupt, Senator Christopher Dodd, one of their big boosters and political beneficiaries, declared: "What's important are facts—and the facts are that Fannie and Freddie are in sound situation . . . They have more than adequate capital. The're in good shape."[60]

Public confidence has an impact on a recession. The more people fear the recession, the more prudent businesses will be in producing and investing, and the least likely the banks will want to lend. In the autumn of 2008, the most frightful time in the recent recession, the government was not really reassuring people in a way to boost confidence and counter the cascade of pessimism. On the contrary, it fuelled the ambient pessimism, acted in a very disorderly fashion, and adopted public policies that had the potential of making everything worse. The protectionist clauses in the Bush stimulus package fuelled protectionism in the world—although the worst was avoided on this front. When George Bush said, on September 24, 2008, "We're in the midst of a serious financial crisis, and the federal government is responding with decisive action,"[61] he probably intensified fears, except to the extent that the federal government is perceived as omnipotent. Another example of how governments worsened the confidence during the economic crisis was the British government's political coup in the Icelandic banking crisis. In response to the demise of Landsbanki, an Icelandic bank in which many British residents had deposited money, the UK government invoked antiterrorist legislation to seize the local subsidiary of *another*, more solid Icelandic bank, Kaupthing, on which the hope of saving Iceland's banking system rested. This incredible act of arbitrary power probably destroyed any hope of restoring confidence in the Icelandic banking system.[62]

Why do state actors run with the crowd? Why would the state inflate bubbles instead of deflating them? As Arnold Kling notes, the record shows that "regulators were subject to the same cognitive shortcomings as private sector participants."[63] There is no reason to expect politicians and bureaucrats to be better at identifying and countering fads and bubbles. Not only are they ordinary individuals, but they might have incentives not to burst bubbles. The politician doesn't want to stop the party that his electors are enjoying— buying and flipping houses with cheap money, for example. The bureaucrat is safe if he commits the same mistake as everybody else, while he would be frowned upon if he played the contrarian and ended up being wrong: it's better for him to be wrong with the crowd than right against it. Like the politician, the typical bureaucrat is likely to benefit from a crisis as it will provoke cries for more bureaucratic control.

Politicians and bureaucrats can use propaganda to hide the risks of their policies and stress the need for further intervention when they fail. In Orwell's *Nineteen Eighty Four*, the Ministry of Truth, charged with propaganda, proclaims three slogans: "war is peace," "freedom is slavery," "ignorance is strength."[64] There is nothing so extreme in our democracy, but note how the 1992 law mandating new HUD-imposed housing goals for Fannie Mae and Freddie Mac was christened the "Federal Housing Enterprises Financial Safety and Soundness Act." Risk and weakness were called safety and soundness. The whole government enterprise of convincing people to take on mortgages that they could not afford is replete with false propaganda. Rationally ignorant, the typical citizen does not notice these lies or rapidly forgets them in the avalanche and complexity of policy proposals in bulk. As Thomas Sowell suggests, it is certainly true that many less sophisticated buyers during the housing boom did not fully understand how, for example, their mortgage payments would raise when their teaser rates reset to market rates.[65] But as electors, they did not understand better the thick web of financial, mortgage and housing interventions and regulations that had been woven around them during the preceding decades, nor the activities of the jungle of federal bureaus: FHA, HUD, VA, RHS, PIH, Fannie Mae, Freddie Mac, Ginnie Mae, OFHEO, FHFB. A tiny proportion of the voters had read or understood the multiple government reports that look like big footnotes. Virtually none of them had any incentive to learn what all that meant and which consequences could follow.

Legal theorists Cass Sunstein and Adrian Vermeule have recently proposed government intervention to control the false information that conspiracy theorists spread—for example, the idea that the U.S. government organized 9/11.[66] Cass Sunstein, a well know Harvard University law professor, is an interesting analyst in many respects: he is one of the inventors of cascade theory, meant to explain why and how fads develop, why people so often follow the herd.[67] He was (and still is at the time of writing) the Director of the Office of Information and Regulatory Affairs in the Obama Administration, the so-called regulatory czar.[68] After an interesting analysis of the problems and dangers of conspiracy theories,[69] Sunstein and Vermeule argue that the government should engage in "cognitive infiltration designed to break up the crippled epistemology of conspiracy-minded groups."[70] The naiveté and danger of this proposal is somewhat attenuated by the authors' admission of their starting assumption: "Throughout, we assume a well-motivated government that aims to eliminate conspiracy theories, or draw their poison."[71] In other words, they assume that the government will only attack false ideas.

There is no basis for such an assumption, especially if the state gets more power to manipulate opinion. The more powerful the state, the greater the likelihood it will spread false ideas. As Lord Acton famously said, "Power tends to corrupt, and absolute power corrupts absolutely."[72] The history of banking, financial, and housing intervention illustrates how the state can worsen bad fads instead of correcting them.

Inefficiency

Efficiency is more difficult to define than it appears at first sight. Ideally, it means that all individuals benefit from the intervention considered. This is impossible in practice, for at least some individuals will be harmed—except perhaps in the broadest and most abstract activities like the maintenance of a general context of peace.[73] The concept I will focus on here is simpler and less techincal: a state intervention will be called efficient or inefficient according to whether or not its consequences are in line with its official goal. Now, if a certain type of intervention constantly misses its official goal, if it is continually inefficient, we must conclude that its real motivation is different from its official goal. Otherwise, the inefficiency would be corrected. The supposed "law of unintended consequences" does not exist—except perhaps, if I can play Keynes a bit, in the short run. If a state intervention with unintended consequences is continuously repeated, there can be only two explanations: politicians and bureaucrats are stupid and there is no political entrepreneur to launch the needed reform; or the real objective of the intervention differs from its professed goal. The second explanation is more realistic. Words are cheap, and the goal of an actor—including a politician or a bureaucrat—is to be deducted from what he does rather than from what he says. Economists call this approach "revealed preference." When the real motivation of a state intervention differs from its official justification, it will appear to constantly miss its objective. In fact, it achieves its real objective.

We have seen many examples of this sort of government inefficiency (where interventions do not really target their official goals but instead satisfy personal interests in the public or private sector) in the run-up to the recent economic crisis. Securities regulation imposed short-termism in corporate outlooks and false investor confidence, but allowed the state to maintain a tight control on the economy. The corporate income tax system encouraged corporate financing by debt as opposed to equity, thereby subsidizing risk, but raised revenues without the taxes appearing to fall on individual voters. The regulation of mortgage loans, the loosening of credit standards and the general encouragement of home ownership led to the market debacle, but created vast public and quasi public bureaucracies, including the GSEs, and allowed the politicians to cater to certain electoral clienteles. Burdensome banking regulations led banks to hold MBSs instead of standard mortgages and fuelled the shadow banking system, but were required to control the moral hazard generated by previous regulations backed by their beneficiaries. A network of regulatory bureaus vied for their turf, evicted private rules and undermined free enterprise, but opened new avenues to regulatory capture and justified fresh interventions by politicians and bureaucrats. The Business-Welfare State offered implicit guarantees against failure to large companies and thus subsidized their risk taking, but created a regulatory-financial complex in which banks and other financial institutions, as good creatures of the state, held large quantities of government securities to finance the growth of their master. The general increase in regulation and public expenditures weakened the economy but boosted the power of politicians and bureaucrats and the benefited their preferred clienteles.

Never underestimate the naked interests of the state and its courtiers. When the state invokes social or economic order, look for the real interests lurking behind. French president Nicholas Sarkozy provided a good illustration. "The monetary disorder in the world has become unacceptable," he said in January 2010, as he vowed to help "put an end to currency disorder." He explained what he meant: "European companies will not gain competitiveness when the dollar is losing 50 per cent of its value."[74] The order to be imposed was thus the satisfaction of private interests important to the state. Sarkozy wanted to protect French exporters, hurt by the appreciation of the euro. The mercantilist state relies on a coalition of producers interested in high prices for their products on the world market, instead of being an association of consumers looking for low-priced imports. Producers win over consumers because their interests are more concentrated and they can more efficiently lobby and influence politicians like Sarkozy.

The political market itself can generate a business cycle, suggest the new theories of the "political business cycle" developed since the 1970s.[75] Before elections, incumbent politicians find in their interest to implement fiscal and monetary policies that will temporarily—but only temporarily—boost employment at the cost of future inflation and future crises, betting that the voters will have forgotten who is responsible when the future comes. There is some evidence that central banks yield to political pressure to accommodate the political business cycle with more a more inflationary policy as election time approaches.[76] If the electorate is polarized (even, presumably, along the small differences between the Democrats and the Republicans), it can be in the interest of the politicians to bring some ideology in their policies. There is some evidence to the effect that from 1948 to 2001, Democratic presidents have focused on fighting unemployment at the cost of inflation, while Republican presidents have been more concerned about inflation. Can the politicians fool all the people all the time with policies that have deleterious consequences in the long run? Can presidents regularly run expansive policies during their first terms in order to assure their reelection, and then restrictive policies to fight inflation and control deficits during their second term, thus fuelling a political business cycle? Yes if the voters are not perfectly informed. The Public Choice idea that voters are rationally ignorant (and thus always imperfectly informed) reinforces this conclusion.

The inefficiency of government intervention is anchored in the disconnect between the state's grandiloquent discourse and the private interests it serves—the interests of those who work in, or influence, the state. The service of private interests by the state grows with its power and capacity to satisfy demands expressed by its clienteles. Inefficient interventionism is part of the animal spirits of the state.

Collectivism

Hard collectivism hit a wall when the Berlin wall fell in 1989 and as the USSR disintegrated a few years later. But a soft collectivism had already impregnated people's minds in what was still called the free world. (People have since, and for very good reasons indeed, become more prudent with the label.) Analysts like Karl Popper and Friedrich Hayek had already denounced the creeping collectivism, which was continuing its progression even in America.

The last section of the last chapter of George Akerlof and Robert Shiller's book *Animal Spirits* is entitled "What We Must Do." The authors claim that "people" are asking questions like:

> How can we allow people of varying abilities and financial sophistication to express their preferences for investments without making them vulnerable to salespeople selling "snake oil"? How can we allow people to take account of their deep intuition about investing opportunities without inviting speculative bubbles and bursts? How can we decide who should be "bailed out" and when? How shall we handle cases of individuals and institutions who have been victimized and wronged?[77]

Assuming that all these *we* do not represent the would-be rulers (the authors and their friends), they must be the people's *we.* They imply that the collectivity should make these decisions and that what this collective wants can be unambiguously determined. "As a society, we . . . ," writes Joseph Stiglitz in the same vein.[78] Although we should expect better from seasoned economists, they are not the only ones to abuse the collective *we.*

In the financial regulatory reforms he proposed on June 17, 2009, President Barack Obama said he sought "to put in place rules that will allow our markets to promote innovation while discouraging abuse."[79] I have already noted how the drift from "the market" to "our markets" suggests a shift away from the impersonal Hayekian society, the Great Society, which is just the framework in which individuals act, toward an organization that belongs to somebody and can be controlled by its owners. The "our," of course, refers to the collective *we.* In his January 27, 2010, State of the Union address, Obama claimed that, in America, "we chose to move forward as one nation, and one people." Switching to a less inclusive *we,* he talked about "investment in our people," as if people were his capital whose value he wanted to preserve. Apparently switching back to the people's inclusive *we,* he said he wanted to protect "our jobs" against foreigners and, in the same breath acknowledged "our First Lady."[80] Are we very far from the ridiculous "our women" uttered by some Russian politician?[81]

Like liberals (in the American sense), conservatives love to say "we." In 2002, as part of the housing crusade, President George W. Bush declared: "We can put light where there is darkness, and hope where there's despondency in this country. And part of this is working together as a nation to encourage folks to own their own home."[82] The "together as a nation" emphasizes the collective *we* and is philosophically close to Obama's "one nation." Bush's second inaugural speech of January 20, 2005, contained 37 *we* in about 2000 words, one *we* for every 55 words.[83]

This collectivist mindset is so widespread, the Hayekian ideal of the Great Society is so ignored, that even people favorable to free markets are infected. Alan Greenspan, who sometimes defined himself as a libertarian, does not always deserves the label as he believes in the necessity of a central bank, deposit insurance, and other regulations inconsistent with laissez-faire. Yet, he was probably the closest to libertarian ideas in the federal establishment. But even he slipped on the banana skin of "our markets."[84]

Who is included in these collective *we* invoked by Akerlof, Shiller, Stiglitz, Obama, Bush, and scores of others? In a small group assembled to achieve a specific task toward an agreed-upon goal, the *we* has a discernable meaning. Any single individual in the group identifies with the goal that he has chosen as demonstrated by his freely becoming a member. He can say, in relation with the group's task and goal: "we do this . . ." or perhaps even "we think that . . . ". The *we* is then a sort of collective *I*. This meaning vanishes when the group is a large group, especially if it is the largest of all groups, the one that includes all others, and has not been assembled for any specific goal—that is, when the group is society. In the larger society each individual or group pursues his own goals. In this context, saying *we* can mean only "we who think similarly and are pursuing the same goal" or, alternatively, "I who am conscripting others in the pursuit of my own goals." *We* either include those who choose to be included or else it is a totalitarian *we* incorporating some individuals who don't want to be part of it. This suggests that the "public interest" is not a well-defined concept, except perhaps for very broad benefits like a general context of peace; in most case, it amounts to nothing more that the private interest of a subset of society.

These ideas have been formalized by the Impossibility Theorem of Kenneth Arrow, winner of the 1972 Nobel Prize in economics. The question is, can we aggregate, add up in some way, the preferences of any number of individuals and obtain "social preferences"—a social interest as it were—that would allow society to say "we" just as an individual says "I"? (If so, the state would be society's collective mouth besides being its armed fist.) Arrow proved that, if we don't restrict the domain of individual preferences, the answer is no.[85] So-called social preferences are either the preferences of a subset of society, that is, they are imposed by certain individuals on others, or else they are inconsistent. Inconsistency means that society will sometimes prefer A to B and, at other times, B to A (A and B being two alternative goods, two alternative policies or two alternative states of the world). This inconsistency—the only alternative to authoritarianism—comes from the coexistence in society of individuals with different preferences that can't be overruled if social preferences are to be an aggregation of all individual preferences.[86] We can't properly say that "society prefers this or that," except by a dangerous metaphor. There is no non-dictatorial way (except perhaps through traditional mores) to aggregate different individual preferences and fuse them into one set of super-individual preferences—just as there is no way to fuse all individuals into a composite super-individual.

The collectivist ideal has a long intellectual history, going back to Plato, the Greek philosopher who, in the fourth century B.C., proposed a hierarchical and totalitarian social model based on the denial of individual autonomy.[87] This ideal was borrowed by many philosophers and writers up to modern socialists and communists. But, as we just saw, society cannot be ruled by a literal collective of all its members; it can only be ruled by a subset of them. A collectivist society is necessarily dictatorial. Collectivism is not necessarily communist nor even socialist. Mussolini attacked the nineteenth century as "a century of individualism" and wished the twentieth would be "the century of collectivism and hence the century of the State."[88] His hopes were realized.

The mixed economy represents a mild form of collectivism. Individuals take benefits, subsidies and handouts from the state, and become more and more dependent on it. Everybody is encouraged to exploit the collective, that is, everybody else; every individual is thus forced to serve everybody else. This is the ideal. In reality, some individuals are more equal than others. At any rate, the collective self-interest that characterizes this system has nothing to do with individualism as a political and economic system. Individuals always behave in their own self-interest, under socialism, capitalism or whatever, so that self-interest is not a defining characteristic of a special sort of social or economic regime. What defines an individualist social order is the primacy of the individual, which is the exact opposite of collectivism.

What happens in a collectivist social system, whether hard or soft, is that the state hides behind the collective to impose the preferences of its clienteles on other individuals. The collectivist rhetoric helps the disadvantaged people swallow the pill. It is easier to impose sacrifices under the name of the collective good than under the banner of privileged subgroups. Collectivism hides state power behind a fake collective and a false collective interest.

Power and Hubris

The state—"government"—benefits from a special feature that allows it to do much more, for good or evil, than any other organization in society. This special feature is power, not power in the vague sense of influence, but power in the strong sense of using force with virtually no challenge from other parts of society. State power is never absolute, even in dictatorial or totalitarian regimes, as the state needs at least a tacit consent from a minimum proportion of the population.[89] But this does not change the central feature of the state. Even in democratic regimes, state intervention depends, at least partly, on coercive power. Laws are not pious wishes, but decrees enforced by armed men.

Armed with this power, the state naturally yields to hubris, an arrogant and misplaced trust in its social-engineering capabilities. It tries to remodel society according to the preferences of some individuals. Social engineering breaks the delicate equilibriums of social institutions and generates unknown consequences. Friedrich Hayek argues that this hubris may lead to nothing less than the destruction of civilization.[90] It can certainly lead to economic catastrophes, as the recent crisis has shown. This crisis was born out of the American state's long intervention in banking and finance, its recently exacerbated whim to increase the proportion of homeowners, and its misguided monetary policy, which combined to produce an unsustainable housing bubble.

What I have called the animal spirits of the state—greed, faddish behavior, inefficiency, collectivism, power, and hubris—makes this institution the most dangerous systemic risk in society. The recent economic crisis was an actualization of that risk.

The constant meddling of the authorities in society not only threatens prosperity, it also undermines the rule of law. The arbitrary powers of the Fed are one aspect of this deeper problem, which Friedrich Hayek had warned about: a government that wants to plan the economy needs arbitrary power.[91] A striking example of the use of arbitrary power in a mixed economy was the use of antiterrorist legislation by the British government to freeze the assets of an Icelandic bank during the economic crisis.[92] But many other cases have been observed. Specially dangerous are retroactive laws, which impose new obligations after the fact and thus prevent individuals to know whether they are or not in compliance with the law, since today's law can be modified by a future retroactive law. When Paulson decided to refinance the banks in late 2008, he forced the largest nine of them to accept capital from TARP (some of them like Wells Fargo did not want the money), arguing that if they did not all take the money, the market would learn which were the most threatened. Later, the government imposed retroactive conditions, like wide controls on executive remuneration, on those who had received the money. Wells Fargo's Chairman Richard Kovacevich complained:

> Is this America—when you do what your government asks you to do and then retroactively you also have additional conditions? If we were not forced to take the TARP money, we would have been able to raise private capital at that time . . . [93]

That the state can itself become a humongous systemic risk is illustrated by modern wars, often waged or at least started for reasons of state aggrandizement. Not only do states kill foreigners and conscripts in times of war, but they have a distressing record of killing their own citizens or residents in civil wars, ethnic cleansing, et cetera. Professor Rudolph Rummel of the University of Hawaii estimates that, during the twentieth century, states have killed 262,000,000 of their own citizens or residents, from communist China and the USSR to Cambodia, Turkey, North Korea, and others.[94] When Leviathan runs loose, dire consequences follow.

One does not need to go that far to realize that the state is a serious systemic danger, even in our democratic countries. It is indeed because the state is such a systemic danger that constitutional or quasi-constitutional rules are required. This was the task that the Founding Fathers set upon to accomplish. The quote from Madison's *Federalist* No. 51 that I gave at the beginning of this chapter continues by emphasizing this point:

> If men were angels, no government would be necessary. If angels were to govern men, neither external nor internal controls on government would be necessary. In framing a government which is to be administered by men over men, the great difficulty lies in this: you must first enable the government to control the governed; and in the next place oblige it to control itself. A dependence on the people is, no doubt, the primary control on the government; but experience has taught mankind the necessity of auxiliary precautions.[95]

We can now go back to the original question of this chapter. Assume that economic crises are a product of the free market—or of whatever freedom remains in the economy. Would it then be a good idea to put some authority in charge of the business cycle, to give the state even more power on the economy than it had at the beginning of 2007? Nothing is perfect but however imperfect the market is, the state is even more imperfect. There is no reason to believe that politicians and bureaucrats would efficiently control the business cycle and prevent economic crises. The more power they have, the bigger mess they will do. To paraphrase Keynes again, a man who tyrannizes over his bank balance is very innocuous compared with the state's animal spirits.

Conclusion: The Emperor's New Clothes

So off went the Emperor in procession under his splendid canopy. Everyone in the streets and the windows said, "Oh, how fine are the Emperor's new clothes! Don't they fit him to perfection? And see his long train!" Nobody would confess that he couldn't see anything, for that would prove him either unfit for his position, or a fool. No costume the Emperor had worn before was ever such a complete success. "But he hasn't got anything on," a little child said.

—*Hans Christian Andersen*[1]

The recent recession is rich in lessons, but they are not necessarily those that the intelligentsia and the political class, dressed in Keynes's old clothes, want us to believe. The most interesting lessons relate to political authority and economic crises in general. We are back to the original question of this book: do we need somebody in charge to control economic crises?

If my argument in this book is correct, the answer is no. There is no need for "somebody in charge," "adult supervision," and new czars to control the business cycle and prevent recessions, for two broad reasons. First, in a modern economy and in a free society, nobody can be literally in charge. The economy is too complex. Nobody has the information that would be needed to control it. In a free society, no authority marshals the power necessary to be in charge. Only in a tribe or in a very simplified organization can some authority literally be in charge. After a few centuries of economic analysis, we are far from understanding the business cycle, let alone being able to control it. There are good reasons to believe that long-lasting recessions or depressions are unlikely to happen on a free market, and John Maynard Keynes was not successful in trying to prove the contrary. The second reason why "somebody in charge" is not a solution is that whoever tries to fill these shoes is more likely to worsen than to improve the situation. This was demonstrated quite clearly by the 2007–2009 recession. On the eve of the crisis, we lived in a mixed economy, and most of the contributing factors to the recent recession are traceable to the actions of those in authority: the heavy regulatory burden of banking and finance, the attempts of the social engineers in authority to manipulate the housing market, the partial nationalization of the mortgage market, and imprudent monetary policies. And this has little to do with those who were in power in the decades preceding the crisis. The nature and work- ings of the state make it an unreliable institution to solve complex economic problems. The state is not manned by angels any more than the market. But the market, at least, is decentralized (in a way that even a federal state can never be), so that systematic mistakes with systemic consequences are more difficult to sustain than the sort of damage that politicians and bureaucrats can do.

The recent economic crisis demonstrates no failure of laissez-faire for the simple reason that there was no such thing. On the eve of the crisis, we were, in America as elsewhere in the West, deep into the mixed economy. There was no deficit of authority, but on the contrary too much of it, and it had been growing for several decades. Somebody was certainly trying to be in charge. Let's recall some broad figures. In the United States, between 1929 and 2007, total public expenditure per capita had been multiplied by 18 in constant dollars. The budgets of the main federal regulatory bureaus had increased by a factor of 14 in the short period between 1960 and 2007; excluding home- land security, the multiplication factor was 11. Regulation had invaded our lives to the point where there was little that did not fall under some form of government reporting or licensing requirement, under some government control and surveillance. Tocquevillian regulation also burdened banking and finance. As John Taylor notes, the New York Fed had hundreds of regulating bureaucrats actually on the premises of large banks.[2] The Welfare State and the Corporate Welfare State had grown continuously. In 2007, social expen- ditures made up 60 percent of total public expenditures compared with less than 40 percent half a century ago. George W. Bush was a good spokesman for the mixed economy when he claimed that "when somebody hurts, govern- ment has got to move."[3] Since there is always somebody who hurts, the state has been growing nonstop. The more the state grew, the more people hurt because that was the way to put one's spoon in the collective gravy. There was little difference between Democrats and Republicans: *The Economist* notes that George W. Bush presided over "the biggest expansion in the American state since Lyndon Johnson's in the mid 1960s."[4] By 2007, many large cor- porations knew they could count on corporate welfare support if they failed: no wonder they took too much risk.

Except for the interests of the politicians, the bureaucrats, and their courtiers, there was little justification for that level of government interven- tion. Government intervention responds to what I have called the animal spirits of the state. For the vagaries of aggregate demand, Keynes blamed the businessmen's animal spirits related to "our innate urge for activity ... often falling back for our motive on whim or sentiment or chance."[5] In fact, this inefficient urge for activity is more the domain of politicians and bureaucrats, who often have an incentive to do anything rather than nothing in order to be seen as playing their role as "the authorities" and to satisfy the demands of their clienteles. Art sometimes confirms science, as shown by the political syllogism of the famous TV series *Yes, Minister:* "Something must be done, this is something, therefore we must do it."

The market—that is, the network of voluntary exchange—is generally more efficient than state intervention. "Thus," James Barth, Gerard Caprio, and Ross Levine conclude in their well-documented study, "the evidence pushes inexorably toward the conclusion that the most successful role for government supervisors is to support the market rather than supplant it in overseeing banks—at least, as James Madison might have said, until angels govern."[6] "[O]ur findings suggest," they write, "that the all too common recommendation by official supervisors to rely on official supervision is misguided, at least 'Till Angels Govern.'"[7] It is not market participants and ordinary individuals who need "adult supervision" but politicians and bureaucrats. Talking about the capital regulations imposed on banks, a senior international official was quoted as saying: "It does read a bit as if it has been written without adult supervision."[8]

In the run-up to the 2007–2009 economic crisis, private businesses and individuals did make errors. There is no liberty without errors—although the errors tend to be less dangerous than when guided from the center. American consumers and businesses had become overleveraged, and were taking too much risk. Banks were relying on faulty models of risk evaluation. Domestic and foreign holders of MBSs were overoptimistic. But note that all these people were following the incentives transmitted or reinforced by public policies. Gary Gorton may be right that a bank run occurred in the shadow banking system, but its origin was in the demise of MBSs, a market dependent on government intervention. Markets are not perfect, but neither are politicians and bureaucrats. In the recent crisis, it is difficult to find private risk taking that was not generated or worsened by public policies. *There was somebody in charge, and that was the problem.*

The same authorities are likely to be at the origin of the next crisis. As I write these lines in the summer of 2010, public authorities in the United States and elsewhere are strengthening the very factors that caused the crisis: regulation of banking and finance is intensified, the government's grip on the mortgage and housing markets shows no sign of relaxation, and the Fed is intent on keeping short-term interest rates very low. John Taylor argues that the 2,319-page Dodd-Frank financial reform bill is a threat to economic growth. This law, he notes, "vastly increases the power of government in ways that are unrelated to the recent crisis and may even encourage future crises."[9] The two sponsors of this so-called financial reform, Senator Christopher Dodd and Representative Barney Frank, whom we have met a few times in this book, were among the major artisans of the mortgage and housing interventions that generated the 2007–2009 crisis.

What will happen now? Extrapolating the recent crisis and its aftermath, one future scenario runs as follows. The size of government continues to increase, regulation and control are expanded, the housing and mortgage markets fall even more in the federal government's hands, and more sectors of the economy become dependent on government. Everybody claims they are too nice to fail, and the most powerful among them get government assistance. The mixed economy becomes even more biased toward socialism and away from economic liberalism. As Hayek had foreseen, the authorities in charge are granted more and more arbitrary power. Investors become more fearful of unexpected, arbitrary interventions. Just as Roosevelt (and Hoover) sowed the interventions that grew into the causes of the 2007–2009 crisis, new regulations and controls set the stage for the future crisis. This scenario may, in the short run, lead to the second dip of what would be seen as a longer recession or depression that started in 2007. Richard Posner's forecast would be vindicated, but for reasons opposite to what he thought.

This scenario is a bit banal. The future is never exactly an extrapolation of the past; it brings surprises, which is what makes it difficult to forecast. Perhaps something else will happen, in continuity with what we have seen but on the surprising side of the future. Perhaps there is a different crisis brewing. In France, where two sets of railroad tracks often run parallel, you may see at railroad crossings a sign warning that "one train can hide another one" *(Un train peut en cacher un autre)*. A nonmoving train may be hiding another one that is coming on the parallel railroad tracks behind. The 2007–2009 crisis looks like the nonmoving train behind which another crisis is coming. We got a glimpse of the second train in the late winter of 2010.

Before the crisis started in 2007, most states in the Western world were burdened with structural deficits that were continuously adding to a bloated public debt. They had little leeway to face any emergency, except with more deficit financing and more borrowing. This is exactly what happened during the 2007–2009 economic crisis: the deficit and the public debt soared. The CBO explains the combination of factors that increased the federal public debt:

The recent increase in debt has been the result of three sets of factors: an imbalance between federal revenues and spending that predates the recession and the recent turmoil in financial markets, sharply lower revenues and elevated spending that derive directly from those economic conditions, and the costs of various federal policies implemented in response to the conditions.[10]

Investors started worrying that the profligate states would not be able to reimburse the money they were borrowing. The Greek state was the first one to hit the wall, and had to be rescued by the European Community and the IMF. But Spain, Portugal, Ireland, Italy, even France and the United Kingdom, were raising concerns. Jonathan Clionna of Barclays Capital observed, "Sovereign risk has supplanted regulatory risk as the primary focus of bank bondholders."[11] Suddenly, sovereign debt (the debt of sovereign states) did not appear totally safe, contrary to what bank regulators had claimed. In February 2010, the price of CDSs had risen on nearly all countries' sovereign debt.[12] "Sovereign risk is out of the bottle," wrote *The Economist,* in an article subtitled "Governments used to worry about their banks. Now the reverse is true."[13]

Many governments are likely to default on their debts, as happened several times in history. A default can take the form of stopping interest payments or principal reimbursements, rescheduling payments, or more indirect tricks. Carmen Reinhart and Kenneth Rogoff have documented more than 300 cases of default by governments on external or internal debt since 1800. Just counting defaults on foreign-held debt, the government of Greece defaulted (including rescheduling) five times, France eight times, Spain 13 times—among other defaults in Europe, South America, and Asia. In the last few decades, the state defaulted on foreign-held debt in Poland (1981), Romania (1981, 1986), Russia (1991, 1998), Turkey (1978, 1982), Indonesia (1998, 2000, 2002), Myanmar (2002), the Philippines (1983), and Sri Lanka (1980, 1982), not counting a host of defaults in Africa and South America.[14]

Since the adoption of the Constitution, the U.S. federal government never directly defaulted on its debt, although it did reschedule payments on states' colonial era debts in 1790 and, in 1933, Roosevelt repealed the optional reimbursement in gold after devaluating the dollar.[15] Several state governments defaulted in the nineteenth century, and Arkansas did it in 1933.[16] Now, the federal government has been running deficits and accumulating debt for several decades. During the 38 years from 1970 to 2007, the federal government's budget showed surpluses in only four years.[17] Contrary to what Keynes envisioned—surpluses during the booming phase of the cycle and deficits during slowdowns—central governments in the United States and in other countries have lived off continuous, structural deficits, which only grow worse during recessions. Public Choice theorists explained this phenomenon three decades ago by noting how tempting it is for politicians to offer goodies to their electors without apparently asking them to pay. Deficit financing, they predicted, would become the rule unless some constitutional or quasi-constitutional constraint prevents it. The informal zero-deficit rule that prevailed until Keynes and his disciples destroyed it was such a quasi-constitutional constraint. Once the constraint was brushed aside, it was to be expected that deficit financing would become the rule in booms as well as in recessions.[18] The Budget Enforcement Act of 1990, a feeble attempt at preventing continuous deficits, was not renewed by Congress when it expired in 2002,[19] confirming the staying power of deficit financing. Now, the CBO forecasts that, as far as its crystal ball can see, the federal government will never run a balanced budget.[20] The 2007–2009 recession, with its massive deficit-financed government intervention, just exacerbated this humongous government failure.

During the recession, government expenditures increased while revenues fell, thereby deepening the debt problem. Between FY 2007 and FY 2010, the annual U.S. federal deficit has gone from $161 billion to $1,342 billion. Total federal debt held by the public has increased from $5.0 trillion (36 percent of GDP) to $9 trillion (62 percent of GDP).[21] (The debt held by the public excludes intragovernmental debt. In the long run, the debt held by the public matches the sum of annual deficits.) Some foreign countries face worse problems, but in some respects—like the years to maturity and the structural deficit—the debt situation in the United States is more worrying.[22] The CBO forecasts that, from 2011 to 2020, the federal government's cumulative annual deficits will add another $6 trillion to the public debt. To get an idea of the order of magnitude of this figure, consider that, in 2010, the annual expenditures of the federal government amount to $3.5 trillion, and the annual deficit to $1.3 trillion. And these projections assume that there won't be another recession.

The federal government can finance a deficit either by borrowing or by printing money. Thus far in the crisis, it appears that the new federal deficits have been financed by borrowing, not by money creation. Professor Jeffrey Hummel notes that about one-half of the new Treasury securities issued between 2007 and the third quarter of 2009 has been gobbled up by foreign buyers, about one-fourth by the household (and nonprofit) sector, and the rest by the Fed. But in doing so, the Fed only brought its holdings of Treasury securities to what they were before 2008.[23]

The deficit and debt problem reminds us that, even during a recession, there is no such thing as a free lunch: whatever the government spends to stimulate the economy, even if successful, has to be taken from the economy in some way, now or in the future. The debt will have to be reimbursed or, at the very least, must not increase more than the taxpayers' capacity and willingness to pay the interest. If it is not reimbursed, it has to be rolled over, that is, refinanced continuously as government securities mature. Refinancing rests on the lenders' confidence that there will be no defaults.

Jeffrey Hummel convincingly argues that default by the federal government is a realistic possibility. He speaks of "the U.S. government's potential bankruptcy,"[24] perhaps even in the present decade. The federal government's budget expenditures now stand at around 24 percent of GDP (states and local government add about 12 percent more as a percentage of GDP), and are projected not to decrease below 23 percent in 2020. This projection, like budget and public debt figures in general, does not take into account the longer-term problems of the Welfare State with the increases in Social Security and Medicare expenditures as the population ages, nor does it include the interest on government debt. Including Social Security and Medicare, the CBO estimates that federal expenditures will reach 35 percent of GDP in 75 years; including interest payments on the debt, the ratio would jump to between 44 percent and 75 percent of GDP. Now, consider the revenue side. Since World War II, the federal government has never been able to raise its (tax) revenues over 20 percent of GDP. Even during that war, federal revenues did not reach 24 percent of GDP. The CBO forecasts that federal tax revenues will not exceed 20 percent of GDP over the next decade, and 26 percent over the next 75 years.[25] Hummel reckons that, in line with historical experience, the federal government will not be able to force American taxpayers to pay more than 20 percent or at most 25 percent of GDP in taxes; consequently, default by the federal government remains the only feasible outcome. Once Medicare runs out of money in 2017, suggests Hummel, "the unwinding could move very fast, much like the sudden collapse of the Soviet Union."

Other economists agree with this dire outlook. Laurence Kotlikoff of Boston University has calculated that the fiscal gap—the present value of the difference between all future projected spending, including interest on the debt, and all future revenues—is nearly as much as today's total federal expenditures, which implies that solving the deficit problems from the revenue side would require doubling forever the amount of all federal taxes paid by Americans. Postponing this solution would require larger tax increases in the future. Kotlikoff concludes that "the U.S. is in worse fiscal shape than Greece."[26] He wrote in the *Financial Times* that "[t]he U.S. is one foot away from a deep and permanent economic grave."[27] The CBO itself admits that, under one of its two scenarios, there is "a clear threat of a fiscal crisis during the next two decades."[28]

Investors have already shown sporadic signs of concern about federal securities. At the beginning of 2009, financial markets were evaluating the federal government's probability of default over ten years at something like 6 percent.[29] Alan Greenspan noted that, in March 2010, the market required a higher yield on ten-year Treasury notes than the swap rate for a comparable maturity, indicating that investors trusted cash flows from private securities more than cash flows from federal securities.[30] The outlook later improved but the alerts suggest that investors' doubts are not far below the surface.

To summarize, the solutions to the federal government's debt crisis are: (1) increasing taxes, which, as we just saw, is unlikely to be feasible as long as America is America; (2) decreasing expenditures, which would be very difficult since a large and growing chunk is made of entitlements and interest payments; and (3) running the printing press, that is, having the Fed lend new money to the federal government—"monetizing the debt" as the technique is called. This inflationary solution also appears unfeasible. The ensuing inflation would automatically increase certain public expenditures, notably Medicare, Medicaid, interest on indexed bonds and, as investors realize the problem, the interest on any federal debt that is rolled over. According to the CBO, the inflation-generated increase in expenditures would cancel out any advantage the federal government would gain in monetizing the debt. Solution No. 4 is default.

A default on federal debt would have major consequences. About half of the publicly held federal debt is held in foreign countries;[31] the other half is owed to American financial institutions, pension funds, and other American institutions and individuals. A formal or informal default on the federal debt would have wide-ranging effects on the country and tragically demonstrate how Americans have become dependent on their own government. It would vividly demonstrate the limits of authority.

The causes and legacy of the economic crisis of 2007–2009 reveal a deeper underlying crisis, which is a crisis of authority. The political authorities have been unable to control the growth of state power, which, during most of the twentieth century, has undermined the rule of law, individual liberty and, in its recent flare, the prosperity to which we have become accustomed. In order to keep the people's support during what Mussolini called "the century of the state," the authorities have made foolish promises that they are unable to keep. Not only have these authorities, the "somebody in charge," created the conditions for the recent recession, but they have also made a mess in trying to solve it, and laid the conditions for much worse crises in the future. To add insult to injury, they have been trying to make us believe that somebody else—"laissez-faire," the speculators, "Wall Street"—was responsible for their failure. We are now facing the reality that these authorities have been unable to control their huge and growing budgets, that they are bankrupt. The emperor's new clothes don't exist. The czar is naked.

There is some hope, especially in America. If the current crisis helps people discover that the emperor is naked, the ordeal will not have been useless. Repairing the mess won't be easy, but seeing through the emperor's nonexisting clothes is a prerequisite to any real solutions. We must also understand that simply changing one czar for another won't do, that we don't need somebody else in charge. What is needed is not another czar reigning over the mixed economy but, on the contrary, more individual liberty and economic freedom. Our own Berlin wall still has to fall. Wickteed's car of collectivism must be stored on a sidetrack. After the little child's reflection, Andersen's tale continues:

> "Did you ever hear such innocent prattle?" said its father. And one person whispered to another what the child had said, "He hasn't anything on. A child says he hasn't anything on."
>
> "But he hasn't got anything on!" the whole town cried out at last.[32]

Notes

Introduction

1. As told by an insider.
2. *The Economist* (2007). See also Greenlaw et al. (2008), pp. 12–14; Taylor (2009), pp. 15–17 and 46–47; Calomiris (2009), pp. 66–67; and Barth et al. (2009), pp. 75–78.
3. Lowenstein (2008).
4. See Barth et al. (2009), pp. 157, 164, and *passim*; and Calomiris (2009), p. 21.
5. Dowd (2009), p. 146.
6. Jabłecki and Machaj (2009), p. 32 1. See also Nathan Kopel et al., "Judge Limits Credit Firms' 1st Amendment Defense," *Wall Street Journal,* September 4, 2009.
7. Greenlaw et al. (2008), p. 15.
8. Lowenstein (2008).
9. Barth et al. (2009), p. 76.
10. Posner (2009), p. 315.
11. Friedman and Schwartz (1963), p. 15.
12. Data from BEA, BLS (bureau of labour statistics), NBER, and Friedman and Schwartz (1963).
13. Norberg (2009), pp. 3, 12.
14. *The Economist,* October 18, 2007, quoted by Norberg (2009), p. 15.
15. "Market Meltdown, Tone on Campaign Trail Top the Week's News," *Online News Hour,* October 10, 2008, at http://www.pbs.org/newshour/bb/politics/july-dec08/speconomy_10–10.html (accessed April 17, 2010).
16. "The London Summit: Multiple Perspectives on the G20," Chatham House, April 1, 2009, at http://www.chathamhouse.org.uk/files/13782_010409g20.pdf (accessed February 26, 2010).
17. Krugman (2009), p. 106.
18. See, for example, Suzy Jagger and Christine Seib, "Barack Obama Lays into SEC for Its Lack of 'Adult Supervision,'" *Times,* December 19, 2008, at http://business.timesonline.co.uk/tol/business/industry_sectors/ banking_and_finance/article5367764.ece (accessed December 22, 2009); and "Was 'Adult Supervision' Needed on Wall Street?" *National Public Radio,* September 17, 2008, at http://www.npr.org/templates/story/story.php?storyId=94686428 (accessed December 22, 2009).

19. Nye (2009).
20. The French Academy has much less control on the French language than many foreigners think. I give one example in my "In Defense of the French," *National Post,* June 9, 2005, at http://www.pierrelemieux.org/artfrench.html. Updating the example makes it even more telling: as of June 19, 2010, Google gives 10,600 web pages where *portemonnaie* is written the way suggested by the French Academy, and 5,930,000 where it is written the traditional way (*porte-monnaie*).
21. Andrew Osborn, "Hands off our women, Russian nationalist MP tells foreigners," *Independent,* June 12, 2005, at http://www.independent.co.uk/news/world/europe / hands-off-our-women-russian-nationalist-mp-tells-foreigners-493879.html (accessed April 17, 2010).
22. SEC (2006), p. 2.
23. Obama (2010).

Chapter 1

1. Smith (1759), Part 6, Vol. 2.
2. BEA (2009).
3. See the BEA's input-output tables, at http://www.bea.gov/industry/iotables/table_list.cfm?anon=111691&CFID=1655339&CFTOKEN=891cfc241a759683-29C5E6E8-0F9A-E9A0-1062F1CB458750E4&jsessionid=a03029d405837bab5dc074427462975748a7 (accessed November 24, 2009).
4. Read (1958).
5. Hayek (1945), pp. 85–86.
6. Fed (2009a).
7. Thanks to Professor Jeff Hummel of San Jose State University for providing a very convenient summary table of "The Country's Balance Sheet," compiled from the Flows of Funds Accounts at http://www.federalreserve.gov/releases/z1/default.htm (accessed June 20, 2010).
8. Fed (2009a), p. 8.
9. Leibenluft (2008).
10. Fed (2009b), p. 8.
11. Jon Hilsenrath, "Bernanke Fights for Second Term," *Wall Street Journal,* December 4, 2009.
12. Barth et al. (2009), p. 248.
13. Barth et al. (2009), pp. 232–233.
14. Kroszner (1997), p. 41.
15. World Bank (2001), p. 37. See also Norberg (2009), p. 131.
16. Brenner (2001).
17. See de Jouvenel (1945), de Jasay (1985), and Wintrobe (1998).
18. See McGuire and Olson (1996) and Olson (1993).
19. Grossman (1967), pp. 69–72 and *passim.*
20. See Hayek (1935) and Hayek (1948a).
21. Caplan (2004).

22. Quoted in Hayek (1944), p. 91.
23. Kling (2009), p. 37.
24. Barth et al. (2009), p. 219.
25. Sowell (2009), p. 80.
26. "A 40-Year Wish List," *Wall Street Journal,* January 28, 2009.
27. Sowell (2009), p. 88.
28. Barth et al. (2009), p. 219.
29. Barth et al. (2009), p. 275.
30. Hummel (2009a).
31. Landefeld, Seskin and Frauneni (2008), p. 213.
32. Friedman and Schwartz (1963a), p. 15.
33. Walter (2005).
34. Calomiris (2000), pp. 4, 7.
35. Lahart (2009).
36. CBO data retrieved on December 15, 2009. The fiscal year now runs from October 1 of the preceding year to September 30 of the identified year; until 1976, it started on July 1. Technically, federal expenditures as measured in the federal budget are called "outlays," but we don't need to be concerned with this distinction in this book. For background, see CBO (2009b).
37. Quoted in Rothbard (1963), p. 169.
38. Sowell (2009), pp. 130 ff.
39. Friedman and Schwartz (1963a, 1963b).
40. *The Economist* (2008).
41. Rustici (2010).
42. See Shlaes (2008).
43. Shlaes (2008), p. 148.
44. Sowell (2009), pp. 130ff.
45. Sowell (2009), p. 139.
46. Excerpts at http://www.bobsuniverse.com/BWAH/33-Truman/19460220a.pdf (accessed April 20, 2010).
47. Quoted in Snowdon and Vane (2005), p. 146.
48. Norberg (2009), pp. 86–87; Bhidé (2009), p. 236.
49. *The Economist* (2008c); Bhidé (2009), p. 236.
50. Louise Turnbull, "The Dangers of Health-and-Safety Hysteria," *Spiked,* March 16, 2010, at http://www.spiked-online.com/index.php/site/printable/8311/ (accessed April 20, 2010).
51. *The Economist* (2010h).
52. Scott McCartney, "Miles for Nothing: How the Government Helped Frequent Fliers Make a Mint," *Wall Street Journal,* December 7, 2009.
53. See Smith (1759).
54. Smith (1776), Book 4, Chapter 2, Paragraph 9.
55. Gifford (2009).
56. *The Economist* (2010b); see also Jenny Strasburg and Scott Patterson, "A Hedge-Fund King Comes Under Siege," *Wall Street Journal,* November 19, 2009.

57. Greenlaw et al. (2008), p. 35.
58. See "The SEC vs. Goldman," *Wall Street Journal*, April 19, 2010; and Carrick Mollenkamp et al., "SEC Probes Other Soured Deals," *Wall Street Journal*, April 19, 2010.
59. Barth et al. (2009), pp. 163, 466.
60. Boudreaux (2008).
61. Keynes (1936), p. 374.
62. Keynes (1936), p. 317.
63. *The Economist* (2010h).
64. Keynes (1936), pp. 161–162.
65. Sargent (2008).
66. Akerlof and Shiller (2009), p. 42.
67. Akerlof and Shiller (2009), p. 3.
68. Akerlof and Shiller (2009), p. 59 and *passim*.
69. Akerlof and Shiller (2009), p. 111. As an anonymous reviewer noted, my criticism of Joseph A. Akerlof's macroeconomics should not be taken as a negation of his contribution to microeconomics. He, A. Michael Spence, and Joseph E. Stiglitz were awarded the 2001 Nobel Prize in economic sciences "for their analyses of markets with asymmetric information"— see http://nobelprize.org/nobel_prizes/economics/laureates/2001/ (accessed June 21, 2010).
70. Lemieux (2003).
71. See, for example, Akerlof (2001).
72. Lee and McKenzie (1999).
73. Taleb's ideas are summarized in two econtalk.org podcasts: Taleb (2007, 2009). The econtalk podcasts, realized by Russ Roberts, cover a large number of topics in economics; they are of a very high quality and all worth listening to. See also Taleb (2005, 2007b).
74. *The Economist* (2008b); Barth et al. (2009), pp. 67–69.
75. Buffett (2008).
76. Gregory Zuckerman, "Fun Boss Made $7 Billion in the Panic," *Wall Street Journal*, December 21, 2009.
77. *The Economist* (2009b).
78. *The Economist* (2010e).
79. Hudson City Bancorp (2009), and Hudson City Bancorp (2009b), pp. 1, 4, and *passim*. However, the bank did own MBSs guaranteed by the GSEs.
80. Yahoo Finance (accessed January 12, 2010).
81. Carrick Mollenkamp et al., "SEC Probes Soured Deals," *Wall Street Journal*, April 19, 2010.
82. Gregory Zuckerman and Tom Lauricella, "How a Texan Bagged Europe," *Wall Street Journal*, February 24, 2010.
83. Hayek (1973–1979).
84. Obama (2009b).
85. Obama (2009c).

86. Roosevelt (1933), p. 7.
87. Estimates from Angus Maddison reported in Snowdon and Vane, p. 581.
88. Cited in Snowdon and Vane (2005), p. 354.
89. Snowdon and Vane (2005), pp. 580–582. See also Turchin (2009), p. 3.
90. See the compilation of estimates by the Minnesotans for Sustainability at http://www.mnforsustain.org/pop_world_historical_estimates_-10000-1950.htm (accessed November 29, 2009).
91. Krugman (2009), p. 27.
92. Snowdon and Vane (2005), pp. 638–640.
93. Olson (1982), p. 177.
94. Cited by Edwin Cannan in his preface of Smith (1776), at http://www.econlib.org/library/Smith/smWN0.html#anchor_n67 (accessed August 17, 2010).
95. Smith (1759), Part 6, Vol. 2.

Chapter 2

1. Huxley (1932), pp. 41–42.
2. Fisher (1932), p. 5.
3. Smith (1776), p. 13.
4. See article "Jean-Baptiste Say" in Henderson (2008), accessed September 9, 2009.
5. Mill (1848), Book 3, Chapter 14.
6. All John Stuart Mill quotes from Mill (1848), Book 3, Chapter 14.
7. See http://www.oanda.com/site/euro.shtml (accessed September 8, 2009).
8. *Le nouveau Petit Robert de la langue française 2007,* CD.
9. Friedman (1980), p. 250; see also p. 252.
10. Friedman (1980), pp. 281–282.
11. Aftalion (1987), pp. 101–141.
12. Friedman (1980), pp. 253–264.
13. Friedman and Schwartz (1963a), pp. 676–677 and *passim.*
14. Hanke (2009).
15. Jane Fields, "Zimbabwe Inflation Rate Soars to 66,000%," *News.scotsman.com,* February 15, 2008, at http://news.scotsman.com/latestnews/A-loaf-hits—78.3781428.jp (accessed March 20, 2010).
16. Kindleberger and Aliber (2005), p. 24.
17. Marshall (1920), p. 591.
18. Marshall (1920), pp. 591–592.
19. Fisher (1933), p. 341.
20. Fisher (1933), p. 348.
21. Fisher (1933), p. 347.
22. Fisher (1933), p. 349.
23. Quoted in Snowdon and Vane (2005), p. 23.
24. Fisher (1932), p. 6.
25. Keynes (1936), p. 370.
26. Huxley (1932), pp. 41–42, 209.

27. Keynes (1936), p. 207.
28. Keynes (1936), p. 162.
29. "The Greater of Two Evils," *The Economist,* May 7, 2009.
30. Snowdon and Vane (2005), pp. 19–20.
31. For example, see the evidence reported in Akerlof (2001), p. 378.
32. Margo (1993), p. 43.
33. Data from the BLS at http://www.bls.gov/eag/eag.us.htm (retrieved December 7, 2009).
34. Snowdon and Vane (2005), pp. 380–396.
35. Christian Calmès reviews the literature in Calmès (2003).
36. Some of the evidence given by Akerlof (2001), p. 378, is from other countries.
37. Margo (1003), p. 43.
38. This argument is made by Rothbard (1963), p. 51. See also pp. 45–46.
39. Rothbard (1963), pp. 236–238.
40. Technically: the marginal value.
41. BEA (2010).
42. See Hayek (1952) and Higgs (2010).
43. Quoted by Snowdon and Vane (2005), p. 676.
44. Hayes (2009). Images of MONIAC are easily available on the web.
45. Krugman (2009), p. 101.
46. Keynes (1936), p. 50.
47. de Jouvenel (1945), p. 9.
48. David Wessel, "Medicine is Working, but U.S. Economy Isn't Healthy Yet," *Wall Street Journal,* August 13, 2009.
49. *The Economist* (2009f).
50. See among others: Hayek (1973–1979), Vol. 1, pp. 52–54; and de Jouvenel (1945), pp. 57–66.
51. Prévost (2009), pp. 204–215, and *passim.*
52. The hypothesis that information is the stuff of which the whole universe is made (see *The Economist,* 2010j) makes Hayek's thesis even more fascinating.
53. Sowell (2009), pp. 134–140.
54. Norberg (2009), p. 101.
55. Keynes (1936), p. 129.
56. Higgs (1997).
57. Becker et al. (2010).
58. *The Economist* (2010k).
59. See Henderson and Hummel (2008), and Selgin (2008).
60. Friedman and Schwartz (1963).
61. Friedman (1980), pp. 266–267.
62. Quoted in Snowdon and Vane (2005), p. 213. For a nontechnical presentation, se also Friedman (1980), Chapter 9.
63. Louise Radnofsky, "Bulk of Stimulus Spending Yet to Come," *Wall Street Journal,* February 17, 2010. See also Bragues (2009).
64. Sowell (2009), p. 88.

65. See a good summary in Snowdon and Vane (2005), Chapter 5.
66. Snowdon and Vane (2005), p. 295.
67. Snowdon and Vane (2005), p. 338. See also Prescott (2004).
68. Royal Swedish Academy of Sciences (2004).
69. Quoted by Snowdon and Vane (2005), p. 437.

Chapter 3

1. Wicksteed (1910), Book 1, Chapter 9, Paragraph. 49.
2. Grossman (1967), p. 112.
3. Quoted in Vatter (1979), p. 314.
4. Vatter (1979).
5. Vatter (1979), p. 307.
6. Vatter (1979), p. 297.
7. Vatter (1979), p. 301.
8. Vatter (1979), p. 325.
9. Vatter (1979), pp. 298–299.
10. Wicksteed (1910), Book 1, Chapter 9, Paragraph 49.
11. Mussolini (1932).
12. Maier (1987), p. 81.
13. Hayek (1944), p. 137.
14. Hayek (1944), p. 66.
15. Robbins (1934), pp. 59–60.
16. Robbins (1934), p. 60.
17. Robbins (1934), p. 194.
18. Posner (2009).
19. Posner (2009), p. 306.
20. Posner (2009), p. 306.
21. Posner (2009), p. 238.
22. Posner (2009), p. 118.
23. Posner (2009), pp. 113, 296–297.
24. Posner (2009), p. 240.
25. Tanzi and Schuknecht (2000), Table 1.1. The data cover 13 large Western countries plus Japan.
26. Tanzi and Schuknecht (2000), p. 6.
27. BEA, National and Product Accounts (NIPA), Tables 3.2 and 1.1.5. "Total government expenditures" is defined as total current expenditures plus gross investment.
28. BEA, National and Product Accounts (NIPA), Tables 3.2, 1.1.4 and 1.1.5, at http://www.bea.gov (retrieved December 15, 2009). The population figures are from the Census Bureau at http://www.census.gov (retrieved December 15, 2009). "Total government expenditures" is defined as total current expenditures plus gross investment.
29. de Tocqueville (1840), Vol. 2, Section 4, Chapter 6.

30. Gary Fields, "In Criminal Trials, Venue Is Crucial But Often Arbitrary," *Wall Street Journal,* December 30, 2004.
31. *The Economist* (2010a).
32. Cooney (1997), p. 386.
33. For other examples, see Bovard (1994).
34. "SEC Boss Defiant on Corporate Reforms," *Guardian,* September 20, 2004.
35. Scott Thurm and Mylene Mangalindan, "Trying to Remember New Passwords Isn't As Easy as ABC123," *Wall Street Journal,* December 9, 2004.
36. Freeman (2009a).
37. At http://www.fasb.org/jsp/FASB/Page/SectionPage&cid=1176154526495 (accessed August 18, 2009).
38. Bhidé (2009).
39. *The Economist* (2009d).
40. *Wall Street Journal,* December 30, 2004.
41. In the 1970s according to http://www.fdic.gov/regulations/laws/rules/8000-7950.html (accessed July 6, 2010).
42. For example, see Swire (1999).
43. de Rugy and Warren (2009).
44. I am grateful to Véronique de Rugy, of the Mercatus Center, who provided the original annual data.
45. *The Economist* (2010a).
46. See Lemieux (2008).
47. BEA, NIPA Tables 3.12 and 3.1 (retrieved March 2, 2010).
48. BEA, NIPA Table 3.17 (retrieved March 2, 2010). This data is only available back to 1959.
49. Buchanan (2005).
50. *The Economist* (2010a).
51. de Jouvenel (1952), p. 72.
52. Calomiris (2000), pp. 164 ff., 193 ff.
53. Obama (2009). See also Lemieux (2009).
54. "France and UK Seek Hedge Fund Deal," *Financial Times,* March 11, 2010, at http://www.ft.com/cms/s/0/3a2d919e-2d1e-11df-8025-00144feabdc0.html (visité le 5 mai 2010).
55. Keynes (1936), p. 372.
56. Keynes (1936), p. 377.
57. Keynes (1936), p. 219.
58. Keynes (1936), p. 164.
59. Keynes (1936), p. 325.
60. Keynes (1936), p. 376.
61. Keynes (1936), p. 378.
62. Keynes (1936), p. 379.
63. Keynes (1936), p. 378.
64. Keynes (1936), p. 374.
65. Keynes (1936), p. 380.

66. Keynes (1936), p. 374.
67. Quoted by Norberg (2009), p. 153.
68. Keynes (1936), p. 380.
69. Raico (2008).
70. Quoted by Raico (2008), p. 170.
71. John Maynard Keynes, quoted by Johan Norberg (2009), p. 107.
72. Loretta Chao, "China Sets New Rules For Music Sold Online," *Wall Street Journal,* September 5, 2009.
73. Aaron Black, "Alibaba Upset With Yahoo," *Wall Street Journal,* January 17, 2010.
74. *The Economist* (2009h).
75. *The Economist* (2010a).
76. *The Economist* (2009i).

Chapter 4

1. Sarkozy (2008).
2. Posner (2009), p. 306.
3. Sarkozy (2008).
4. IMF (2009), p. 22.
5. IMF (2009), p. 24.
6. At http://www.sec.gov/about/laws/sea34.pdf (accessed January 4, 2009).
7. Freeman (2009b).
8. SEC (2006), p. 2.
9. Cari Tuna, "Corporate Blogs and 'Tweets' Must Keep SEC in Mind," *Wall Street Journal,* April 27, 2009.
10. Boudreaux (2008).
11. See my little essay, Lemieux (1991).
12. See Calomiris (2000), pp. 1–92.
13. Number of banks in 1928: see U.S. Department of Commerce (1929), p. 264. Calomiris (2000, p. 190) reports the numbers of banks at the end of 1932 was 17,796.
14. Calomiris (2009), p. 34.
15. Hummel (2010).
16. Sowell (2009), p. 125.
17. Calomiris (2009), pp. 7 ff.; see also Sowell (2009), p. 125.
18. Calomiris (2009), p. 19.
19. The Banker's Academy at http://www.bankersacademy.com/bankingregs.php (accessed April 3, 2010).
20. Krugman (2009), p. 161.
21. ICI (2009), p. 1. See also Hanke (2010).
22. Jesse Westbrook, "Fed to Get Role in Setting Investment Banks' Capital (Update 3)," *Bloomberg.com,* July 7, 2008, at http://www.bloomberg.com/apps/news?pid=20601103&sid=a5ekn3jxkP.0&refer=news# (accessed April 6, 2010).

23. SIGTARP (2009), p. 131.
24. ICI (2009).
25. Posner (2009), p. 145.
26. See Shabab (2007).
27. Norberg (2009), pp. 109–112.
28. Quoted by Norberg (2009), p. 110.
29. Kindleberger and Aliber (2005), p. 46.
30. See Suzanne Barlyn, "How the Rules Developed," *Wall Street Journal,* March 30, 2009; and "Important Banking Legislation," FDIC, at http://fdic.gov/regulations/laws/important/index.html (accessed August 18, 2010).
31. Peter Lattman and Damian Paletta, "Funds Get Freer Hand in Buying Bank Stakes," *Wall Street Journal,* September 23, 2008.
32. Fed (2009c), pp. 11–12.
33. See Shull (2007), pp. 11–13.
34. "Debt Watchdogs: Tamed or Caught Napping," *New York Times,* November 7, 2008, at http://www.nytimes.com/2008/12/07/business/worldbusiness/07iht-07rating.18454861.html (accessed May 16, 2010).
35. Calomiris (2000), p. 58.
36. de Rugy and Warren (2008).
37. BEA, Value Added by Industry as a Percentage of Gross Domestic Product, April 28, 2009, at http://www.bea.gov/industry/gpotables/gpo_action.cfm?anon=499070&table_id=24753&format_type=0 (accessed April 3, 2009).
38. BEA, National Income and Product Accounts, Table 1.5.3, at http://www.bea.gov/national/nipaweb/SelectTable.asp?Selected=N (accessed January 4, 2009).
39. Gilbert (1986).
40. Calomiris (2000), p. 49.
41. Shull (2007).
42. Calomiris (2000), and Suzanne Barlyn, "How the Rules Developed," *Wall Street Journal,* March 30, 2009.
43. Henderson and Hummel (2008), pp. 4–5.
44. Kloner (2001).
45. Ferguson and Johnson (2009), p. 13.
46. Posner (2009), p. 270.
47. Calomiris (2000), pp. xxviii–xxix.
48. Shull (2007), p. 6.
49. Shull (2007), p. 7.
50. Shull (2007), p. 12.
51. Alessandri and Haldane (2009), pp. 6, 26.
52. Capie (1997), pp. 24–25.
53. See Barth, Caprio and Levine (2006), pp. 123, 125, 128, 131, and *passim.* What follows in this paragraph is quoted from the questions asked by the survey in each country.
54. Barth, Caprio and Levine (2006), p. 72.
55. Barth, Caprio and Levine (2006), pp. 93, 96.
56. Perry (2009).

57. Freeland (2010).
58. "Tracking Bank Failures: Bank Seizures Reach 133 This Year," *Wall Street Journal,* December 15, 2009; and Robin Sidel, "Bank, Credit Union Are First Failures of 2010," *Wall Street Journal,* January 9, 2010.
59. See, for example, Theresa Tedesco and John Turley-Ewart, "Canadian Banks: A Better System" *Financial Post,* April 3, 2009, at http://www.financialpost.com/story.html?id=1461341 (accessed July 21, 2010).
60. Royal Bank, CIBC, Bank of Montreal, Bank of Nova Scotia, Toronto, and Dominion Bank. National Bank, a smaller Schedule I bank, and a credit union have a large share of the market in the province of Québec.
61. World Bank data at http://econ.worldbank.org/WBSITE/EXTERNAL/EXTDEC/EXTRESEARCH/0,,contentMDK:20345037~pagePK:64214825~piPK:64214943~theSitePK:469382,00.html (accessed August 20, 2009).
62. As of October 31, 2008; see National Bank of Canada (2008).
63. See http://www2.fdic.gov/qbp/grgraph.asp (accessed August 18, 2010).
64. As of December 18, 2009; see FDIC (2009).
65. Brewer et al. (2008), and private correspondence with Dr. Larry Wall (August 2009).
66. Barth, Caprio and Levine (2006), p. 305.
67. Barth, Caprio and Levine (2006).
68. Gorton (2010), p. 11.
69. Gorton (2010), p. 7.
70. Calmès and Théoret (2009), pp. 4–5.
71. Alessandri and Haldane (2009), pp. 6, 26.
72. Calomiris (2000), p. xxii.
73. Posner (2009), p. 46.
74. Krugman (2009), pp. 62–68 and *passim.*
75. Quoted by Norberg (2009), p. 144.
76. Posner (2009), pp. 271–273, 281, 297 and passim.
77. Posner (2009), p. 289.
78. *The Economist* (2010a).
79. Udell (1989); Barth, Caprio and Levine (2006), p. 96.
80. On economic and financial crises in history, see also Reinhart and Rogoff (2009).
81. Barth, Caprio and Levine (2006), pp. 214–224.
82. Barth, Caprio and Levine (2006), p. 224.
83. Bhidé (2009), pp. 242–243.
84. Roosevelt (1933), p. 5.
85. Barth et al. (2009), p. 184.
86. Posner (2009), p. 238.
87. Posner (2009), p. 235.
88. Posner (2009), p. 260.
89. Ferguson and Johnson (2009), p. 11.
90. Ferguson and Johnson (2009), p. 20.
91. Krugman (2009), p. 164.
92. Posner (2009), p. 113.

93. Posner (2009), p. 134.
94. Posner (2009), p. 274.
95. Posner (2009), p. 292.
96. Posner (2009), p. 310.
97. Norberg (2009), p. 133, citing Véronique de Rugy.

Chapter 5

1. Quoted by Sowell (2009), p. 107.
2. James R. Hagerty, "U.S. Home-Financing System Has Fans and Foes," *Wall Street Journal*, July 12, 2004.
3. Quoted by Barth et al. (2009), p. 30.
4. Quoted by Norberg (2009), p. 37.
5. Quoted by Sowell (2009), p. 50.
6. Barth et al. (2009), p. 354.
7. Quoted in "Blaming Bank of America," *Wall Street Journal*, February 6, 2010.
8. "Prosecutor, Charge Thyself," *Wall Street Journal*, February 6, 2010.
9. Mozilo (2003), slide 5.
10. Martinez (2003).
11. Quoted in Sowell (2009), p. 49.
12. Sowell (2009), p. 33.
13. See Sowell (2009), p. 34; and Barth et al. (2009), p. 72.
14. James R. Hagerty, "U.S. Home-Financing System Has Fans and Foes," *Wall Street Journal*, July 12, 2004.
15. Sowell (2009), p. 11.
16. Sowell (2009), p. 18.
17. Sowell (2009), p. 108.
18. Sowell (2009), p. 109.
19. Cited by Sowell (2009), p. 114, with reference on p. 175.
20. Barth et al. (2009), pp. 50, 72, and 356.
21. Norberg (2009), p. 8.
22. Barth et al. (2009), pp. 67–69.
23. FHA (2009), p. 3.
24. http://www.fanniemae.com/aboutfm/charter.jhtml?p=About+Fannie+Mae (accessed November 20, 2009).
25. http://www.ginniemae.gov/about/about.asp?Section=About and http://www.ginniemae.gov/about/history.asp?subTitle=About (accessed November 20, 2009).
26. Congleton (2009), p. 290.
27. See http://www.fhlbanks.com/ and http://www.fhlbdm.com/au_system.htm (accessed January 30, 2010). Moreover, the government mortgage agencies did not face the branching restrictions that private banks were subjected to. Thanks to Jeff Hummel for pointing this out.
28. See Fannie Mae (2007) and Freddie Mac (2007).

29. Congleton (2009), p. 295.
30. Barth et al. (2009), p. 179.
31. Freddie Mac (2007).
32. See the epigraph to Chapter 3.
33. Fannie Mae (2007), Freddie Mac (2007).
34. Barth et al. (2009), pp. 350, 15 ff.
35. Steven A. Holmes, "Fannie Mae Eases Credit to Aid Mortgage Lending," *New York Times,* September 30, 1999, at http://www.nytimes.com/1999/09/30/business/fannie-mae-eases-credit-to-aid-mortgage-lending.html?pagewanted=1 (accessed April 9, 2010).
36. Wallison (2009), p. 367.
37. Wallison (2009), p. 367.
38. Sowell (2009), p. 102.
39. Sowell (2009), p. 106.
40. Sowell (2009), p. 107.
41. See the epigraph of this chapter.
42. Sowell (2009), p. 36 sq.
43. Sowell (2009), p. 66.
44. Barth et al. (2009), pp. 47, 291.
45. Barth et al. (2009), p. 21.
46. Sowell (2009), pp. 42–43.
47. Wallison (2009), p. 470.
48. Quoted in Barth et al. (2009), p. 56.
49. Edward M. Gramlich quoted in Barth et al. (2009), p. 57.
50. Bart (2009), pp. 53–54.
51. Statistics Canada, CANSIM, Table 176-0043 (accessed December 5, 2009).
52. Steven A. Holmes, "Fannie Mae Eases Credit to Aid Mortgage Lending," *New York Times,* September 30, 1999, at http://www.nytimes.com/1999/09/30/business/fannie-mae-eases-credit-to-aid-mortgage-lending.html?pagewanted=1 (accessed April 9, 2010).
53. Quoted by Norberg (2009), p. 31.
54. Barth et al. (2009), pp. 61–62, and 350.
55. Barth et al. (2009), p. 352.
56. At http://www.ginniemae.gov/about/history.asp?subTitle=About (accessed May 11, 2010).
57. Norberg (2009), p. 47. See also Barth et al. (2009), p. 445.
58. Krugman (2009), p. 149.
59. Barth et al. (2009), p. 23.
60. Barth et al. (2009), p. 350.
61. Barth et al. (2009), p. 180.
62. Greenlaw et al. (2008), p. 35.
63. Kling (2009), p. 25.
64. Barth, Caprio and Levine (2006), pp. 53–54.
65. Kling (2009), p. 23. See also Jabłecki and Machaj (2009), pp. 302 ff.

66. Kling (2009), p. 26.
67. Quoted in Kling (2009), p. 24.
68. Courville (2008).
69. Kling (2009), p. 42.
70. IMF (2009c), p. 85.
71. Barth et al. (2009), p. 350.
72. *The Economist* (2010i).
73. Barth et al. (2009), p. 271.
74. Not corrected with the regulatory risk weighs, which did not exist until the Basel accords in the late 1990s.
75. Barth et al. (2009), p. 167.
76. Calomiris (2009), p. 13.
77. Calomiris (2009), p. 20. According to Gary Gorton, there was also a demand for highly rated securities from the repo market; see Gorton (2010).
78. Kling (2009), p. 22; Calomiris (2009), pp. 16–17.
79. Barth et al. (2009), p. 400.
80. Kling (2009), pp. 26–34.
81. Barth et al. (2009), pp. 348–349.
82. Wallison (2009), p. 371 and passim.
83. Barth et al. (2009), pp. 26–28; Kling (2009), pp. 25, 26, 36 et passim.
84. IMF (2009c), p. 85. See also *The Economist* (2010a).
85. Barth et al. (2009), p. 113.
86. For example, see Liz Rappaport and Nathan Becker, "Ohio Files Suit Against Credit Raters," *Wall Street Journal,* November 20, 2009.
87. Rick Brooks, "Raters Sued by Calpers Over Losses," *Wall Street Journal,* July 15, 2009; Joseph A. Giannone, "Calpers Sues Rating Agencies Over Losses," Reuters, July 15, 2009, at http://www.reuters.com/article/business News/idUSTRE56E4D420090715?sp=true (accessed April 9, 2010).
88. Barth et al. (2009), p. 353.
89. Greenlaw et al. (2008), p. 35.
90. Data from Barth et al. (2009), p. 163. As this book is going to press, the Fed's disclosures of December 1, 2010, reveal that all large banks voluntarily contracted big loans from the Fed over and above what they were compelled to accept under TARP.
91. Wallison (2009), p. 373.
92. Norberg (2009), p. 6.
93. Calomiris (2009), p. 10.
94. Barth et al. (2009), p. 356.
95. Barth et al. (2009), p. 211.
96. Congleton (2009), p. 300.
97. Steve Ladurantaye, "U.S. Housing Crisis Hits New Level," *Globe and Mail,* November 19, 2009, at http://www.theglobeandmail.com/report-on-business/us-housing-crisis-hits-new-level/article1370396/ (accessed May 12, 2010).
98. Wallison (2009), p. 372.

99. Sowell (2009), p. 27.
100. Barth et al. (2009), p. 253.
101. Quoted by Sowell (2009), p. 50.
102. Sowell (2009), p. 74.
103. As of the first quarter of 2008; see Barth et al. (2009), p. 92.
104. Sowell (2009), p. 66.
105. "Democracy is the theory that the common people know what they want, and deserve to get it good and hard." Quoted from *A Mencken Chrestomathy* (1949) at http://en.wikiquote.org/wiki/H._L._Mencken (accessed April 9, 2010).
106. Quoted in Sowell (2009), p. 74.
107. Kling (2009), p. 5.
108. Sowell (2009), p. 144.
109. Gorton (2010).

Chapter 6

1. Quoted by Evans-Pritchard (2008).
2. Friedman and Schwartz (1963).
3. Menger (1871).
4. Mises (1912).
5. On the Austrian theory of the business cycle, see among other sources Garrison (2005), Mises (1912), and O'Driscoll and Shenoy (1976). I owe much to the Garrison article for the present summary.
6. Garrison (2005), p. 491.
7. Garrison (2005), pp. 504, 513, 500.
8. See Higgs (2010).
9. O'Driscoll and Shenoy (1976), par. 3.7.25.
10. Garrison (2005), p. 514.
11. Rothbard (1963b).
12. See White (1999) and Hayek (1978).
13. See, for example, Kroszner (1997).
14. Friedman and Schwartz (1963b).
15. Rothbard (1963).
16. Keeler (2001), p. 331.
17. Keeler (2001), pp. 345–346, 349–350, and *passim*.
18. It is not completely clear in my mind why this implication is justified.
19. Keeler (2001), p. 350. It may be that macroeconomic statistics, born in the wake of Keynes's theory, have been designed in function of Keynesian, as opposed to Austrian, concepts and categories.
20. See Barth et al. (2009), pp. 39, 75; and S&P Case-Shiller Home Price Indices at http://www.standardandpoors.com/indices/sp-case-shiller-home-price-indices/en/us/?indexId=spusa-cashpidff–p-us- - - - (accessed February 13, 2010).
21. As does Austrian theorist Robert Murphy (2008) of the Mises Institute.
22. Greenspan (2009); and Greenspan (2010), especially pp. 37 ff.

23. See the MORTG series at the Federal Reserve Bank of St. Louis, at https://research.stlouisfed.org/fred2/series/MORTG?cid=114 (accessed February 13, 2010).
24. See the AAA series at the Federal Reserve Bank of St. Louis, at https://research.stlouisfed.org/fred2/series/AAA?cid=119 (accessed February 13, 2010).
25. See Greenspan (2008), pp. 385–388, and Wolf (2008), Chapter 4.
26. O'Driscoll (2009).
27. Taylor (2009), p. 75; White (2008).
28. White (2008).
29. Taylor (2009), p. 4.
30. Taylor (2009), pp. 31, 61.
31. Henderson and Hummel (2008), p. 3.
32. Henderson and Hummel (2008), p. 3. See the M2 series at the Federal Reserve Bank of St. Louis, at https://research.stlouisfed.org/fred2/graph/?chart_type=line&s[1][id]=M2&s[1][transformation]=ch1 (accessed February 14, 2010). The M1 series can be found at https://research.stlouisfed.org/fred2/graph/?chart_type=line&s[1][id]=M1&s[1][transformation]=ch1 (accessed February 14, 2010).
33. Calomiris (2009), pp. 9, 12 and *passim*.

Chapter 7

1. Akerlof and Shiller (2009), p. 173.
2. Keynes (1936), pp. 160–163.
3. Keynes (1936), p. 270.
4. Madison (1788).
5. On Public Choice economics, see Lemieux (2004) and the references cited therein.
6. Lemieux (2004) provides more detailed explanations on the economics of voting.
7. Damian Paletta and Robin Sidel, "House Strikes at Wall Street," *Wall Street Journal,* December 12, 2009.
8. Jonathan Weisman, Siobhan Gorman and Evan Perez, "President Says U.S. Missed Key Bomb Clues," *Wall Street Journal,* January 7, 2009.
9. Tom Braithwaite, "FDIC Chief Blames Fed for Crisis," *Financial Times,* January 14, 2009; and Bair (2009).
10. Calomiris (2000), pp. 177–179, 200–201.
11. Calomiris (2009), pp. 200–201, 200–201. See also Barth, Caprio and Levine (2006), p. 220.
12. Quoted in *The Economist* (2008).
13. See Norberg (2009), pp. 118–126, and Sowell (2009), p. 80.
14. See "House Approves Extending 'Cash for Clunkers'," *MSNBC.com,* July 31, 2009, at http://www.msnbc.msn.com/id/32228179/ns/business-autos/; and "Cash for Clunkers to end on Monday," *MSNBC.com,* August 20, 2009, at http://www.msnbc.msn.com/id/32490342/ns/business-us_business//.

15. See Chapter 2.
16. See Chapter 1.
17. As of October 21, 2009.
18. SIGTARP (2009), p. 48 and *passim*.
19. See Chapter 1.
20. Pelosi (2009).
21. Data as of October 30, 2009 relating to the February 2009 stimulus package; see Revovery.gov at http://www.recovery.gov/Transparency/RecipientReportedData/Pages/RecipientLanding.aspx (accessed January 16, 2009).
22. Stigler (1971).
23. Congleton (2009), pp. 309–310.
24. Jennifer Niemela, "Regulator to InterBank: Boost Capital—or Else," *Minneapolis/St. Paul Business Journal,* July 13, 2009, at http://twincities.bizjournals.com/twincities/stories/2009/07/13/story1.html.
25. See http://www.fhlbdm.com/Docs/Products_Services/MPP/Subprime%20Change%202007%2012%2012%20-%202008%2008.pdf.
26. At http://www.fnb-hartford.com/a_history.htm (accessed January 30, 2010).
27. *The Economist* (2010l).
28. Cited in Sowell (2009), p. 54.
29. Sowell (2009), p. 59.
30. Mian, Sufi and Trebbi (2010).
31. Congleton (2009), pp. 287–295.
32. See Sowell (2009), p. 55; and John R. Emshwiller, "Senate VIP Loans Mount," *Wall Street Journal,* July 15, 2010.
33. John R. Emshwiller, "153 'VIP' Loans to Fannie Cited," *Wall Street Journal,* July 21, 2010.
34. Brennan and Buchanan (1980).
35. de Jasay (1985).
36. Buchanan (1975).
37. Quoted in Prévost (2009), p. 3. On the idea of the "total 'statistization' of fociety," see p. 191.
38. Jennifer Niemela, "Regulator to InterBank: Boost Capital—or Else," *Minneapolis St. Paul Business Journal,* July 10, 2009.
39. Norberg (2009), pp. 97–98.
40. *The Economist* (2009e).
41. Higgs (1987).
42. "A 40-Year Wish List," *Wall Street Journal,* January 28, 2009.
43. Jeff Zeleny, "Obama Weighs Quick Undoing of Bush Policy," *New York Times,* November 10, 2008.
44. Sowell (2009), p. 143. Emphasis in original.
45. See Chapter 1.
46. Al Yoon and Walden Siew, "Financial Regulation Fight is a 'Just War': Geithner," *Reuters,* October 27, 2009, at http://www.reuters.com/article/idUSTRE59Q4PU20091027 (accessed April 12, 2010).

47. Roosevelt (1933), p. 8.
48. Roosevelt (1933), p. 7.
49. Obama (2010).
50. de Jouvenel (1945).
51. Hayek (1944).
52. See Chapter 1.
53. Akerlof and Shiller (2009), p. 155.
54. See the epigraph at the beginning of this chapter.
55. Quoted in Barth et al. (2009), p. 65.
56. Quoted in Barth et al. (2009), p. 66.
57. Stiglitz, Orszag, and Orszag (2002), p. 5.
58. "Systemic Risk and Fannie Mae," *Wall Street Journal,* December 1, 2009.
59. I have reproduced it at http://www.pierrelemieux.org/stiglitzrisk.pdf.
60. Quoted by Barth et al. (2009), p. 173.
61. Bush (2008).
62. Norberg (2009), pp. 97–98.
63. Kling (2009), p. 44.
64. Orwell (1949), p. 27.
65. Sowell (2009), p. 26.
66. Sunstein and Vermeule (2008).
67. Lemieux (2003b).
68. Jonathan Weisman and Jess Bravin, "Obama's Regulatory Czar Likely to Set a New Tone," *Wall Street Journal,* January 8, 2009.
69. On this topic, see Lemieux (2003).
70. Sunstein and Vermeule (2008), p. 29.
71. Sunstein and Vermeule (2008), p. 15.
72. Lord Acton (1907), Appendix.
73. See Lemieux (2006).
74. "Sarkozy Says World Currency Disorder Unacceptable," *Globe and Mail,* January 7, 2009, at http://www.theglobeandmail.com/report-on-business/sarkozy-says-world-currency-disorder-unacceptable/article1421894/ (accessed April 12, 2010).
75. Snowdon and Vane (2005), pp. 525–556.
76. White (1999), p. 186.
77. Akerlof and Shiller (2009), p. 175.
78. Stiglitz (2010), Kindle version, locations 164–73.
79. Obama (2009d).
80. Obama (2010).
81. See the Introduction of this book.
82. Quote in Jo Becker et al., "White House Philosophy Stoked Mortgage Bonfire," *New York Times,* December 21, 2008, at http://www.nytimes.com/2008/12/21/business/21admin.html (accessed April 12, 2010).
83. Bush (2005).
84. Greenspan (2008), p. 523.

85. Arrow (1951).
86. A more formal demonstration is given in Lemieux (2008), p. 317–318.
87. On Plato, see Karl Popper (1945).
88. Mussolini (1932).
89. See Wintrobe (1998).
90. Hayek (1988).
91. Hayek (1944).
92. Norberg (2009), pp. 97–98.
93. "Wells Fargo Assails TARP, Calls Stress Test 'Asinine'," *bloomberg.com,* March 16, 2009, at http://www.bloomberg.com/apps/news?pid=20601110& sid=ayqseC8JU2.I# (accessed January 12, 2010). As this book is going to press, the Fed's disclosures of December 1, 2010, reveal that all large banks, including Wells Fargo, borrowed from the Fed over and above what they were obliged to accept under TARP. This may dampen our sympathies for the bankers caught in a debacle that was not of their own making. And it reminds us how the state is easily captured by powerful interests.
94. See http://www.hawaii.edu/powerkills/20TH.HTM (accessed January 28, 2010).
95. Madison (1788).

Conclusion

1. Andersen (1837).
2. Taylor (2010).
3. *The Economist* (2010a).
4. *The Economist* (2010a).
5. Keynes (1936), p. 163.
6. Barth, Caprio and Levine (2006), p. 14.
7. Barth, Caprio and Levine (2006), p. 316.
8. Quoted by Dowd (2009), p. 160.
9. Taylor (2010).
10. CBO (2010d), p. 1.
11. *The Economist* (2010c).
12. *The Economist* (2010g).
13. *The Economist* (2010c).
14. Reinhart and Rogoff (2009), pp. 95–97, 111, and *passim.*
15. Ip (2009).
16. *The Economist* (2010m).
17. CBO (2010), p. 126.
18. Buchanan and Wagner (1977).
19. Norberg (2009), p. 20.
20. Ferguson (2010), CBO (2010c).
21. CBO (2010a, 2010e).
22. *The Economist* (2010d).

23. Private correspondence of February 25, 2010. See also Fed (2009b), Table L.209, p. 89.
24. Hummel (2009b).
25. Besides Hummel (2009b), see CBO (2010).
26. Kotlikoff (2010).
27. Kotlikoff (2010b).
28. CBO (2010d), p. 3.
29. Ip (2009).
30. Greenspan (2010). Greenspan explains the (private) swap rate as "the fixed interest rate required of a private bank or corporation to be exchanged for a series of cash flow payments, based on floating interest rates, for a particular length of time."
31. OMB (2009), p. 236.
32. Andersen (1837).

Bibliography

Aftalion, Florin (1987), *L'économie de la Révolution française* (Paris: Hachette).

Akerlof, George A. (2001), *Behavioral Macroeconomics and Macroeconomic Behavior,* Nobel Prize Lecture, December 8, 2001, at http://nobelprize.org/nobel_prizes/economics/laureates/2001/akerlof-lecture.pdf (accessed June 23, 2010).

Akerlof, George A., and Robert J. Shiller (2009), *Animal Spirits: How Human Psychology Drives the Economy and Why It Matters for Global Capitalism* (Princeton NJ and Oxford UK: Princeton University Press).

Alessandri, Piergiorgio, and Andrew G. Haldane (2009), *Banking on the State,* Bank of England, November 2009, at http://www.bankofengland.co.uk/publications/speeches/2009/speech409.pdf (accessed January 22, 2009).

Andersen, Hans Christian (1837), "The Emperor's New Clothes," in *The Complete Andersen,* translated by Jean Hersholt (New York: The Limited Editions Club, 1949), at http://www.andersen.sdu.dk/vaerk/hersholt/TheEmperorsNewClothes_e.html.

Arrow, Kenneth J. (1951), *Social Choice and Individual Values,* 2nd Edition (New Haven CT and London: Yale University Press, 1963).

Barth, James R., et al. (2009), *The Rise and Fall of the U.S. Mortgage and Credit Markets: A Comprehensive Analysis of the Market Meltdown* (Hoboken NJ: Wiley).

Barth, James R., Gerard Caprio, Jr., and Ross Levine (2006), *Rethinking Bank Regulation: Till Angels Govern* (New York: Cambridge University Press).

BEA (2009), *National Income and Product Accounts,* Bureau of Economic Analysis, at http://www.bea.gov/national/Index.htm (accessed December 17, 2009).

BEA (2010), *2010 Satellite Account Underscores Importance of R&D,* News Release, June 30, 2010, at http://www.bea.gov/newsreleases/general/rd/2010/pdf/R&DSA_2010.pdf (accessed August 18, 2010).

Becker, Gary S., Steven J. Davis, and Kevin M. Murphy (2010), "Uncertainty and the Slow Recovery," *Wall Street Journal,* January 4, 2010.

Bernanke, Ben (2009), "The Right Reform for the Fed," *Washington Post,* November 29, 2009, at http://www.washingtonpost.com/wp-dyn/content/article/2009/11/27/AR2009112702322.html (accessed August 18, 2010).

Bhidé, Amar (2009), "An Accident Waiting to Happen," *Critical Review,* 21:2–3, pp. 211–247.

BLS (2009), *Employee Costs for Employee Compensation,* Bureau of Labor Statistics, September 2009, at http://www.bls.gov/news.release/pdf/ecec.pdf (accessed December 12, 2009).

Boudreaux, Don (2008), *On Greed,* October 4, 2008, at http://lists.powerblogs.com/pipermail/marketcorrection/2009-February/001382.html (accessed February 19, 2010).

Bovard, James (1994), *Lost Rights: The Destruction of American Liberty* (New York: St. Martin's Press).

Bragues, George (2009), "Pointless Stimulation," *Financial Post,* October 6, 2009, at http://network.nationalpost.com/NP/blogs/fpcomment/archive/2009/10/06/pointless-stimulation.aspx (accessed April 13, 2010).

Brennan, Geoffrey, and James M. Buchanan (1980), *The Power to Tax. Analytical Foundations of a Fiscal Constitution* (Cambridge: Cambridge University Press), at http://www.econlib.org/library/Buchanan/buchCv9c0.html (accessed August 18, 2010).

Brenner, Reuven (2001), *The Financial Century: From Turmoils to Triumphs* (Toronto: Stoddart).

Brewer, Elijah III, George G. Kaufman, and Larry D. Wall (2008), "Bank Capital Ratios across Countries: Why Do They Vary?," Federal Reserve Bank of Atlanta, *Working Paper Series* No. 2008–27, December 2008, at http://www.frbatlanta.org/filelegacydocs/wp0827.pdf (accessed April 13, 2010).

Buchanan, James M. (1975), *The Limits of Liberty: Between Anarchy and Leviathan* (Indianapolis: Liberty Fund, 1999), at http://www.econlib.org/library/Buchanan/buchCv7.html (accessed June 12, 2010).

Buchanan, James M. (2005), "Afraid to Be Free: Dependency ad Desideratum," *Public Choice,* 124, pp. 19–31.

Buchanan, James M., and Richard E. Wagner (1977), *Democracy in Deficit: The Political Legacy of Lord Keynes* (Indianapolis IN: Liberty Fund, 1999), at http://www.econlib.org/library/Buchanan/buchCv8.html (accessed April 13, 2010).

Buffett, Warren E. (2008), "Buy American. I am," *New York Times,* October 17, 2008, at http://www.nytimes.com/2008/10/17/opinion/17buffett.html (accessed April 13, 2010).

Bush, George W. (2005), *Second Inaugural Address,* January 20, 2005, at http://www.presidentialrhetoric.com/speeches/01.20.05.html (accessed April 12, 2010).

Bush, George W. (2008), *Our Economy Is in Danger,* September 24, 2008, CNN Politics.com, at http://www.cnn.com/2008/POLITICS/09/24/bush.transcript/index.html (accessed April 12, 2010).

Calabria, Mark A. (2009), *Did Deregulation Cause the Financial Crisis?,* Cato Policy Report 31:4 (July/August 2009), at http://www.cato.org/pubs/policy_report/v31n4/cpr31n4-1.pdf (accessed April 13, 2010).

Calmès, Christian (2003), *Poignée de main invisible et persistance des cycles économiques: une revue de la littérature,* Working Paper 2003–40, Bank of Canada, December 2003, at http://www.bankofcanada.ca/en/res/wp/2003/wp03-40.pdf (accessed August 18, 2010).

Calmès, Christian, and Raymond Théoret (2009), *Off-Balance-Sheet Activities and the Shadow Banking System: An Application of the Hausman Test with Higher Moments Instruments,* Cahier de recherche 09-2009, EST UQAM, at http://www.repad.org/ca/qc/uq/uqo/dsa/endo092009.pdf (accessed August 5, 2010).

Calomiris, Charles W. (2000), *U.S. Bank Deregulation in Historical Perspective* (Cambridge UK and Cambridge MA: Cambridge University Press).

Calomiris, Charles W. (2009), "The Subprime Turmoil: What's Old, What's New, and What's Next," *Journal of Structured Finance,* 15:1 (Spring 2009), pp. 6–52.

Capie, Forrest (1997), "The Evolution of Central Banking," in Cabrio and Vittas (1997), pp. 22–34.

Caplan, Bryan (2004), "Is Socialism Really 'Impossible'," *Critical Review,* 16:1, pp. 33–52.

Caplan, Bryan (2005), "Bait and Switch: The Cynic's Argument for Gas," *Library of Economics and Liberty,* September 12, 2005, at http://econlog.econlib.org/archives/2005/09/bait_and_switch.html (accessed April 13, 2010).

Caprio, Gerard, Jr., and Dimitri Vittas, Eds. (1997), *Reforming Financial Systems: Historical Implications for Policy* (Cambridge UK: Cambridge University Press).

CBO (2009a), *The Budget and Economic Outlook: An Update,* Congressional Budget Office, August 2009, at http://www.cbo.gov/ftpdocs/105xx/doc10521/08-25-BudgetUpdate.pdf (accessed February 21, 2010).

CBO (2009b), *The Treatment of Federal Receipts and Expenditures in the National Income and Product Accounts,* Congressional Budget Office, June 2009, at http://www.cbo.gov/ftpdocs/102xx/doc10298/06-29-NIPAs.pdf (accessed August 13, 2010).

CBO (2010a), *The Budget and Economic Outlook: Fiscal Years 2010 to 2020,* Congressional Budget Office, January 2010, at http://www.cbo.gov/ftpdocs/108xx/doc10871/01-26-Outlook.pdf (accessed February 21, 2010).

CBO (2010b), *An Analysis of the President's Budgetary Proposals for Fiscal Year 2010,* Congressional Budget Office, April 2010, at http://www.cbo.gov/ftpdocs/112xx/doc11231/BudgetProjections.pdf (accessed July 3, 2010).

CBO (2010c), *The Long-Term Budget Outlook, Congressional Budget Office,* Congressional Budget Office, June 2010, at http://www.cbo.gov/ftpdocs/115xx/doc11579/06-30-LTBO.pdf (accessed July 4, 2010).

CBO (2010d), *Federal Debt and the Risk of a Fiscal Crisis,* Congressional Budget Office, July 27, 2010, at http://www.cbo.gov/ftpdocs/116xx/doc11659/07-27_Debt_FiscalCrisis_Brief.pdf.

CBO (2010e), *The Budget and Economic Outlook: An Update,* Congressional Budget Office, August 2010, at http://www.cbo.gov/ftpdocs/117xx/doc11705/08-18-Update.pdf (accessed August 31, 2010).

CEA (2009), *Economic Indicators, May 2009,* Council of Economic Advisers, at http://frwebgate.access.gpo.gov/cgi-bin/getdoc.cgi?dbname=economic_indicators&docid=f:00my09.txt.pdf (accessed February 22, 2010).

CEA (2010), *Economic Report of the President,* Council of Economic Advisers, at http://www.gpoaccess.gov/eop/2010/2010_erp.pdf (accessed February 22, 2010).

Congleton, Roger D. (2009), "On the Political Economy of the Financial Crisis and Bailout of 2008–2009," *Public Choice,* 140, pp. 287–317.

Cooney, Mark (1997), "The Decline of Elite Homicide," *Criminology,* 35:3 (August 1997), pp. 381–405.

Courville, Léon (2008), "Socialized Risk," *Financial Post,* October 17, 2008, at http://network.nationalpost.com/np/blogs/fpcomment/archive/2008/10/17/leon-courville-socialized-risk.aspx (accessed November 29, 2009).

De Jasay, Anthony (1985), *The State* (Indianapolis IN: Liberty Fund, 1998), at http://www.econlib.org/library/LFBooks/Jasay/jsyStt.html (accessed August 18, 2010).

De Jouvenel, Bertrand (1945), *On Power: The Natural History of Its Growth* (Indianapolis IN: Liberty Fund, 1993).

De Jouvenel, Bertrand (1952), *The Ethics of Redistribution* (Indianapolis IN: Liberty Press, 1990).

De Rugy, Véronique, and Melinda Warren (2008), *Regulatory Agency Spending Reaches New Height: An Analysis of the U.S. Budget for Fiscal Years 2008 and 2009* (Arlington VA, and St. Louis MO: Mercatus Center and Weidendbaum Center, October 2009), at http://mercatus.org/sites/default/files/publication/1-regulatoryagency20080807_wc-regulators_budget_09.pdf (accessed April 13, 2010).

De Rugy, Véronique, and Melinda Warren (2009), *Expansion of Regulatory Budgets and Staffing Continues in the New Administration: An Analysis of the U.S. Budget for Fiscal Years 2009 and 2010* (Arlington VA, and St. Louis MO: Mercatus Center and Weidendbaum Center, October 2009), at http://regbudget.mercatus.org/wp-content/uploads/2009/10/Regulators-Budget-Report-Final-Version-October-29.pdf (accessed April 13, 2010).

De Tocqueville, Alexis (1835–1840), *Democracy in America* (London: Longmans, Green, and Co., 1899), at http://xroads.virginia.edu/~HYPER/DETOC/toc_indx.html (accessed November 29, 2009).

De Tocqueville, Alexis (1856), *L'Ancien Régime et la Révolution,* 7th Edition (Paris: Michel Lévy Frères, 1866), at http://oll.libertyfund.org/index.php?option=com_staticxt&staticfile=show.php%3Ftitle=2024&Itemid=27 (accessed November 29, 2009).

Dolan, Edwin G. (1976), *The Foundations of Modern Austrian Economics* (Kansas City KS: Sheed and Ward, Inc.), at http://www.econlib.org/library/NPDBooks/Dolan/dlnFMA.html (accessed April 13, 2010).

Dowd, Kevin (2009), "Moral Hazard and the Financial Crisis," *Cato Journal,* 29:1 (Winter 2009), pp. 141–166, at http://www.cato.org/pubs/journal/cj29n1/cj29n1-12.pdf (accessed April 13, 2010).

Evans-Pritchard, Ambrose (2008), "Anna Schwartz Blames Fed for Sub-prime Crisis," *The Telegraph,* January 13, 2008, at http://www.telegraph.co.uk/

finance/comment/ambroseevans_pritchard/2782488/Anna-Schwartz-blames-Fed-for-sub-prime-crisis.html (accessed April 9, 2010).

Fannie Mae (2007), *2006 Annual Report,* at http://www.fanniemae.com/ir/pdf/annualreport/2006/2006_annual_report.pdf (accessed November 29, 2009).

FDIC (2007), *Annual Report 2006,* Federal Deposit Insurance Corporation, at http://www.fdic.gov/about/strategic/report/2006annualreport/ar06final.pdf (accessed April 13, 2010).

FDIC (2008), *Annual Report 2007,* Federal Deposit Insurance Corporation, at http://www.fdic.gov/about/strategic/report/2007annualreport/ar07final.pdf (accessed April 13, 2010).

FDIC (2009), *Bank Failures in Brief,* Federal Deposit Insurance Corporation, at http://www.fdic.gov/bank/historical/bank/index.html (accessed January 7, 2009).

Fed (2009a), *Flow of Funds Accounts of the United States: Flows and Outstandings, Second Quarter 2009,* Board of Governors of the Federal System, September 17, 2009, at http://www.federalreserve.gov/releases/z1/20090917/z1.pdf (accessed April 13, 2010).

Fed (2009b), *Flow of Funds Accounts of the United States: Flows and Outstandings, Third Quarter 2009,* Board of Governors of the Federal System, December 10, 2009, at http://www.federalreserve.gov/releases/z1/20091210/z1.pdf (accessed April 13, 2010).

Fed (2009c), *Policy Statement on Equity Investments in Banks and Bank Holding Companies,* September 2008, at http://www.federalreserve.gov/newsevents/press/bcreg/bcreg20080922b1.pdf (accessed April 13, 2010).

Ferguson, Niall (2010), "A Greek Fiscal Crisis Is Coming to America," *Financial Times,* February 10, 2010, at http://www.ft.com/cms/s/0/f90bca10-1679-11df-bf44-00144feab49a.html (accessed February 22, 2010).

Ferguson, Thomas, and Robert Johnson (2009), "Too Big to Fail: The 'Paulson Put', Presidential Politics, and the Global Financial Meltdown – Part 1: From Shadow Financial System to Shadow Bailout," *International Journal of Political Economy,* 38:1 (Spring 2009), pp. 3–34.

FHA (2009), *Annual Management Report Fiscal Year 2009,* Federal Housing Administration, at http://www.hud.gov/offices/hsg/fhafy09annualmanagementreport.pdf (accessed April 8, 2010).

Fisher, Irving (1932), *Booms and Depressions: Some First Principles* (New York: Adelphi Company).

Fisher, Irving (1933), "The Debt-Deflation Theory of Great Depressions," *Economica,* 1:3, pp. 337–357, at http://fraser.stlouisfed.org/docs/meltzer/fisdeb33.pdf (accessed April 13, 2010).

Freddie Mac (2007), *2006 Annual Report,* at http://www.freddiemac.com/investors/ar/pdf/2006annualrpt.pdf (accessed April 13, 2010).

Freeland, Chrystia (2009), "What Toronto Can Teach New York and London," *Financial Times,* January 29, 2010, at http://www.ft.com/cms/s/2/db2b340a-0a1b-11df-8b23-00144feabdc0.html (accessed April 13, 2010).

Freeman, James (2009a), "The Supreme Case Against Sarbanes-Oxley," *Wall Street Journal,* December 7, 2009.

Freeman, James (2009b), "Is Silicon Valley a Systemic Risk?," *Wall Street Journal*, April 9, 2009.

Friedman, Milton, and Anna J. Schwartz (1963a), *A Monetary History of the United States 1867–1960* (Princeton NJ: Princeton University Press).

Friedman, Milton, and Anna J. Schwartz (1963b), *The Great Contraction* (Princeton NJ: Princeton University Press).

Friedman, Milton, and Anna J. Schwartz (1982), *Monetary Trends in the United States and the United Kingdom: Their Relation to Income, Prices, and Interest Rates* (Chicago IL and London: University of Chicago Press).

Friedman, Milton, and Rose (1980), *Free to Choose: A Personal Statement* (San Diego CA: Hartcourt).

Garrison, Roger W. (2005), "The Austrian School," in Snowdon and Vane (2005), pp. 474–516.

Gifford, Dan (2009) "Hollywood Receives Government Help – Why No Salary Caps?," *Big Hollywood,* November 3, 2009, at http://bighollywood.breitbart.com/dgifford/2009/11/03/national-public-hollywood/#comments (accessed April 13, 2010).

Gilbert, R. Alton (1986), "Requiem for Regulation Q: What It Did and Why It Passed Away," *Federal Reserve Bank of St. Louis Review*, February 1986, pp. 22–37, at http://research.stlouisfed.org/publications/review/86/02/Requiem_Feb1986.pdf (accessed April 13, 2010).

Gorton, Gary (2010), *Question and Answers about the Financial Crisis,* Prepared for the US Financial Crisis Inquiry Commission, February 20, 2010, at http://online.wsj.com/public/resources/documents/crisisqa0210.pdf (accessed March 1, 2010).

Greenlaw, David et al. (2008), *Leverage Losses: Lessons from the Mortgage Market Meltdown,* Proceedings of the U.S. Monetary Policy Forum 2008, at http://research.chicagogsb.edu/igm/docs/USMPF_FINAL_Print.pdf (accessed February 1, 2010).

Greenspan, Alan (2008), *The Age of Turbulence: Adventures in a New World* (New York: Penguin Books).

Greenspan, Alan (2009), "The Fed Didn't Cause the Housing Bubble," *Wall Street Journal,* March 11, 2009.

Greenspan, Alan (2010), *The Crisis,* April 15, 2010, at http://www.brookings.edu/~/media/Files/Programs/ES/BPEA/2010_spring_bpea_papers/spring2010_greenspan.pdf (accessed May 15, 2010).

Grossman, Gregory (1967), *Economic Systems* (Englewood Cliffs NJ: Prentice- Hall).

Gup, Benton E., Ed. (2007), *Corporate Governance in Banking: A Global Perspective* (Cheltenham UK and Northampton MA: Edward Elgar).

Hanke, Steve H. (2009), *R.I.P. Zimbabwe Dollar,* Cato Institute, February 9, 2009, at http://www.cato.org/zimbabwe (accessed September 11, 2009).

Hanke, Steve H. (2010), "Money Dominates," *Globe Asia,* August 2010, pp. 20–24, at http://www.cato.org/pub_display.php?pub_id=12001 (accessed July 26, 2010).

Hayek, Friedrich A. (1935), "Socialist Calculation II: The State of the Debate," in Hayek (1948b), pp. 148–180.

Hayek, Friedrich A. (1944), *The Road to Serfdom* (Chicago IL: University of Chicago Press, 2007).

Hayek, Friedrich A. (1945), "The Use of Knowledge in Society," *American Economic Review*, 35:4 (September), pp. 519–530; reproduced in Hayek (1948b), pp. 77–91.

Hayek, Friedrich A. (1948a), "Socialist Calculation I: The Nature of the Problem," in Hayek (1948b), pp. 119–147.

Hayek, Friedrich A. (1948b), *Individualism and Economic Order* (Chicago IL: Henry Regnery).

Hayek, Friedrich A. (1952), *The Counter-Revolution of Science. Studies on the Abuse of Reason* (Indianapolis IN: LibertyPress, 1979).

Hayek, Friedrich A. (1973–1979), *Law, Legislation and Liberty*, 3 Vol. (Chicago IL: University of Chicago Press).

Hayek, Friedrich A. (1978), *Denationalisation of Money*, 2nd Edition (London: Institute of Economic Affairs).

Hayek, Friedrich A. (1988), *The Fatal Conceit* (Chicago IL: University of Chicago Press).

Hayes, Brian (2009), "Everything Is Under Control," *American Scientist* 97:3 (May/June), pp. 186–191.

Henderson, David R., Ed. (2008), *The Concise Encyclopedia of Economics* (Indianapolis IN: Liberty Fund), at http://www.econlib.org/library/CEE.html.

Henderson, David R., and Jeffrey Rogers Hummel (2008), "Greenspan's Monetary Policy in Retrospect: Discretion or Rules?," *Cato Institute Briefing Papers* No. 109, November 3, 2008, at http://www.cato.org/pubs/bp/bp109.pdf (accessed May 15, 2010).

Higgs, Robert (1987), *Crisis and Leviathan: Critical Episodes in the Growth of American Government* (New York: Oxford University Press).

Higgs, Robert (1997), "Regime Uncertainty: Why the Great Depression Lasted so Long and Why Prosperity Resumed after the War," *The Independent Review*, 1:4, pp. 561–590, at http://www.independent.org/pdf/tir/tir_01_4_higgs.pdf (accessed April 13, 2010).

Higgs, Robert (2008), "Higgs on the Great Depression," Podcast, *econtalk.org*, December 15, 2008, at http://www.econtalk.org/archives/2008/12/higgs_on_the_gr.html (accessed January 12, 2009).

Higgs, Robert (2009), "Hummel, Henderson, the Fed, and the Housing Bubble," *The Beacon,* April 18, 2009, at http://blog.mises.org/archives/009810.asp (accessed April 13, 2009).

Higgs, Robert (2010), "Recession and Recovery: Six Fundamental Errors of the Current Orthodoxy," *The Independent Review*, 14:3 (Winter), pp. 465–472, at http://www.independent.org/pdf/tir/tir_14_03_et_higgs.pdf (accessed April 13, 2010).

Hudson City Bancorp (2009a), *Hudson City Bancorp's Chairman and CEO Reaffirms Positive Outlook,* Press release, March 18, 2009, at https://www.hcsbonline.com/documents/pr_03_18_09.pdf (accessed January 12, 2010).

Hudson City Bancorp (2009b), *Annual Report 2008,* at http://www.hcsbonline.com/documents/hcbk_annual_report_2008.pdf (accessed January 12, 2010).

Hummel, Jeffrey Rogers (2009a), "Latest GDP Revisions," *History News Network,* August 3, 2009, at http://hnn.us/blogs/entries/109277.html (accessed November 26, 2009).

Hummel, Jeffrey Rogers (2009b), "Why Default on U.S. Treasuries is Likely," *Library of Economics and Liberty,* August 3, 2009, at http://www.econlib.org/library/Columns/y2009/Hummeltbills.html (accessed May 29, 2010).

Hummel, Jeffrey Rogers (2010), "Breaking Up Big Banks?," *History News Network,* March 29, 2010, at http://hnn.us/blogs/entries/124968.html (accessed April 13, 2010).

Huxley, Aldous (1932), *Brave New World* (Toronto: Vintage Canada), at http://www.huxley.net/bnw/index.html (accessed April 13, 2010).

IMF (2005), *World Economic Outlook: Building Institutions* (Washington DC: International Monetary Fund, September 2005), at http://www.imf.org/external/pubs/ft/weo/2005/02/ (accessed April 13, 2010).

IMF (2009a), *United States: Selected Issues,* IMF Country Report No. 09/229 (Washington DC: International Monetary Fund, July 2009), at http://www.imf.org/external/pubs/ft/scr/2009/cr09229.pdf (accessed August 6, 2009).

IMF (2009b), *Global Financial Stability Report: Responding to the Financial Crisis and Measuring Systemic Risks* (Washington DC: International Monetary Fund, April 2009), at http://www.imf.org/External/Pubs/FT/GFSR/2009/01/pdf/text.pdf (accessed April 13, 2010).

IMF (2009c), *Global Financial Stability Report: Navigating the Financial Challenges Ahead* (Washington DC: International Monetary Fund, October 2009), at http://www.imf.org/External/Pubs/FT/GFSR/2009/02/pdf/text.pdf (accessed April 13, 2010).

IMF (2009d), *World Economic Outlook: Sustaining the Recovery* (Washington DC: International Monetary Fund, October 2009), at http://www.imf.org/external/pubs/ft/weo/2009/02/pdf/text.pdf (accessed April 13, 2010).

ICI (2009), *Report of the Money Market Working Group* (Washington DC: Investment Company Institute, March 17, 2009), at http://www.ici.org/pdf/ppr_09_mmwg.pdf (accessed February 17, 2010).

Ip, Greg (2009), "We're Borrowing Like Mad. Can the U.S. Pay It Back?," *Washington Post,* January 11, 2009, at http://www.washingtonpost.com/wp-dyn/content/article/2009/01/09/AR2009010902325.html.

Jabłecki, Juliusz, and Mateusz Machaj (2009), "The Regulated Meltdown of 2008," *Critical Review,* 21:2–3, pp. 301–328.

Keeler, James P. (2001), "Empirical Evidence on the Austrian Business Cycle Theory," *The Review of Austrian Economics* 14:4, pp. 331–351.

Keynes, John Maynard (1926), *The End of Laissez-Faire,* in *The Collected Writings of John Maynard Keynes,* Vol. 9 (London and Basingstoke UK: Macmillan, 1972), available at http://www.panarchy.org/keynes/laissezfaire.1926.html (accessed April 13, 2010).

Keynes, John Maynard (1936), *The General Theory of Employment, Interest and Money* (London, Macmillan, 1967), reproduced at http://www.marxists.org/reference/subject/economics/keynes/general-theory/ (accessed April 13, 2010).

Kindleberger, Charles P., and Robert Aliber (2005), *Manias, Panics, and Crashes* (Hoboken NJ: John Wiley & Sons).

Kling, Arnold (2009), *Not What They Had in Mind: A History that Produced the Financial Crisis of 2008* (Arlington VA: Mercatus Center, September 2009), at http://www.mercatus.org/PublicationDetails.aspx?id=28118 (accessed April 13, 2010).

Kloner, Dean (2001), "The Commodity Futures Modernization Act of 2000," *Securities Regulation Law Journal*, 29:3 (Fall), pp. 287–297.

Kotlikoff, Laurence (2010a), "U.S. Is Banrkupt and We Don't Even Know It," *bloomberg.com,* August 10, 2010, at http://www.bloomberg.com/news/2010-08-11/u-s-is-bankrupt-and-we-don-t-even-know-commentary-by-laurence-kotlikoff.html (accessed August 11, 2010).

Kotlikoff, Laurence (2010b), "Uncle Sam Has Worse Woes Than Greece," *Financial Times,* July 25, 2010.

Kroszner, Randall S. (1997), "Free Banking: The Scottish Experience as a Model for Emerging Economies," in Caprio and Vittas (1997), pp. 41–57.

Krugman, Paul (2009), *The Return of Depression Economics and the Crisis of 2008* (New York and London: W.W. Norton & Company).

Lahart, Justin (2009), "Central Banks Are Creatures of Financial Crises," *Wall Street Journal,* January 27, 2009.

Landefeld, Steven J., Eugene P. Seskin, and Barbara M. Fraumeni (2008), "Taking the Pulse of the Economy: Measuring GDP," *Journal of Economic Perspectives*, 22:2 (Spring), pp. 193–216.

Lee, Dwight R., and Richard B. McKenzie (1999), *Getting Rich in America: Eight Simple Rules for Building a Fortune – and a Satisfying Life* (New York: HarperCollins).

Leibenluft, Jacob (2008), "$596 Trillion!," *Slate,* October 15, 2008, at http://www.slate.com/id/2202263/ (accessed February 28, 2010).

Lemieux, Pierre (1991), *Apologie des sorcières modernes* (Paris: Les Belles Lettres).

Lemieux, Pierre (2003a), "Following the Herd," *Regulation*, 26:4 (Winter 2003–04), pp. 16–21, at http://www.cato.org/pubs/regulation/regv26n4/v26n4-2.pdf (accessed February 1, 2010).

Lemieux, Pierre (2003b), "The Pros and Cons of Conspiracy Theories," *Laissez-Faire Electronic Times,* February 3, 2003, at http://www.pierrelemieux.org/artconspire.html (accessed February 1, 2010).

Lemieux, Pierre (2004), "The Public Choice Revolution," *Regulation*, 27:3 (Fall), pp. 22–29, at http://www.cato.org/pubs/regulation/regv27n3/v27n3-2.pdf (accessed February 1, 2010).

Lemieux, Pierre (2006), "Social Welfare, State Intervention, and Value Judgments," *The Independent Review*, 11:1 (Summer), pp. 19–36, at http://www.independent.org/pdf/tir/tir_11_01_02_lemieux.pdf (accessed February 1, 2010).

Lemieux, Pierre (2008a), "Public Health Insurance under a Nonbenevolent State," *Journal of Medicine and Philosophy*, 33:5, pp. 416–426.

Lemieux, Pierre (2008b), *Comprendre l'économie: Ou comment les économistes pensent* (Paris: Belles Lettres).

Lemieux, Pierre (2009), "Obama's Reform: Systemic Danger Once Again," *Western Standard,* June 24, 2009, at http://www.westernstandard.ca/website/article.php?id=2996 (accessed December 20, 2009).

Lord Acton (1907), *Historical Essays and Studies* (John N. Figgis and Reginald V. Laurence, Eds.) (London: Macmillan), at http://oll.libertyfund.org/title/2201/203934 (accessed April 12, 2010).

Lowenstein, Roger (2008), "Triple-A Failure," *New York Times,* April 27, 2008, at http://www.nytimes.com/2008/04/27/magazine/27Credit-t.html (accessed January 11, 2010).

Madison, James (1788), *The Structure of the Government Must Furnish the Proper Checks and Balances between the Different Departments,* The Federalist No. 51, at http://www.constitution.org/fed/federa51.htm (accessed March 3, 2010).

Maier, Charles S. (1987), *In Search of Stability: Explorations in Historical Political Economy* (Cambridge: Cambridge University Press).

Margo, Robert A. (1993), "Employment and Unemployment in the 1930s," *Journal of Economic Perspectives,* 7:2, pp. 41–59.

Marshall, Alfred (1920), *Principles of Economics,* 8th Edition (London: Macmillan), at http://www.econlib.org/library/Marshall/marPCover.html (accessed April 13, 2010).

Martinez, Mel (2003), *Statement of the Honorable Mel Martinez before the United States House Committee on Small Business,* Department of Housing and Urban Development, March 11, 2003, at http://www.hud.gov/offices/cir/test31103respa.cfm (accessed March 3, 2010).

McGuire, Martin C., and Mancur Olson (1996), "The Economics of Autocracy and Majority Rule: The Invisible Hand and the Use of Force," *Journal of Economic Literature,* 34, pp. 72–96.

Menger, Carl (1871), *Principles of Economics* (Auburn AL: Ludwig von Mises Institute, 2004), at http://mises.org/Books/Mengerprinciples.pdf (accessed May 15, 2010).

Mian, Atif, Amir Sufi, and Francesco Trebbi (2010), *The Political Economy of the Subprime Credit Expansion,* voxeu.org, July 11, 2010, at http://www.voxeu.org/index.php?q=node/5288 (accessed August 6, 2010).

Mill, John Stuart (1848), *Principles of Political Economy with Some of Their Applications to Social Philosophy* (London: William J. Ashley, 1909), at http://www.econlib.org/library/Mill/mlPCover.html (accessed March 19, 2010).

Mises, Ludwig von (1912), *The Theory of Money and Credit* (Indianapolis IN: Liberty Fund, Inc., 1981), at http://www.econlib.org/library/Mises/msT.html (accessed February 12, 2010).

Mises, Ludwig von (1949), *Human Action: A Treatise on Economics,* 3rd Edition (San Francisco CA: Fox & Wilkes, 1963), at http://mises.org/resources/3250 (accessed February 12, 2010).

Mozilo, Angelo R. (2003), *The American Dream of Homeonership: From Cliché to Mission,* Presentation at the Joint Center for Housing Studies of Harvard University, February 4, 2009, at http://www.jchs.harvard.edu/publications/homeownership/M03-1_mozilo.pdf (accessed March 19, 2010).

Murphy, Robert P. (2008), "Did the Fed Cause the Housing Bubble?," *Mises Daily,* April 14, 2008, at http://mises.org/daily/2936 (accessed February 12, 2010).

Mussolini, Benito (1932), "Fascism," in *Italian Encyclopaedia,* reproduced at http://www.fordham.edu/halsall/mod/mussolini-fascism.html (accessed December 19, 2009).

National Bank of Canada (2008), *Annual Report 2008,* at http://www.nbc.ca/bnc/files/bncpdf/en/2/e_ri_QGJqbrZtpRlM.pdf (accessed April 3, 2010).

Norberg, Johan (2009), *Financial Fiasco: How America's Infatuation with Home-ownership and Easy Money Created the Economic Crisis* (Washington DC: Cato Institute).

Nye, John (2009), "Nye on the Great Depression, Political Economy, and the Evolution of the State," Podcast, *econtalk.org,* September 14, 2009, at http://www.econtalk.org/archives/2009/09/nye_on_the_grea.html (accessed January 12, 2010).

Obama, Barack (2009a), *Remarks by the President on 21st Century Financial Regulatory Reform,* White House, June 17, 2009, at http://www.whitehouse.gov/the_press_office/Remarks-of-the-President-on-Regulatory-Reform/ (accessed January 28, 2010).

Obama, Barack (2009b), "President Obama's Nobel Reaction," *New York Times,* October 9, 2009, at http://www.nytimes.com/2009/10/09/us/politics/09obama-text.html (accessed November 29, 2009).

Obama, Barack (2009c), "Obama's Nobel Prize Acceptance Speech," *Wall Street Journal,* December 10, 2009.

Obama, Barack (2009d), "Obama's Remarks on Financial Regulatory Reform: The Official Transcript – President Barack Obama's Remarks at the White House on Financial Regulatory Reform," *Wall Street Journal,* June 17, 2009.

Obama, Barack (2010), "Obama's Full State of the Union Address," *Wall Street Journal,* January 27, 2010.

O'Driscoll, Gerald P., and Sudha R. Shenoy (1976), "Inflation, Recession, and Stagflation," in Dolan (1976), Part 3, Essay 7, at http://www.econlib.org/library/NPDBooks/Dolan/dlnFMA13.html#Part%203,%20Essay%207 (accessed March 19, 2010).

O'Driscoll, Gerald P. (2009), "What Savings Glut?," *Wall Street Journal,* March 27, 2009.

Olson, Mancur (1982), *The Rise and Decline of Nations: Economic Growth, Stagflation, and Social Rigidities* (New Haven CT and London: Yale University Press).

Olson, Mancur (1993), "Dictatorship, Democracy, and Development," *American Political Science Review,* 87:3 (September), pp. 567–576.

OMB (2009), *Analytical Perspectives, Budget of the U.S. Government – Fiscal Year 2010,* Office of Management and Budget, at http://www.whitehouse.gov/sites/default/files/omb/budget/fy2011/assets/spec.pdf (accessed August 13, 2010).

Orwell, George (1949), *1984* (New York: New American Library, 1961).

Pelosi, Nancy (2009), *American Recovery and Reinvestment Act As Signed Into Law: Updated Overview,* Office of Speaker Nancy Pelosi, February 18, 2009, at http://www.majorityleader.gov/docUploads/EconomicRecoverySignedbyPresident Overview021809.pdf (accessed March 19, 2010).

Perry, Mark (2009), "Banks and Housing Markets: Canada VS U.S.," *Daily Markets,* at http://www.dailymarkets.com/economy/2009/05/08/banks-and-housing-markets-canada-vs-us/ (accessed August 8, 2009).

Popper, Karl (1945), *The Open Society and Its Enemies,* Vol. 1: *The Spell of Plato* (Princeton NJ: Princeton University Press, 1971).

Posner, Richard A. (2009), *A Failure of Capitalism: The Crisis of '08 and the Descent into Depression* (Cambridge MA: Harvard University Press).

Prescott, Edward C. (2004), *The Transformation of Macroeconomic Policy and Research,* Nobel Prize Lecture, December 8, 2004, at http://nobelprize.org/nobel_prizes/economics/laureates/2004/prescott-lecture.pdf.

Prévost, Jean-Guy (2009), *A Total Science: Statistics in Liberal and Fascist Italy* (Montréal and Kingston ON: McGill-Queen's University Press).

Raico, Ralph (2008), "Was Keynes a Liberal," *The Independent Review,* 13:2 (Fall), pp. 165–188, at http://www.independent.org/pdf/tir/tir_13_02_1_raico.pdf (accessed April 13, 2010).

Read, Leonard (1958), *I, Pencil: My Family Tree as Told to Leonard E. Read* (Irvington-on-Hudson: Foundation for Economic Education, 1999), at http://www.econlib.org/library/Essays/rdPnclCover.html (accessed April 13, 2010).

Reinhart, Carmen M., and Kenneth S. Rogoff (2009), *This Time is Different: Eight Centuries of Financial Folly* (Princeton NJ and Oxford UK: Princeton University Press).

Robbins, Lionel (1934), *The Great Depression* (Freeport NY: Books for Libraries Press), at http://mises.org/books/depression-robbins.pdf (accessed April 13, 2010).

Roosevelt, Franklin D. (1933), *Inaugural Address of the President,* March 4, 1933, at http://www.archives.gov/education/lessons/fdr-inaugural/ (accessed April 13, 2010).

Rothbard, Murray N. (1963a), *America's Great Depression* (Sheed and Ward).

Rothbard, Murray N. (1963b), *What Has Government Done to Our Money?* (Auburn AL: Praxeology Press, 1990), at http://mises.org/books/whathasgovernmentdone.pdf (accessed April 13, 2010).

Royal Swedish Academy of Sciences (2004), *Fin Kydland and Edward Prescott's Contribution to Dynamic Macroeconomics: The Time Consistency of Economic Policy and the Driving Forces Behind Business Cycles,* October 11, 2004, at http://nobelprize.org/nobel_prizes/economics/laureates/2004/ecoadv.pdf (accessed December 8, 2009).

Rustici, Thomas (2010), "Rustici on Smoot-Hawley and the Great Depression," Podcast, *econtalk.org,* January 4, 2010, at http://www.econtalk.org/archives/2010/01/rustici_on_smoo.html (accessed April 12, 2010).

Sargent, Thomas J. (2008), "Rational Expectations," *The Concise Encyclopedia of Economics,* at http://www.econlib.org/library/Enc/RationalExpectations.html (accessed April 13, 2010).

Sarkozy, Nocolas (2008), *International Financial Crisis,* Speech of September 25, 2008, at http://www.ambafrance-uk.org/president-sarkozy-speaks-to-French.html (accessed August 18, 2010).

SEC (2006), *2006 Performance and Accountability Report,* Securities and Exchange Commission, at http://www.sec.gov/about/secpar/secpar2006.pdf (accessed January 4, 2009).

Selgin, George, "Guilty as Charged," *Mises Daily,* November 7, 2008, at http://mises.org/story/3200 (accessed February 15, 2010).

Shabab, Houman B. (2007), "The Challenge of Hedge Fund Regulation," *Regulation,* 30:1 (Spring), pp. 36–41, at http://www.cato.org/pubs/regulation/regv30n1/v30n1-1.pdf (accessed January 4, 2009).

Shlaes, Amity (2008), *The Forgotten Man: A New History of the Great Depression* (New York: Harper).

Shull, Bernard (2007), "Corporate Governance, Bank Regulation and Activity Expansion in the United States," in Gup (2007), pp. 1–17.

SIGTARP (2009), *Quarterly Report to Congress,* Office of the Special Inspector General for the Troubled Asset Relief Program, October 21, 2009, at http://www.sigtarp.gov/reports/congress/2009/October2009_Quarterly_Report_to_Congress.pdf (accessed April 13, 2010).

Smith Adam (1759), *The Theory of Moral Sentiments* (London: A. Millar, 1790), at http://www.econlib.org/library/Smith/smMSCover.html (accessed November 27, 2009).

Smith, Adam (1776), *An Inquiry into the Nature and Causes of the Wealth of Nations* (New York: Modern Library, 1937), at http://www.econlib.org/library/Smith/smWNCover.html (accessed November 27, 2009).

Snowdon, Brian, and Howard R. Vane (2005), *Modern Macroeconomics: Its Origins, Development and Current State* (Cheltenham UK and Northampton MA: Edward Elgar).

Sowell, Thomas (2009), *The Housing Boom and Bust* (New York: Basic Books).

Stigler, George J. (1971), "The Theory of Economic Regulation," *Bell Journal of Economics and Management Science,* 2:1, pp. 3–21.

Stiglitz, Joseph E. (2010), *Freefall: America, Free Markets, and the Sinking of the World Economy* (New York: W.W. Norton & Company).

Stiglitz, Joseph E., Jonathan M. Orszag, and Peter R. Orszag (2002), "Implications of the New Fannie Mae and Freddie Mac Risk-based Capital Standard," *Fannie Mac Papers* 1:2 (March).

Sunstein, Cass R., and Adrian Vermeule (2008), *Conspiracy Theories,* Harvard Public Law Working Paper No. 08-03, University of Chicago Public Working Paper No. 199, University of Chicago Law & Economics Olin Working Paper No. 387, January 15, 2008, at http://papers.ssrn.com/sol3/papers.cfm?abstract_id=1084585 (accessed April 13, 2010).

Swire, Peter P. (1999), "Financial Privacy and the Theory of High-tech Government Surveillance," in Anthony M. Santomero and Robert E. Litan, Eds., *Brookings-Wharton Papers on Financial Services: 1999* (Washington DC: Brookings Institution Press), pp. 391–442.

Taleb, Nassim Nicholas (2005), *Fooled by Randomness: The Hidden Role of Chance in Life and in the Markets,* 2nd Edition (New York: Random House).

Taleb, Nassim Nicholas (2007a), "Taleb on Black Swans," Podcast, *econtalk.org,* April 30, 2007, at http://www.econtalk.org/archives/2007/04/taleb_on_black.html (accessed April 13, 2010).

Taleb, Nassim Nicholas (2007b), *The Black Swan: The Impact of the Highly Improbable* (New York: Random House).

Taleb, Nassim Nicholas (2009), "Taleb on the Financial Crisis," Podcast, *econtalk.org,* March 23, 2009, at http://www.econtalk.org/archives/_featuring/nassim_taleb/ (accessed April 13, 2010).

Tanzi, Vito, and Ludger Schuknecht (2000), *Public Spending in the 20th Century: A Global Perspective* (Cambridge UK: Cambridge University Press).

Taylor, John B. (2009), *Getting Off Track: How Government Actions and Interventions Caused, Prolonged, and Worsened the Financial Crisis* (Stanford CA: Hoover Institution Press, 2009).

Taylor, John B. (2010), "The Dodd-Frank Financial Fiasco," *Wall Street Journal,* July 1, 2010.

The Economist (2007), "Bankers' Mistrust," August 18, 2007.

The Economist (2008a), "The Battle of Smoot-Hawley," December 18, 2008.

The Economist (2008b), "John Templeton," Obituary, July 19, 2008.

The Economist (2008c), "Wall Street's Bad Dream," September 18, 2008.

The Economist (2009a), "Thriving on Adversity," October 1, 2009.

The Economist (2009b), "Brand Loyalty," November 26, 2009.

The Economist (2009c), "A Load to Bear," November 26, 2009.

The Economist (2009d), "Return of the Trustbusters," August 27, 2009.

The Economist (2009e), Banking on the Banks, October 15, 2009.

The Economist (2009f), "A Reluctant Patient," July 23, 2009.

The Economist (2009g), "Saving the Oligarchs," December 3, 2009.

The Economist (2009h), "The Rise of the Hybrid Company," December 3, 2009.

The Economist (2010a), "Leviathan Stirs Again," January 21, 2010.

The Economist (2010b), "Model Behaviour," January 21, 2010.

The Economist (2010c), "The Safety-Net Frays," February 11, 2010.

The Economist (2010d), "Not So Risk-Free," February 11, 2010.

The Economist (2010e), "A Matter of Principle," February 11, 2010.

The Economist (2010f), "Fingers in the Dike," February 11, 2010.

The Economist (2010g), "Domino Theory," February 18, 2010.

The Economist (2010h), "Bearers of Bad News," February 18, 2010.

The Economist (2010i), "Number-crunches Crunched," February 11, 2010.

The Economist (2010j), "A Physicist Argues that Information Is at the Root of Everything," April 22, 2010.

The Economist (2010k), "Obama v BP," June 17, 2010.

The Economist (2010l), "Not All on the Same Page," July 1, 2010.

The Economist (2010m), "Can Pay, Won't Pay," June 17, 2010.

Turchin, Peter (2009), "Long-Term Population Cycles in Human Societies," in *Annals of the New York Academy of Sciences* 1162, pp. 1–17.

Udell, Gregory F. (1989), "Loan Quality, Commercial Loan Review and Loan Officer Contracting," *Journal of Banking and Finance*, 13, pp. 367–382.

US Department of Commerce (1929), *Statistical Abstract of the United States 1929* (Washington DC: US Government Printing Office), at http://www2. census.gov/prod2/statcomp/documents/1929-01.pdf (accessed April 13, 2010).

Vatter, Harold G. (1979), "Perspectives on the Forty-sixth Anniversary of the U.S. Mixed Economy," *Explorations in Economic History*, 16, pp. 297–330.

Wallison, Peter J. (2009), "Cause and Effect: Government Policies and the Financial Crisis," *Critical Review*, 21:2–3, pp. 365–376.

Walter, John R. (2005), "Depression-Era Bank Failures: The Great Contagion or the Great Shakeout?," *Federal Reserve Bank of Richmond Economic Quarterly*, 91:1 (Winter), at http://www.unc.edu/~salemi/Econ423/Depression_Era_Bank_ Failures.pdf.

White, Lawrence H. (1999), *The Theory of Monetary Institutions* (Malden MA and Oxford UK: Blackwell).

White, Lawrence H. (2008), "What Really Happened?," *Cato Unbound*, December 2, 2008, at http://www.cato-unbound.org/2008/12/02/lawrence-h-white/what-really-happened/ (accessed April 13, 2010).

Wicksteed, Philip H. (1910), *The Common Sense of Political Economy* (London: Macmillan), available at http://www.econlib.org/library/Wicksteed/wkCSCover. html (accessed April 13, 2010).

Wintrobe, Ronald (1998), *The Political Economy of Dictatorship* (Cambridge: Cambridge University Press).

Wolf, Martin (2008), *Fixing Global Finance* (Baltimore MD: John Hopkins University Press).

World Bank (2001), *Finance for Growth: Policy Choices in a Volatile World* (New York: Oxford University Press).

Index